Taharah Kahalachah

The Practical Laws of
Taharas Hamishpachah

Compiled by
Rabbi Yekusiel Farkash

Translated by
Rabbi Yehuda Altein

Jerusalem
5784

Table of Contents

ב"ה

APPROBATIONS
ON THE AUTHOR'S PREVIOUS WORKS
ON THE LAWS OF
TAHARAS HAMISHAPACHAH

מורי ורבי הרב שמואל הלוי ואזנר זצ"ל

כבוד תלמידי חביבי הרב הגאון המושלם מאד בתורה ויראה כש"ת הרב ר'
יקותיאל בן כבוד הרבני היקר המופלג ר' גרשון פרקש שליט"א - רב ומו"צ בעיה"ק
ירושלים תוב"ב - הראה לי כתבי יד תורה . . מסודר על הלכות נדה, באופן מעשי
נפלא מאד בלישנא קלילא ובירורי הלכה יסודיים - על יסודות איתן פסקי גדולי
הפוסקים דורות הקודמים עד היום הזה - בלשון קל והכרעה ברורה, וגם נושא ונותן
באמונה ומעיר ובא בדברי גדולי הפוסקים והכל על מקומו הראוי. והבולט בזה, גודל
ידיעותיו ויגיעותיו למען בירור האמת.

על כן גם ידי תכון עמו . . וישתמשו בו מבקשי תורה והלכה פסוקה.

הגאון הרב מנשה קליין זצ"ל
אבדק"ק אונגוואר בעמ"ח שו"ת משנה הלכות

הן הובא לפני . . הלכות נדה וטהרתה מאת ידידי הרב הגאון וו"ח כו' כש"ת מוה"ר
יקותיאל פרקש שליט"א מו"צ בעיה"ק ירושלים ת"ו.

והנני מכיר את המחבר ואת שיחו מאד חשוב בתורה, ודברתי אתו כמה פעמים
וראיתיו קולע אל השערה ולא יחטא ונהירין ליה שבילין דהלכה, וכמעט כל ההלכות
עברתי עליהם וראיתי דברים נחוצים . . כרך דכולי ביה . . והנני מבקש מידידי ותלמידי
בפרט ולומדי תורה בכלל, הביאו ברכה בבתיכם ספר חשוב הזה . .

הגאון הרב משה שטערן זצ"ל
אב"ד דעברעצין בעמ"ח שו"ת באר משה

הן הובא לפני . . הלכות נדה וטהרתה מאת הרב הגאון המופלא ומופלג חריף
ובקי עצום כש"ת מו"ה יקותיא-ל פארקאש שליט"א מו"צ בעיה"ק ירושלים
תובב"א . . והי' לי לשמחת הנפש לראות איך מברר ומפרש ענינים עמוקים ומסובכים
בדרך הישר . . ואשרי לו ואשרי חלקו שזכה לכך . . ובטוח אני שכל רואיו בעודו בכפו
יבלענו . .

הגאון הרב פינחס הירשפרונג זצ"ל
אב"ד מאנטריאל קנדה

. . ועייינתי בהספר ומצאתיו מלא דבר ה' זו הלכה אשר מברר ומלקט הדינים
המפוזרים, והנני מחזיק טובה להרב הנ"ל על אשר מברר ומלבן הדינים הנ"ל וראויים
הם לאדפוסי אידרא ולפוץ מעינותיו חוצה . .

Introduction

I offer praise and thanksgiving to the Almighty who has enabled me in his everlasting kindness to publish the present book, an English edition of **Taharah Kahalachah**. This book details the laws of *taharas hamishpachah*—family purity—that have been treated at length in the two-volume Hebrew series with this name I have had the privilege of authoring (henceforth referred to as "the *sefer*"). In those volumes, the practical laws of *taharas hamishpachah* have been presented in a concise and easy-to-read format, enabling them to be understood by all, including those unfamiliar with the distinctive style of the *Shulchan Aruch* and halachic codifiers.

Indeed, the Almighty has granted me the great merit of seeing this set of Hebrew books become a staple in thousands of homes, and it is used prolifically by many rabbis who rule in these matters. The *sefer* has been reprinted numerous times, and it has proven itself as the most detailed and up-to-date work dealing with this important area of Jewish life.

Nevertheless, the *sefer* does not meet the needs of all those who desire to familiarize themselves with the details of *taharas hamishpachah*. The numerous pressures and obligations of daily life cause many to find it difficult to peruse a book of such lengthy style, especially if Hebrew is not one's mother tongue.

Because of this concern, I have been requested by numerous individuals to present the laws of *taharas hamishpachah* in a format that is even more concise, suiting the needs of those who are unable to study the *sefer* in its entirety. In addition to a Hebrew edition, an English edition is being presented as well for those who are more at ease with the English language.

❧

Some details about the structure of this book:

1. On the one hand, the scope of this book is not limited to the essentials of *taharas hamishpachah* alone, in which the majority of laws are not addressed. Conversely, it does not include every possible circumstance and detail either. The book attempts to create somewhat of a compromise between the two: laws that are uncommon have been omitted, while those important to be aware of have been included. Similarly, differences of opinion between halachic authorities have generally been omitted. Instead, wherever necessary, the reader is directed to refer to a competent rabbi to determine the halachic decision.

2. For technical reasons, the order of the chapters in this book differs from their order in the two-volume Hebrew edition. A footnote noting the corresponding chapter in the *sefer* accompanies the title of each chapter, enabling the reader to expand his knowledge by referring to the relevant chapter in the *sefer* and its footnotes and addenda.

3. It is important to note that many laws have been added in the present book that have not been cited in the *sefer*. I thank the various rabbis and *taharas hamishpachah* instructors who drew my attention to these laws and suggested that they be added. Another unique addition is the inclusion of an entirely new chapter dedicated to the laws of *yichud*.

4. The majority of the footnotes found in the *sefer*, which direct the reader to the sources of the laws and outline the various relevant opinions, have not been included in this book. However, in certain places, a need was felt for specific information to be brought to the reader's attention, and the pertinent footnotes were then quoted.

5. Certain laws that may be difficult to grasp at first are accompanied by examples that illustrate the case and applicable law. These examples have been set off in italics to aid the reader in identifying them.

6. It is self-understood that nothing can replace a systematic study of the laws of *taharas hamishpachah*. Nonetheless, if a question arises, one may not always remember the exact location of the relevant law. For this purpose, a comprehensive table of contents has been included to enable one to easily locate particular laws as needed.

Additionally, a glossary has been appended to provide background information for those unfamiliar with the Hebrew terms used in the book.

7. Wherever a referral is made to "the *sefer*," the object of the reference is the two-volume Hebrew edition of *Taharah Kahalachah*.

It is important to emphasize the obvious: even if one feels confident that they have fully mastered the laws of *taharas hamishpachah*, a competent rabbi **must** be consulted whenever they are in doubt, however minor the doubt seems to be.

~~◈~~

I would like to thank the many individuals who were instrumental in the preparation of this book:

Rabbi Yehuda Altein, who translated the book from the Hebrew and arranged the table of contents and glossary. His tireless efforts and superb work were apparent in every step of the book's preparation, and numerous laws were clarified and revised thanks to his valuable comments and suggestions. May the Almighty bless him with revealed good both physically and spiritually, and may he find success in all his endeavors.

Rabbis Yosef Yitzchak Vigler, Pesach Schmerling, and Yehoram Ulman who spent much precious time reviewing the book and repeatedly added many valuable comments and suggestions. Additionally, numerous other individuals reviewed and commented on sections of the book. May the merit of their holy work bring them blessings beyond measure, accompanied by health, long life, and much nachas from their offspring.

My esteemed and scholarly father Rabbi Aharon Gershon of blessed memory, and my mother Leah Rochel of blessed memory, daughter of Rabbi Elimelech Goldstein of blessed memory (author of the three-volume series *Amirah Yafah*), who have brought me to where I am today. And first and foremost, my wife Rochel, who with great self-sacrifice has enabled me to devote my life to Torah study, although this entails the relinquishing of certain comforts of life on her part. Indeed, the Almighty has blessed us with children and grandchildren who are involved in spreading Torah and Yiddishkeit and give us much *nachas*. May He continue to shower His blessings upon us, and may we experience an abundance of good and blessings together forevermore.

I would also like to express my heartfelt appreciation to a number of noble individuals (who wish to remain anonymous) who have always stood at my side and supported me, enabling me to devote my time to advancing the study and fulfillment of Jewish law. May the Almighty repay them physically and spiritually and fulfill their hearts' desires for the good.

I hope and pray that this work will assist in increasing purity within the Jewish community at large. May we merit to receive an added measure of purity from Above,[1] and to experience the deliverance of the Jewish nation from exile with the coming of Moshiach speedily in our days.

Rabbi Yekusiel Farkash

Jerusalem, 24 Teves 5775

---

1. See *Yoma* 8:9.

Comprehensive Table of Contents[1]

---

1. The symbol preceding the references (§) indicates a section within the chapter.

(Tissue, unwoven cotton: §54. Nylon: §55. Cloth smaller than three *etzba'os*: §56. Pads: §57. Using pads during *shivah nekiyim*: §58.)

Kesamim discovered in special circumstances: §§59–61.

After marital relations or urinating: §59.

On day of *veses*: §60.

During first three days of *shivah nekiyim*: §61.

Medical procedures: §§1–10.

Insertion of medical instrument into uterus: §§1–5.

(HSG, ultrasound: §4. Speculum, finger: §5.)

Blood discharged as the result of a medical procedure: §§6–7.

(Grasping cervix with tongs: §7.)

Suppositories: §8.

Artificial insemination, contraception, abortion: §9.

Yichud when visiting a physician: §10.

Vaginal wounds: §§11–15.

(Consulting a rabbi: §§11–12; §15. Physician's credibility: §§13–14.)

Blood discharged when urinating: §§16–18.

(Consulting a rabbi: §§16–17. Examining tissues used when wiping: §18.)

Fundamentals of *harchakos*: §§1–5.

(Definition of *harchakos*: §1. Types of *tum'ah*: §1. Doubtful *tum'ah*: §2. Acting stringently: §3. Binding on both spouses: §4. Acting leniently due to embarrassment or personal judgment: §5.)

Frivolity: §§6–6*.

(Affectionate expressions: §6.)

Forbidden touch: §§7–9.

(Clothing: §§7–8. Blanket: §7. Blowing: §9.)

Passing and throwing: §§10–11.

(*Kvater*: §11.)

Touching an object the other is holding: §§12–13.

(Child: §12. Bench or bed: §13.)

she has no white undergarments: §47. If she continued wearing her previous undergarments: §47. Bloodstained garments or sheets: §48. Colored undergarments or non-*mekabel tum'ah* items: §49. If she must begin counting *shivah nekiyim* anew: §50. If *hefsek taharah* was performed on Shabbos: §51. On Yom Tov preceding Shabbos: §52.)

Method and correct time of performing *bedikos*: §§1–7.

(Vaginal rings: §2. Time of *bedikos*: §3. If second *bedikah* was delayed until bein hashmashos: §4. Examining undergarments and sheets: §5. Examining tissues: §6. Rinsing the vagina before *bedikos*: §7. Squirting liquid or inserting suppository into vagina: §7.)

Examining cloth after *bedikah*: §§8–9.

(At night vs. by day: §8. Type of lighting: §8. If the cloth was misplaced: §9.)

If she did not perform all of the *bedikos*: §§10–11.

(First **and** seventh days: §10. First **or** seventh days, middle days: §11.)

Difficulty in performing *bedikos*: §§12–13.

Vaginal wounds: §14.

Separation between *shivah nekiyim* and *tevilah*: §15.

Discharge of blood during *shivah nekiyim*: §§16–17.

Uncertainty how many days were counted: §18.

Change of time zone: §19.

Crossing the International Date Line: §20.

Correct time *lechatchilah*: §§1–2.

Duration: §3.

If performed only at night: §4.

If performed only by day: §§5–7.

Preference of day over night: §8.

If time passed from *chafifah* until *tevilah*: §9.

Chafifah performed at home: §§10–12.

(Leaving to the *mikvah* after nightfall: §12.)

Clarifications regarding *chafifah* on Shabbos and Yom Tov: §12*.

CHAPTER ONE

THE FUNDAMENTALS OF
TAHARAS HAMISHPACHAH

1. The obligation to follow the laws of *taharas hamish-pachah* is stated explicitly in the Torah and by our Sages in numerous locations. Observing the laws of *taharas hamish-pachah* is one of the central precepts of our faith, while lacking to observe them properly is a matter of critical severity.

2. There is an additional element in the fulfillment of these laws: In letters written to couples experiencing problems in *shalom bayis*, the Lubavitcher Rebbe often pinpointed the lack of proper fulfillment of the laws of *taharas hamish-pachah* as one of the key factors behind their marital difficulties. Perhaps, he would add, they acted leniently with regard to the *harchakos* kept when the wife is *temei'ah* or failed to observe one of the crucial steps in the *taharah* process, either by overlooking certain details or by lacking to acquire a comprehensive familiarity with these laws.

3. Essentially, the *taharah* process described in *Shulchan Aruch* is required whenever blood of any kind is discharged from a woman's womb. There is no difference if the blood was part of a regular menstrual cycle which continued for a number of days, if a single drop of blood was found during a *bedikah* or when wiping, or if blood stains were found on her clothing or elsewhere; whenever *halachah* dictates that a woman is *temei'ah*, the entire process must be followed.

4. If a woman tells her husband that she is *temei'ah*, or

if she conducted herself in accordance with the *harchakos* kept when a woman is a *nidah*, she must count *shivah nekiyim* and immerse in the *mikvah*, even if she subsequently retracts, saying that her previous words had merely been stated in jest. Furthermore, if she had said that she was *temei'ah* due to a regular menstrual period (and not just a *kesem*), she must keep any *vestos* that result from this supposed bleeding.

The only exception to this law is if she is able to provide a reasonable explanation why she had previously presented herself as a *nidah*. However, many details apply, and not always can her explanation be accepted. Accordingly, one should be extremely careful in this regard and refrain from creating unnecessary difficulties.

5. In general, the *taharah* process is as follows:

1. Waiting the prescribed amount of days before performing a *hefsek taharah*.

2. Performing a *hefsek taharah* (the *bedikah* performed before *shivah nekiyim* to verify that the menstrual bleeding has stopped).

3. Counting *shivah nekiyim* (beginning with the day following the *hefsek taharah*), during which white undergarments are worn and two daily *bedikos* are performed.

4. Preparing for the *tevilah* by means of a thorough cleansing of all parts of the body known as *chafifah*.

5. Immersing properly in a kosher *mikvah*.

The chapters that follow will explain, with Hashem's help, these steps and their many details, starting from when a woman becomes *temei'ah* and continuing until she becomes completely *tehorah*.

CHAPTER TWO

HOW A WOMAN BECOMES *TEMEI'AH MID'ORAYSA*
(*Hargashah*; *bedikos*;
blood discharged during marital relations)

Hargashah[1]

1. If a woman felt blood being discharged from her uterus and subsequently discovered even a tiny drop of blood,
she is *temei'ah mid'oraysa*. This is true even if the discharge
was caused by an outside factor, such as physical exertion,
a medical procedure, or the like. The color of the garment
upon which the blood was found is of no relevance, nor is it
relevant if the garment is *mekabel tum'ah*.

Requirements When a *Hargashah* is Felt

2. If a woman felt fluid trickling from the uterus, she must
determine if the sensation, known as a *hargashah*, was associated with the discharge of blood or not. She must therefore immediately examine herself with a *bedikah* cloth. If she
discovers a thick fluid of a *tahor* color on the cloth, she is
tehorah. But if no thick fluid is discovered, or if she failed to
perform a *bedikah*, she is *temei'ah* out of doubt. If over two
minutes passed from the time of the *hargashah* until the *bedikah*, a rabbi who is an expert in the laws of *taharas hamishpachah* should be consulted to determine if she can still be
considered *tehorah*.

---

1. Paragraphs 1–11 correspond to Chapter One in the *sefer*.

3. The above *bedikah* should be performed in an identical manner to those performed during *shivah nekiyim* (see Chapter Eight §§19-31). However, **in this scenario**, if she merely wiped herself instead of performing a *bedikah*, it can be relied upon *bedi'eved*. If she did not perform a *bedikah* but was wearing tight undergarments upon which she found a thick fluid of a *tahor* color, an expert rabbi should be consulted to determine if there is room to rule leniently.

Types of *Hargashah*

4. The above law—that she is *temei'ah* if she fails to perform a *bedikah*—applies only when she is **certain** that she experienced a *hargashah*. But if she is in doubt whether or not she felt a *hargashah*, although it is best to perform a *bedikah* in this case as well, she is *tehorah* if she failed to do so.

The definition of a **distinct** *hargashah* is the feeling of fluid trickling from the uterus to the vagina. The feeling of a liquid flow in the vagina is defined as an **uncertain** *hargashah*.

5. Nowadays it is extremely rare for a woman to feel a distinct *hargashah*, and it is questionable if what is generally felt can even be defined as an uncertain *hargashah*. Consequently, although it is customary to perform a *bedikah* upon feeling a *hargashah* nowadays as well, she is *tehorah* if she failed to do so (or if she performed a *bedikah* and no fluid was discovered). She is certainly *tehorah* if she was wearing tight undergarments and found on them a thick fluid of a *tahor* color.

Three Discharges of Clear Fluid

6. If a woman determined three times on three separate occasions (by means of *bedikos* performed immedi-

ately after the *hargashah*) that her *hargashos* are not associated with blood but rather with the discharge of clear fluid, she is never required to perform a *bedikah* again upon feeling such a *hargashah*.

7. If a woman has determined that her *hargashos* are associated with the discharge of clear fluid and she discovers a *kesem* following a *hargashah*, we do not assume that this time the *hargashah* was associated with a discharge of blood. Rather, if the *kesem* can be ruled as *tahor* (as will be explained in the following chapter), she is *tehorah*.

8. Nowadays most women do not feel the flowing of fluid in the vagina, rather the moisture of the blood after it has already been discharged from the body. Accordingly, if a woman discovers a *kesem* following such a *hargashah*, she is *tehorah* if the *kesem* can be ruled as *tahor*, even if she has not determined that her *hargashos* are associated with the discharge of clear fluid.

It is important to clarify that this does not apply to a regular menstrual period. Even if she does not feel a uterine discharge or vaginal flow, if she feels that she has received her period, she is *temei'ah mid'oraysa*, even if the blood was found on a colored or non-*mekabel-tum'ah* garment.

Mesulekes Damim

9. A *mesulekes damim* is a woman who *halachah* establishes as not expecting to experience menstrual periods. Each of the following women is classified as a *mesulekes damim*:

1. A pregnant woman, beginning from the fourth month of her pregnancy (see note for further clarifica-

tions).[2] The pregnancy is calculated as beginning on the *tevilah* night following her latest menstrual period.

2. A nursing woman, for a period of 24 months following birth. Even a woman who is presently not nursing is included in this category, and even one who has not begun to nurse at all (see note for further clarifications).[3] A miscarriage that occurred over 40 days from the beginning of the pregnancy shares the same status as a birth, and the mother is considered as a nursing woman for the next 24 months. The 40 days are calculated from the *tevilah* night following her latest menstrual period.

3. An elderly woman, that is, a woman who has not experienced periods for an extended amount of time, and the evident reason is because of her advanced age (see note).[4]

10. A woman classified as a *mesulekes damim* who felt a *hargashah* and performed a *bedikah* is *tehorah* even if no fluid was discovered. This is true even if she has not determined

---

2. A number of relevant clarifications: (1) The first three months of pregnancy are not calculated according to the calendar but as consisting of **90 days**. (2) Before three months have passed, a woman is not considered a *mesulekes damim* even if she is sure that she is pregnant and even if the fetus is noticeable.

3. A number of relevant clarifications: (1) These 24 months are calculated based on the months of the Hebrew year, in which one month consists of 29 days and the next, of 30. (2) Even though nowadays nursing women frequently experience regular menstrual periods, the same laws continue to apply. See the *sefer* (Chapter Twenty-Four fn. 157) for an elaboration of the topic.

4. The exact definition of an elderly woman in this context is unclear (see the *sefer* Chapter One fn. 23), and an expert rabbi should be consulted when in doubt.

that her *hargashos* are associated with the discharge of clear fluid.

Sudden Trauma

11. A woman who experienced sudden trauma or shock should perform a *bedikah* immediately to determine that no bleeding occurred as a result. However, she is *tehorah* even if she failed to do so, provided that no *kesem* was discovered. She is required to state to her husband clearly that she indeed determined that no blood was discharged (at least by verifying that no *kesem* was discovered).

Bedikos[5]

Blood Found on an Examined *Bedikah* Cloth

12. If a woman discovered blood on the *bedikah* cloth after performing a *bedikah*, she is *temei'ah mid'oraysa* if she had examined the *bedikah* cloth beforehand and it was clean. This applies even if only a tiny drop of blood was found, and even if the cloth she used was colored or not *mekabel tum'ah* (such as a tissue or the like).

Since such a woman is *temei'ah mid'oraysa*, she must calculate the relevant *veses* calculations, just like she must do after a regular menstrual period. (See Chapter Sixteen §§55ff. for the laws that apply if an impure *bedikah* occurred during the *shivah nekiyim*.)

13. A cloth that was stripped off of a washed garment has the same status as a pre-examined cloth. This is true even

---

5. Paragraphs 12–23 correspond to Chapter Two in the *sefer*.

if the cloth was not examined when it was washed or after-ward, provided it was kept in a sheltered location from the time it was washed until the *bedikah*.

14. If she did not examine the cloth properly before per-forming the *bedikah* but just glanced at it quickly, and after the *bedikah* she discovered a minute drop of blood that can only be detected through careful observation, it is as if the cloth was not examined before the *bedikah* (see §16). The same law applies if there was not sufficient lighting when she examined the cloth. However, she may not rely on her own judgment, and the cloth **must** be brought to an expert rabbi to determine its status.

Blood Derived From an External Source

15. The above (§12) applies if the *bedikah* was performed immediately after the cloth was examined, or if the exam-ined cloth was kept until it was used in a place where it could not have become stained. In these cases, it is certain that the blood derived from the woman, and she is therefore *temei'ah mid'oraysa*. Different laws, however, may apply if the cloth was kept in a place where it could have become stained from an external source (see the *sefer* Chapter Two §4 for the rel-evant laws).

Blood Found on an Unexamined *Bedikah* Cloth

16. Different laws apply if blood was found on an un-examined *bedikah* cloth. The *sefer* (ibid. §§5–7) should be consulted for the definition of an unexamined cloth and the relevant laws.

17. If it is uncertain if the cloth was examined before-

hand or not, the cloth is viewed as having the status of an examined cloth.

Misplaced *Bedikah* Cloth

18. An expert rabbi should be consulted if a woman misplaced a *bedikah* cloth with a questionable *mar'eh*. In certain scenarios, he may be able to render it *tehorah*.

19. If a woman misplaced a *bedikah* cloth that she did not examine at all, she is *tehorah*, and we are not concerned that there was a *tamei* color on the cloth. (See Chapter Eight §§43–44 and Chapter Nine §9 for the laws that apply if this occurred after a *bedikah* she was obligated to perform.)

Kinuach—Wiping

20. The *Poskim* differ regarding the law of a *kinuach*, i.e., if she did not insert the *bedikah* cloth deeply into the vagina but merely wiped herself with it.

The Opinion of the Alter Rebbe (and Others):

1. A *kinuach* shares the laws of a **regular *bedikah*** (in which the cloth was inserted deeply into the vagina), and she is *temei'ah mid'oraysa* under all circumstances. However, with regard to *veses* calculations, blood found as a result of a *kinuach* is not reckoned with (see Chapter Sixteen §5). (It should be noted that a *kinuach* cannot take the place of a *bedikah* when *bedikos* must be performed, such as during *shivah nekiyim* and the like.)

2. If a woman performed a *bedikah* and she was found to be *tehorah*, and immediately afterwards she

wiped herself and discovered blood, the *kinuach* has the status of a *kesem* even according to this opinion.

3. If she did not insert the cloth into the vagina itself but merely wiped the surrounding area, an expert rabbi should be consulted to determine if there is room to rule leniently.

The Opinion of Most *Poskim*

Many *Poskim* are of the opinion that a *kinuach* shares the laws of a **kesem**, and she is only *temei'ah* *mid'rabanan*. Consequently, she is *tehorah* if the blood was found on a colored cloth or on a material which is not *mekabel tum'ah* (as will be explained in Chapter Four §§48ff. regarding *kesamim*). **(See the following paragraph.)**

21. Even when a *kinuach* shares the laws of a *kesem*, it is only with regard to blood found on a colored cloth or on a material which is not *mekabel tum'ah*. However, the **size** of the stain is of no consequence, and she is *temei'ah* even if only a tiny drop of blood was found (unlike a *kesem* which is *tahor* if smaller than a *gris ve'od*).

Examining Tissues Used When Wiping

22. It is recommended to avoid looking at the tissues used to wipe the vaginal area (after using the restroom and the like). Instead, she should dispose of them without looking at them. This applies during the *shivah nekiyim* as well.

23. On the other hand, if she did look at them and noticed a questionable *mar'eh*, she may not ignore the matter and dispose of the tissue, rather she must show it to an expert

rabbi. In any event, she should not perform a *bedikah* after discovering the *mar'eh*, as doing so will not better the situation and can possibly complicate matters even more.

Blood Caused by Marital Relations[6]

24. If a woman menstruated three consecutive times as a result of marital relations, the couple may be obligated to divorce, G-d forbid (see *Shulchan Aruch Yoreh Dei'ah* §187). As such, it is imperative that if blood is ever discharged shortly after marital relations even once, an expert rabbi should be approached **immediately** to determine how to proceed, and they should not wait to see if it will happen again. Additionally, an expert doctor in this field should be contacted to assist them in preventing this from repeating itself, before matters become more complicated.

However, blood that was discharged a number of hours after marital relations (and not shortly after) is not an issue.

25. If blood was discharged once or twice immediately after marital relations, the woman must perform a *bedikah* at least before and after the subsequent intercourse (and the husband should wipe himself afterward as well). The same law applies if the husband discovered blood on the cloth with which he wiped himself. Some authorities are of the opinion that *bedikos* are required at the subsequent three intercourses.

The above is true even if they had already performed three sets of *bedikos* to establish that marital relations do not cause her to menstruate (see Chapter Fifteen).

---

6. Paragraphs 24–30 correspond to Chapter Twelve in the *sefer*.

26. If she did not discover the blood immediately after marital relations, *bedikos* do not need to be performed at the subsequent intercourse. However, *bedikos* must be performed if blood was discovered on the cloth with which the husband wiped himself, even if it was discovered a long time after marital relations.

27. In any event, it is of extreme importance that a *bodekes* or observant doctor be contacted to determine the cause of the blood. Often the blood is the result of a wound and the like, and when the relevant details are brought to the attention of an expert rabbi, he may be able to render her completely *tehorah*.

Concern for *Tum'ah* During Marital Relations

To note: It is extremely rare for a *tum'ah* to occur during marital relations, and there is no reason at all for one to worry that such an incident might occur.

28. If a woman experienced a discharge of blood during marital relations, the husband may not withdraw his organ while it is still erect; rather, he must wait until the organ relaxes and only then should he separate. In the interim, he should not lie on her; rather he should support himself on his hands and legs and thrust his toes into the bed. To quote the *Shulchan Aruch*,[7] "he should be overcome by fear from the transgression that has come his way." He should wait in this manner until the organ relaxes and then separate immediately. The wife should similarly lie motionless so as not to cause any movement of the organ.

---

7. *Yoreh Dei'ah* 185:4.

The husband may not withdraw the organ even if he senses that semen will be discharged, resulting in a possible pregnancy from this intercourse.

29. If they did not act in the above manner, a rabbi should be consulted regarding the possible need for atonement.

30. If a couple remembered during marital relations that it was the day of her veses, they may not continue the intercourse. The husband should withdraw the organ immediately even if it is erect, provided there is no concern that this will cause semen to be discharged outside the wife's body. If such a concern does exist, he should wait until the organ relaxes before separating. Similarly, if the wife feels the symptoms associated with her menstrual period, he must wait for the organ to relax before separating.

CHAPTER THREE[1]

MAR'OS

The term "*mar'eh*" refers to a stain found on a *bedikah* cloth, garment, sheet, and the like.

Directing Questionable *Mar'os* to an Expert Rabbi

1. The Torah gives women complete reliance regarding the laws of *nidah* and its *taharah*. However, much expertise is required to differentiate between the various types of colors that can be found on a *mar'eh*, and even an expert rabbi must spend a great deal of time with rabbis proficient in this field to acquire this skill. It is therefore of **paramount importance** that any doubt that arises be resolved exclusively by a rabbi who is an expert in the laws of *taharas hamishpachah*.

Color of *Mar'eh*

2. Any *mar'eh* of a **red** color is *tamei*. This is true even if it merely carries a slight resemblance to the color red, and even if the color is extremely light.

A *mar'eh* that resembles the color **black** must be brought to an expert rabbi to determine whether it is mere residue or an impure *mar'eh* that originated from the uterus.

3. Similarly, a **brown** *mar'eh* must be brought to an expert rabbi to determine if this was indeed the original color of the *mar'eh* or if it was previously red.

---

1. Corresponding to Chapter Six in the *sefer*.

A **white** or **yellow** *mar'eh* is *tahor*, even if it consists of thick mucus.[2]

4. One may not act stringently out of doubt to consider a *mar'eh* as *tamei*, as it is forbidden to delay the *tevilah* by even a single day. Our Sages have extolled the merit of hastening to immerse as soon as possible, and they have emphasized the severity of delaying to do so. It is important to clarify the woman's status even when dealing with the possible addition of only **one impure day**. Obviously, the couple must act stringently as long as they have not yet brought the *mar'eh* under discussion to a rabbi; however, they should hasten to do so as soon as possible.

5. Some authorities recommend the husband as the one who should bring the questionable *mar'eh* to the rabbi, as the woman might be embarrassed at times, resulting in the delaying of her *taharah*, G-d forbid. Many people follow this practice. However, some say that it is better for the woman to be the one to do so.[3]

---

2. If a woman spent a lengthy amount of time in hot water and then found a *mar'eh* consisting of thick white mucus, although some are of the opinion that she is *temei'ah*, many *Poskim* disagree and rule leniently. The Tzemach Tzedek (Responsa §125) concludes that this "custom" (to consider such a woman *temei'ah*) has no basis. This is true even if this occurred during the *shivah nekiyim* (unlike those who rule stringently in such a case).

3. The rationale of the latter opinion is that sometimes the rabbi must inquire specific details from her of which the husband might be unaware. However, nowadays it is possible to contact the wife via telephone if the need arises, even if the husband is the one bringing the *mar'eh* to the rabbi.

Safeguarding the *Mar'eh*

6. The *mar'eh* should be safeguarded in a dry, clean location to ensure that it will not become stained or dirty and that the color does not become distorted. Additionally, it should be brought to the rabbi as soon as possible, and one should not scrape it, shake it off, rub it, or the like. These factors (the length of time that has passed and the mishandling of the *mar'eh*) can change the color and texture of the *mar'eh*, resulting in an improper *halachic* decision, G-d forbid. Accordingly, if particles or pieces were found with a resemblance to red or black, care should be taken that they do not fall off, and one should not press them or remove them before showing the *mar'eh* to an expert rabbi.

7. On the other hand, even if a long time has passed and the *mar'eh* has still not been brought to a rabbi, it can—and should—be brought to him.[4] This is true even

---

4. In principle, *mar'os* are to be judged as they appear upon being emitted from the body, and the fact that the color has since changed is insufficient to render it *tahor*. Therefore:

(1) If one proficient in viewing *mar'os* initially viewed a *mar'eh* as consisting of a **doubtful color,** and then he viewed it a second time and it appeared to be *tahor*, it can be rendered *tahor* if it is possible to explain the previous doubt as having been a result of it having been viewed at night, due to the darkness of the room, or the like.

(2) If the *mar'eh* appeared to be *tamei* **without a doubt** when it was initially viewed, and when viewed a second time it appeared to be *tahor*, it cannot be rendered *tahor*. This is true even if it was initially viewed at night. We do not assume that it had initially appeared to be *tamei* due to a lack of proper lighting; rather we assume that the color had indeed changed, and that at the time of the emission from the body it was indeed *tamei*.

(3) The *sefer* (Chapter Six fn. 19) should be consulted for the law

if the color of the *mar'eh* appears to have changed in the interim.

If the color of the *mar'eh* appears to have changed (either from *tum'ah* to *taharah* or vice versa), one should not decide alone whether it is *tamei* or *tahor*. Many details apply in such a case, and the *mar'eh* must be brought to an expert rabbi.

8. Some practical advice:

1. A moist *mar'eh* should be laid out to dry before it is wrapped or stored in an envelope or bag. If the *mar'eh* remains moist, some of the moisture may adhere to the paper when it is removed, preventing the rabbi from discerning the original color properly. Similarly, if a moist *mar'eh* is stored in a plastic bag, the moisture may smear onto the bag and may even grow mold!

2. It is extremely important to take note of when the *mar'eh* was discovered, i.e., if it was from a *hefsek taharah* or *moch dochuk* or the *bedikah* of a certain day. If the *mar'eh* is from a *bedikah*, one should note if it is from the morning or the evening. If these details are not recorded, a woman may bring various *mar'os* to a rabbi and one might be discovered to be *tamei*. If the date of the *mar'eh* is unknown, we will have to assume that the last *bedikah* was the one that was *tamei*, and she will be unnecessarily considered *temei'ah* for an extra amount of time!

9. The rabbi should be informed of all the details relating to the *mar'eh*, for in certain scenarios, even seemingly unim-

---

that applies if the woman claims that the color has changed (as opposed to someone proficient in viewing *mar'os*).

portant facts can play a role in the final ruling. The following are a number of examples of factors of which the rabbi should be informed:

1. If it is possible that the *bedikah* cloth or garment was unclean before the *mar'eh* was found on it.

2. If the garment had been washed beforehand, and if it had been kept in a guarded place from when it was washed until the *mar'eh* was found.

3. If the *mar'eh* was from a *bedikah*, *kinuach*, or something else.

4. If the color of the *mar'eh* appeared to have changed from when it was found. In such a case, the rabbi should also be informed whether the previous color appeared to have certainly been *tamei*, and if it had previously been viewed at night or by day.

5. If she felt discomfort when doing the *bedikah*.

6. If the *mar'eh* was found when she was *tehorah* or during *shivah nekiyim*. In the latter case, the rabbi should also be informed whether she had been counting due to a *kesem* or a regular menstrual period.

10. An unused *bedikah* cloth is not *muktzeh*, but it is *muktzeh* once it has been used and is no longer needed. Consequently, after performing a *bedikah* on Shabbos, she should dispose of the cloth at the first possible opportunity, unless it must be shown to a rabbi or the like. A rabbi may handle a *mar'eh* on Shabbos if he desires to examine it further or use it to train others who are studying the skill of viewing *mar'os*.

11. A *mar'eh* may be shown to a rabbi even when it is still moist, and there is no need to be concerned that it will change colors once it dries. But if one did notice that the color changed once it dried, the rabbi must be informed, whether it changed from a *tahor* color to a *tamei* color or vice versa. The laws pertaining to such changes are explained in the sefer (Chapter Six §§9ff.).

12. An expert rabbi should be consulted if a *mar'eh* with a questionable color was misplaced, whether it was a *bedikah*, *kesem*, or *kinuach*. (For additional details, see Chapter Two §§18–19, Chapter Four §47, Chapter Eight §§43–44, and Chapter Nine §9.)

Type of Lighting When Examining a Mar'eh

13. It is best to examine the *mar'eh* by daylight, as opposed to candlelight, electric light, and the like. However, if the *mar'eh* was examined by means of alternative forms of light and appeared *tahor*, and it was then misplaced, there is no need to be concerned that it was not *tahor*. Similarly, if the *mar'eh* must be examined at night (for example, with a *bedikah* performed before or after marital relations), it may be examined by means of alternative forms of light. However, one should avoid forms of light that may cause the mar'eh to appear overly white, such as neon, fluorescent, or LED lighting.

14. An expert rabbi should be consulted if the *mar'eh* appeared questionable when examined at night and then appeared *tahor* when examined the following day.

Asking a Second Rabbi

15. If a woman showed a *mar'eh* to one rabbi and he ruled

it *tamei*, she may not show it to a second rabbi unless she informs him that the *mar'eh* had previously been ruled *tamei* by another rabbi. Additionally, the second rabbi must be informed if the first rabbi's decision was given a while earlier and the color may have since changed.

CHAPTER FOUR

KESAMIM

Introduction

A *kesem* is a stain of blood (typically found on a garment or her body) that is not associated with a *bedikah, kinuach,* or regular menstrual period. The laws of *kesamim* consist of many details, and they are divided in the *sefer* into three chapters (Chapters Three, Four and Five):

(1) The methods by which a *kesem* can be rendered *tahor* by attributing the blood to an external source. (2) A *kesem* discovered on a colored garment or on a material which is not *mekabel tum'ah*. (3) *Kesamim* discovered in special circumstances.

This chapter will discuss these laws with relative brevity; as such, the *sefer* should be consulted if one wishes to expand their knowledge of these laws or examine their sources.

General Laws of *Kesamim*[1]

1. If a woman discovered a *kesem* on her body, garments, or linen, she is *temei'ah* even if no *hargashah* was felt (with the exception of the cases listed in §3).

2. The *tum'ah* and *taharah* of a *kesem* are identical to that of a regular menstrual period or unclean *bedikah*. This includes the laws of *harchakos*, waiting five days before count-

---

1. Paragraphs 1–47 correspond to Chapter Three in the *sefer*.

ing *shivah nekiyim*, *hefsek taharah*, *shivah nekiyim*, *chafifah*, and *tevilah*. The only exception is with regard to calculating *vestos* (see Chapter Sixteen §6; §8).

3. Since the *tum'ah* of *kesamim* is *mid'rabanan*, our Sages ruled leniently in the following three scenarios (as will be explained in detail in this chapter): (1) If the *kesem* can be attributed to a source outside of the woman's body. This includes a *kesem* that is smaller than a *gris ve'od* (see §5), which is assumed to have originated from an external source. (2) If the *kesem* was found on a colored garment. (3) If the *kesem* was found on a material which is not *mekabel tum'ah*.

It is important to clarify that this does not apply to a regular menstrual period. Even if she does not feel a uterine discharge or vaginal flow, if she feels that she has received her period, she is *temei'ah mid'oraysa*, even if the blood was found on a colored or non-*mekabel-tum'ah* garment.

4. A woman who discovered a *kesem* should not perform a *bedikah* or wipe herself. An expert rabbi can often rule that a *kesem* is *tahor* (in the cases listed in the previous paragraph); but if even a mere drop of blood is found as the result of a **bedikah**, she will be *temei'ah*. The possibility to attribute such blood to an external source is subject to many limitations, and she is *temei'ah* even if the blood was found on a colored garment or on a garment which is not *mekabel tum'ah*. Since there is no reason to perform a *bedikah*, she should not do so, as this will only complicate matters unnecessarily.

Certain women feel that lacking to perform a *bedikah* to clarify the situation constitutes deception and that they are deliberately disregarding the facts. But this is entirely not the case. The laws of *tum'ah* and *taharah* are based on the decrees of the Torah and are not limited by the human thought process. If the Torah decrees that a woman is *tehorah*, she is *tehorah*, and if she does something that will change her current status, she may create a new situation in which she will be *temei'ah*.

First Exception:
Kesem That Can Be Attributed to an External Source

Kesem Smaller Than a *Gris Ve'od* Discovered on a Garment

(The following section details the laws pertaining to a *kesem* found on a garment, linen and the like. For the laws of a *kesem* found on her body, see §§28ff.)

5. A *kesem* is *tamei* only if it is larger in size than a *gris*. (This is termed in *Shulchan Aruch* and by the *Poskim* as a *gris ve'od*.) In modern dimensions, the size of a *gris ve'od* is as follows: According to the Alter Rebbe, it is slightly larger than a circle with a diameter of 17 mm. or 0.68 in. According to the majority of *Poskim*, it is an area with a diameter of 19–20 mm. or 0.76–0.8 in. (Images portraying the exact dimensions of a *gris ve'od* can be found at the end of the chapter.)

Any *kesem* consisting of a somewhat larger size should be brought to an expert rabbi to determine its exact dimension, and one should not establish its status on their own.

6. The shape of the *kesem* is of no consequence; in any case, if the *kesem* is smaller than a *gris ve'od*, she is *tehorah*. If the *kesem* does not consist of a circular shape, it should be measured as if the blood was assembled to form a circle. If it does consist of a *gris ve'od*, she is *temei'ah* even if it is an

unusual shape. Although one can speculate that if it indeed originated from the uterus it would not have formed such a shape, nevertheless she is *temei'ah* (unless there is an external source to which it can be attributed, as will be explained further).

7. A *kesem* consisting of a thick fluid should be measured as it currently appears (and not as if the fluid was spread across the garment). However, an expert rabbi should be consulted if one discovers an abnormally thick mass.

8. If one discovers numerous *kesamim* on a garment with no contact between them, they should each be measured separately, and if none of them consist of a *gris ve'od* she is *tehorah*. But if there is contact between them, they should be measured together, and if they total a *gris ve'od* she is *temei'ah*.

9. A *kesem* discovered spread over two adjacent articles of clothing should be measured as two separate *kesamim*. If each individual *kesem* does not consist of a *gris ve'od*, she is *tehorah*, even if they would total a *gris ve'od* were they to be measured as a single unit.

10. Similarly, a *kesem* discovered spread over a garment and its lining should be measured as two separate *kesamim*.

11. If a *kesem* was discovered on a thick garment and the *kesem* penetrated the depth of the garment, only the surface of the *kesem* that can be observed is measured.

12. If a *kesem* was spread over a crease but it is clear that the crease was there at the time when the *kesem* was created and that it is a single *kesem*, it is measured as a single unit even if it divides when the crease is smoothed.

13. Similarly, if a *kesem* was discovered on a knitted garment and it is clear that it is a single *kesem*, it is measured as a single unit even if small spaces are formed between the stitches when the garment is stretched.

14. A *kesem* will often consist of various shades of color, not all of which are *tamei*. In such a case, she is *temei'ah* only if the *tamei* shades of color alone total a *gris ve'od*, even if it appears as if all the colors form a single unit. This is true even if she is sure the *tahor* color originated from the uterus, for example, if she commonly discovers clear fluid on her garments. (See the *sefer* Chapter Three §§89–90 for more details concerning this law.)

Locations Where the *Kesem* Was Found

15. A *kesem* is *tamei* if it was discovered on a location where uterine blood was able to drip directly, even if this was only possible if she bent down (exceedingly). Even if she is certain that she did not do so, we are concerned that she bent down without realizing. In general, anywhere on her clothing from the **navel and below** are included in the *tum'ah* of *kesamim*.

16. If she removed her clothing by way of her legs, she is *temei'ah* even if a *kesem* was discovered on the upper part of her clothing, because uterine blood may have dripped there at that time.

17. If a woman discovered multiple *kesamim* and some of them were found in places where uterine blood could not have dripped, she is *tehorah*, even though the other *kesamim* were found in places where such blood could have dripped. We suppose that these latter *kesamim* originated from an un-

known external source just like the former *kesamim* (even if she is unaware of such an external source). However, various conditions and details apply to this law, and the *sefer* (Chapter Three §§85–88) should be consulted for a proper grasp of this subject.

18. If a *kesem* was discovered on her outer garment and her inner garment remained clean, she is *temei'ah* if it is possible that uterine blood dripped on the outer garment without staining the inner one. Examples include if it is possible that the inner garment shifted slightly or if it is possible that the outer garment became stained while the inner one was being removed. If no such possibility exists, she is *tehorah*, as we must conclude that the *kesem* originated from an unknown external source.

19. If a *kesem* was discovered on the portion of the sleeve covering the palm of her hand (until the joint connecting the palm to the arm), she is *temei'ah*. But if it was discovered on the upper portion of the sleeve, she is *tehorah*, unless that part of the sleeve was able to slide down and cover the palm of her hand.

20. If a *kesem* was discovered on the outer surface of a garment, she is *temei'ah* if there is any possibility, however remote, that the garment had folded over and was positioned opposite the vagina. Understandably, such a possibility can only exist with a particularly wide nightgown or the like. (See the following paragraph for another possibility.)

21. If a *kesem* was discovered on undergarments that were worn tightly, she is *tehorah* if it was discovered above the vagina or to the sides, where uterine blood was unable to reach

despite any type of body movement. However, this is only true if she is certain that they got stained while she was already dressed with them (for example, if she inspected them after she got dressed and they were clean). But if it is possible that the blood dripped there while dressing or undressing, she is *temei'ah* no matter where on the undergarments the *kesem* was discovered, and even if it was discovered on their outer surface.

22. If a *kesem* was discovered on a garment that was lying near her on her bed, she is *temei'ah* no matter where on the garment the *kesem* was discovered. It is possible that she or the garment may have moved while she was sleeping in such a way that the garment was positioned opposite her vagina. (See, however, §25.)

23. If a *kesem* was discovered on her kerchief, she is *temei'ah* even if it was still secured to her head when she awoke. It is possible that the kerchief slipped off of her head while she was sleeping and then she secured it once again, even if she doesn't remember having done so. (See, however, §25.) However, she is *tehorah* if she secured it **firmly** to her head before going to sleep and in the morning it was still **firmly** secured.

Bed Linen

24. If a *kesem* was discovered on her sheet, blanket, pillow, and so on, she is *temei'ah*, even if it was discovered far from where she had lain.

If it was discovered on the mattress or mattress cover and the sheet remained clean, she is *tehorah* if the sheet was secured firmly to the mattress from all sides and did not shift while she slept. But if it is possible that it shifted, we are concerned that this is indeed what happened and she is *temei'ah*.

Similar laws apply if the bed was covered with two sheets and a *kesem* was discovered on the inner sheet while the outer sheet remained clean.

25. A *kesem* discovered on her bed linen is *tahor* if she slept with undergarments that were worn tightly, if they definitely did not shift and they remained clean.

Garments of Husband or Children

26. If her husband or children lay with her in bed and a *kesem* was discovered on their clothing, she is *tehorah* unless it is certain that the garment was not stained beforehand, for example, if they were wearing clothing that had just been washed. Even in such a case, she is *temei'ah* only if the *kesem* was discovered when they were still in her bed, but if it was discovered afterward she is *tehorah*.

27. Similar laws apply if the husband discovered a *kesem* on his clothing after marital relations, in one of the following two scenarios: (1) If he wiped his organ and the surrounding area thoroughly after intercourse before donning the garment. (2) If the *kesem* was discovered on an area of the garment that is clean from semen. In any of these two cases, she is *tehorah* unless it is certain that the garment was not stained beforehand and the *kesem* was discovered when he was still in her bed.

The *sefer* (Chapter Five §2) should be consulted for the law in a case where he did not wipe himself thoroughly and the *kesem* was discovered on an area that was soiled with semen.

Kesem Smaller Than a *Gris Ve'od* Discovered on Her Body

28. Many *Poskim* are of the opinion that a *kesem* discovered on a woman's body is *tamei* even if it is **smaller than a gris ve'od** if uterine blood could have reached there directly (as will be explained further). However, it is advisable to consult an expert rabbi in such a case, as he may be able to rule leniently in certain situations.

The stringency of a *kesem* discovered on the body applies when it was discovered only on the body. If it was discovered on her body **and** on her clothing, various details and conditions apply, as explained in the *sefer* (Chapter Three §§16-17).

29. If numerous *kesamim* were discovered on her body that total a *gris ve'od* when measured together, all *Poskim* agree that she is *temei'ah* even if there is no contact between the individual *kesamim* (unlike *kesamim* discovered on her garments—see §8).

Locations Where the *Kesem* Was Found

30. If a *kesem* was discovered anywhere along the entire length of the inner section of her legs—that is, the places that touch each other when she stands with her feet together—she is *temei'ah*. But if it was discovered on the front, back, or sides, she is *tehorah*, because uterine blood could not have reached these areas directly.

31. If a *kesem* was discovered on her heel, she is *temei'ah* if she sometimes sits without socks with her feet folded beneath her, unless she is certain she did not sit in this way at the time the *kesem* may have been created. If a *kesem* was

discovered on the outer section of her heel, she is *tehorah* in either case, because uterine blood could not have reached there directly.

If a *kesem* was discovered on her big toe she is *temei'ah*, but if it was discovered on one of the other toes she is *tehorah*.

If a *kesem* was discovered anywhere on the upper surface of her foot, she is *temei'ah*.

32. If a *kesem* was discovered on her fingers or on the palm of her hand (until the joint connecting the palm to the arm), she is *temei'ah*. However, she is *tehorah* if she is certain that she did not extend her hand between her legs, and we are not concerned that she did so without realizing.

33. Even the *Poskim* who rule that a *kesem* smaller than a *gris ve'od* discovered on the body is *tamei* (see §28) agree that such a *kesem* discovered on her hand is *tahor*. However, if she had previously touched her vagina—for example, if she had performed a *bedikah* or wiped herself—and had not rinsed her hands from then until the *kesem* was discovered, she is *temei'ah* if a *kesem* was discovered on her fingers, even if it was smaller than a *gris ve'od*.

34. If a *kesem* was discovered on any other area of the body, she is *tehorah* unless uterine blood could have dripped there directly.

35. If a woman performed a headstand, handstand, cartwheel, or the like, she is *temei'ah* even if a *kesem* was discovered on the upper part of her body. The *sefer* (Chapter Three §§66; 75) should be consulted for additional details concerning such cases.

36. It may be possible to rule leniently when a *kesem* was discovered on her body if she was wearing tight undergarments, provided she is certain that the stain was not created at a time when she was not wearing them (for example, while using the restroom). An expert rabbi should be consulted in such a case.[2]

Attributing *Kesamim* to Bedbugs

37. In places where bedbugs are widespread, it may be possible to attribute *kesamim* to them. Various details apply in this case, but they have not been enumerated here due to their infrequency. If the need arises, the following sources can be consulted: *Shulchan Aruch Yoreh Dei'ah* 190:29 and commentaries; *Alter Rebbe's Shulchan Aruch* ad loc.; *Piskei Dinim* (*Tzemach Tzedek*) ad loc. at length.

Attributing *Kesamim* to External Sources

Note: In the following paragraphs, whenever the terms "garment" or "clothing" are used, sheets and other bed linen are included as well.

38. If it is possible to **directly** attribute a *kesem* discovered on a garment to an external source instead of to the uterus, she is *tehorah*. However, one cannot assume that perhaps her hands (or the hands of someone who touched her) became stained from dealing with a staining entity and in turn stained her clothing, for doing so would constitute an **indirect** attribution of a *kesem* to an external source.

---

2. It appears that in order to rule leniently, it must also first be verified that her undergarments did not shift to the side, thus allowing for uterine blood to drip onto her body.

If it is **certain** that the hands that touched her clothing had been previously stained, the *kesem* can be attributed to them. Even if the hands are presently clean, we assume that they became clean because the blood wiped onto her clothing.

39. Even if it is not certain that the stained hands touched her clothing, if they belong to people who touch her frequently—for example, her children and the like—the *kesem* can be attributed to them, for we assume that they indeed touched her. But if it is certain that they did not touch her, or if they do not usually do so, the *kesem* cannot be attributed to them.

Kesem Larger Than the External Source

40. If it is certain that the *kesem* on the garment is larger than the external source with which we desire to attribute it, it cannot be attributed to that source. However, the *kesem* can be attributed to the external source if she is in doubt if it is larger or not. In any case, if the section that is larger than the external source is smaller than a *gris ve'od*, she is *tehorah*, for we combine both factors: the blood that originated from an external source and the general attribution of any blood smaller than a *gris ve'od*.

Kesem of a Different Color Than the External Source

41. If it is certain that the *kesem* is of a different color than the external source, it cannot be attributed to that source. However, if she is in doubt, she can attribute the *kesem* to the external source and she is *tehorah*. Furthermore, there is no requirement to bring the *kesem* together with the external source to a Rabbi to determine if the color is the same even if both entities are at hand.

Attributing a *Kesem* to a Wound

42. One can attribute a *kesem* to a wound on her body, even if it is not certain that the wound generally discharges blood. This is true even if the wound has been covered by a layer of skin, provided that it is possible for it to break open and discharge blood if it is scraped or the like. However, various conditions and details apply to this law, as explained in the *sefer* (Chapter Three §§51ff.)

Attributing When In Doubt

43. If it is not certain that a given entity was present from which it is possible that the *kesem* originated, the *kesem* cannot be attributed to that external source. Examples include if a woman is in doubt if she passed through a location where it is possible that blood dripped onto her, or if she is in doubt if a wound was present at the time when the *kesem* was discovered. Additional examples have been brought down by the *Poskim*, some of which have been cited in the *sefer* (ibid. §33).

Garment Worn at an Earlier Time or by Another Woman

44. The laws in the following scenarios involve various details, and since they are relatively uncommon, they are only mentioned here briefly. The laws have been explained in detail in Chapter Three of the *sefer* in the sections indicated below.

1. If a woman donned a garment which she had worn previously at a time when it was more likely for blood to be discharged and the garment had not been cleansed in the interim. Examples include a garment she had worn

during her menstrual period or during *shivah nekiyim* (§§38-42).

2. Under certain conditions, the garment can be assumed to have been stained beforehand even if it had been cleansed in the interim (§§55-57).

3. If a woman discovered a *kesem* on a garment that she had borrowed from another woman (§§43-54).

Attributing a *Kesem* Discovered on the Body

45. A *kesem* discovered only on the body cannot be attributed to a source outside of the body. However, it can be attributed to a source on her body, for example, if it is possible that it originated directly from a wound on her body. Similarly, if her hands were stained, she can presume that she touched the spot where the *kesem* was discovered and she is *tehorah* (see §§38-39 for additional details regarding the attribution of a *kesem* to stained hands).

46. The law of a *kesem* discovered both on her body and on her clothing is identical to that of a *kesem* discovered only on her clothing, and it can be attributed to whatever such a *kesem* can be attributed to (see note).[3] More details concerning this law have been explained in the *sefer* (Chapter Three §36).

Misplaced *Kesem*

47. An expert rabbi should be consulted if a woman misplaced a *kesem* and she is in doubt if it consisted of a *mar'eh*

---

3. However, if the *kesem* was discovered only on her body and on a garment that was worn close to the body, it is unclear if it can be attributed to an outside source, and an expert rabbi should be consulted.

of a *tahor* color or if it consisted of a *gris ve'od* (see the *sefer* [Chapter Three §§92-94]).

Second Exception:
Kesem Discovered on a Colored Garment[4]

48. Our Sages rendered a *kesem tamei* only if it was discovered on a white garment. However, if it was discovered on a colored garment, regardless of the color and even if it was of a light color, she is *tehorah*, even if it consisted of a *gris ve'od*.

49. She is *tehorah* even if the blood is visible despite the color of the garment.

50. The following law applies if a *kesem* was discovered on a garment that was striped, flowered, spotted or the like, and certain sections of the garment were colored and certain sections were white: If a *kesem* was discovered partially on the white section and partially on the colored section, only the portion of the *kesem* located on the white section is measured, and if it does not total a *gris ve'od*, she is *tehorah*. The portion of the *kesem* located on the colored section is not taken into account, even if it is obvious that both portions comprise a single *kesem*.

Advice of Our Sages to Wear Colored Garments

51. In light of the above, our Sages have advised that women should wear colored garments and cover their beds with colored sheets, so as to prevent them from becoming *temei'ah* due to *kesamim*. Even one who commonly discovers

---

4. Paragraphs 48–58 correspond to Chapter Four in the *sefer*.

kesamim may follow this advice. (There is no reason at all to feel that this constitutes deception or the like—see §4.)

52. However, a woman must wear white undergarments and cover her bed with a white sheet during the *shivah ne-kiyim*. A woman who discovers *kesamim* frequently should ask an expert rabbi if her condition allows for a lenient position. (Another suggestion for such a woman can be found in §58.)

Third Exception:
Kesem Discovered on a Garment That is Not *Mekabel Tum'ah*

53. Our Sages rendered a *kesem tamei* only if it was discovered on a garment that is *mekabel tum'ah*. However, if it was discovered on a garment that is not *mekabel tum'ah*, she is *tehorah*, even if it consisted of a *gris ve'od* and there was no external source with which to attribute it.

The *Poskim* disagree with regard to the law of a *kesem* discovered on a garment that is only *mekabel tum'ah mid'ra-banan*. It appears that such a case can be ruled leniently.

Tum'ah Status of Various Materials

54. Tissue is not *mekabel tum'ah*, nor is cotton that has not been woven to form thread. Accordingly, a woman is *tehorah* if she placed tissue or cotton in her undergarments to absorb moisture and a *kesem* was discovered on them.

55. Nylon is not *mekabel tum'ah*. However, a garment made from nylon or another synthetic material is *mekabel tum'ah*.

56. A piece of cloth less than 3 square *etzba'os* (equivalent to 6 sq. cm. or 2.34 sq. in.) is not *mekabel tum'ah*.

The status of the following items has been outlined in the *sefer* (Chapter Four §8): Pottery, a structure attached to the ground, glassware, and plasticware.

57. Most pads commonly used today are made from plastic materials that are not *mekabel tum'ah* (**see note**[5]). This can be determined by ripping off a small portion of the pad; if it breaks into small pieces, the pad is clearly not made from a cloth material (which would not have fallen apart).

58. In light of the above, if a woman was authorized by an expert rabbi to wear colored garments during *shivah nekiyim* due to unique circumstances (see §52), it is preferable that he advise her to use a white pad instead of colored garments. Doing so allows her to fulfill the directive to wear white garments while not becoming *temei'ah* if a *kesem* is discovered.

Kesamim Discovered in Special Circumstances[6]

59. The law of a *kesem* discovered after marital relations or after urinating is equal to that of a regular *kesem*: she is *tehorah* if it can be attributed to an external source (as explained earlier) or if it was discovered on a colored garment or on a garment that is not *mekabel tum'ah*. The law of a *kesem* discovered on the clothing of her husband after marital relations has been outlined above (§27).

---

5. However, certain companies (such as Kotex) manufacture pads that are covered with a layer made out of **100% cotton.** It is therefore important to inspect the pad (as has been described in the text) to verify that it is indeed made out of a plastic material.

6. Paragraphs 58–61 correspond to Chapter Five in the *sefer*.

60. The law of a *kesem* discovered on the day of a *veses* is equal in all its details to that of a regular *kesem*.

61. A *kesem* discovered during the first three days of the *shivah nekiyim* cannot be attributed to an external source, even with attributions that could have been applied if the *kesem* were to have been discovered during any other time. Various details concerning this law can be found in the *sefer* (Chapter Five §§4ff.).

The above is true only if there is a need to attribute the *kesem* to an external source in order to render it *tahor*. However, if the *kesem* was smaller than a *gris ve'od* or was discovered on a colored garment or on a garment that is not *mekabel tum'ah*, she is *tehorah* even if it was discovered during these days.

~⊙~

ADDENDUM

Size of *Gris*

The size of a *gris* is a matter of debate among the *Poskim*:

According to various sources, the Alter Rebbe's opinion is that a *gris* is the size of an old Russian coin known as a *pyatak*, and he would constantly carry such a coin with him to use when measuring *kesamim*. According to the calculations I have made, the diameter of this coin is 17 mm. or 0.68 in. This equals the diameter of an American dime (and of an Israeli new *shekel* coin).

pyatak   dime   1 shekel

According to other *Poskim*, however, the diameter of a *gris* is roughly 19 mm. or 0.76 in. This corresponds to the diameter of an American cent (and of a euro 2cent coin). Others give the size of 20 mm. or 0.8 in., corresponding to an American nickel (and an Israeli 10-*agurot* coin).

1 cent

nickel

2 euro cents

10 agurot

CHAPTER FIVE

MEDICAL-RELATED ISSUES

Medical Procedures[1]

Insertion of Medical Instrument Into Uterus

1. Our Sages established that any activity resulting in the opening of the uterus—whether by means of something that was released from the uterus or inserted within it—will result in a (minute) discharge of blood, and the woman is therefore *temei'ah*. This is true even if she did not notice any blood and even if she performed a *bedikah* and did not discover any blood. Accordingly, a woman in such a situation should not perform a *bedikah*, for doing so will not assist in rendering her *tehorah*.

This rule essentially applies with regard to a *mesulekes damim* as well, i.e., a pregnant, nursing or elderly woman (see Chapter Two §9).

2. In light of the above, if a woman underwent a medical procedure in which a medical instrument was inserted into the vagina, one should ascertain if the instrument was inserted into the uterus. The physician should be asked to clarify the objective of the procedure, the method in which it was performed, the type of instrument used and its diameter. A Rabbi who is also proficient in the medical aspects of these laws should then be consulted to determine if the woman is *temei'ah* as a result.

---

1. Corresponding to Chapter Seven in the *sefer*.

3. Despite the above, an expert rabbi may rule leniently under certain circumstances with regard to a *mesulekes damim*, or with regard to a woman with a *veses kavua* during the days other than the time of her *veses*.

4. An HSG entails the opening of the uterus, and a woman who undergoes such a procedure is *temei'ah* even if no blood was discovered as a result. An ultrasound, by contrast, is not inserted into the uterus, and a woman who undergoes such a procedure is *tehorah*. This is true even with regard to a transvaginal ultrasound, as it is inserted 5-7 cm. into the vagina and does not penetrate the uterus at all.

5. A speculum—used by the physician to open the vagina to enable it to be examined—does not penetrate the uterus, and a woman who undergoes such a procedure is *tehorah*. It is self-evident that procedures performed with the physician's finger do not penetrate the uterus.

Blood Discharged as the Result of a Medical Procedure

6. If blood was discharged as the result of a medical procedure, one cannot rely on a non-observant physician who claims that the blood originated from an external injury caused by the medical instrument (see §13), rather an expert rabbi should be consulted to determine the woman's status.

If possible, the woman should be examined by a *bodekes* or an observant physician or midwife proficient in the field. They can be relied upon—as per the directive of an expert rabbi—if they indeed discover an injury that justifies the discharge of blood.

7. A physician may grasp the cervix with a pair of specialized tongs to enable the insertion of a medical instrument. The rabbi should be notified if this was done, as he may be able to attribute the blood to the wound created by this procedure.

Suppositories

8. Even those suppositories inserted into the vagina by means of a syringe do not penetrate the uterus, and a woman who uses them is *tehorah*.

An important note regarding *bedikos*: The dissolving substance contained within certain suppositories is colored; accordingly, before inserting the suppository (by day), she should rinse the vagina and perform the required *bedikah* (during *shivah nekiyim* and the like).

Artificial Insemination, Contraception and Abortion

9. The issues of artificial insemination, contraception and abortion are extremely serious. They require the decision of a prominent *halachic* authority who will determine in each scenario if *halachah* requires or forbids the use of these methods, and if and how they should be performed.

Yichud When Visiting a Physician

10. If a woman must be examined or be subject to a procedure performed by a male physician, care must be taken that the prohibition of *yichud* is not transgressed. The methods by which one can avoid the problem of *yichud* when visiting a physician have been explained in Chapter Twenty (§§57-58).

Vaginal Wounds
and Blood Discharged When Urinating[2]

Vaginal Wounds

11. A woman cannot presume that blood originated from a vaginal wound, even if she is certain that one is present and it is logical to assume that the blood originated from there. Rather, an expert rabbi must be consulted, as it is not easy to render blood discharged from the vagina as *tahor*. A woman certainly cannot rely on her colleagues who relate that they were found in similar situations and were ruled to be *tahor*, as even a seemingly minor change in the case at hand can result in an entirely different ruling.

12. Even it has been ascertained that blood originated from a vaginal wound, it goes without saying that the wound will eventually heal. One must ask an expert rabbi and/or *bodekes* to determine the length of time one can assume that the wound is still present and if it is necessary to undergo an additional examination to establish that it is still there. Similarly, one must confirm if it is logical to assume that the amount of blood that has been discharged has originated from the wound.

Physician's Credibility

13. A non-observant physician cannot be relied upon with regard to any issue related to *tum'ah* or *taharah*, be it regarding the existence of a wound or regarding its nature (see the *sefer* [Chapter Eight fn. 1]). Accordingly, a woman who believes that she has a vaginal wound must be examined

---

2. Corresponding to Chapter Eight in the *sefer*.

by an **observant** physician or specialist. If this is not possible, an expert rabbi should be consulted to determine if and how the physician can be relied upon (particularly with regard to the discharge of blood that was not accompanied by a *hargashah*).

14. Whatever the case, one cannot suffice with the physician's report but must convey the details of the case and the physician's opinion to an expert rabbi to determine the law.

15. One should be equipped with as many details as possible before consulting the Rabbi:

(1) Was an irregular pain felt at the time the blood was discovered? (2) What caused her to assume that she has a wound? (3) Where does she feel the wound? (4) Does she suffer from a vaginal infection or the like? (5) Has blood been discovered during the time when she was a *mesulekes damim* (see Chapter Two §9) or during the "certain days" (see Chapter Fifteen §6) as well? (6) Was the blood discovered through a *bedikah*, through a *kinuach*, during marital relations, or merely in the form of a *kesem* on her clothing? (7) Was blood discovered on the cloth with which the husband wiped himself following marital relations?

Each of the above details may play a role in determining the law.

Blood Discharged When Urinating

16. If a woman discovered blood when urinating, she cannot assume that she is *tehorah* or rely on her friends who state that rabbis rule leniently in such cases. Even if an observant physician diagnosed her with a urinary tract infec-

tion, she cannot act leniently without consulting an expert rabbi.

17. It is important to take note of the following details and convey them to the rabbi:

(1) Was the blood discovered in a vessel within which she urinated, or was it discovered in a toilet (that is connected to the ground)? (2) Did she feel pain when urinating? (3) Did she wipe herself and discover blood on the tissue as well? (4) Did she discover blood in her urine, or was the urine itself red? (It is sometimes possible to attribute the color of the urine to the consumption of certain foods.) (5) Does she have the status of a *mesulekes damim*?

It is important to take note of each of the above details, as they may play a significant role in determining the law.

18. The above deals with a woman who **discovered** blood in her urine or on the tissue used to wipe herself. However, it is preferable not to look at the tissue used to wipe the vaginal area, as doing so may result in unnecessary complications; rather she should dispose of it without glancing at it at all. The above is true even during *shivah nekiyim*; there is no need to inspect the tissue used to wipe after urination.[3] If,

---

3. What has been stated in the text holds true with regard to wiping oneself after urinating; however, one must look at the tissues used to wipe the rectal area to determine its cleanliness. It is forbidden to recite blessings, prayers and other words that contain sanctity when the rectal area is unclean, and doing so is tantamount to reciting G-d's name in vain. To quote the Alter Rebbe in his *Shulchan Aruch*, based on previous *Poskim*: "One must be exceedingly careful to wipe oneself properly, for [it is forbidden to recite words containing sanctity if even] a minute amount of excrement [is found] in its place...If possible, it is preferable to

however, she did glance at the tissue and noticed a *mar'eh*, she may not ignore it and dispose of it, rather she must bring it to an expert rabbi to determine the law.

rinse [the rectal area] with water" (*Orach Chaim* §3:25). "If excrement is found in its place, i.e., the opening of the rectum, it is forbidden to recite the *Shema* prayer according to all opinions even if it is covered..." (ibid. §76:6. See there for more on this topic, as well as the commentaries to *Shulchan Aruch* ibid. §76:5).

CHAPTER SIX[1]

HARCHAKOS

Fundamentals of *Harchakos*

1. The husband and wife must adhere to a certain method of conduct when she is *temei'ah* until she immerses in a *mikvah*, which involves various types of separations, referred to by the *Poskim* as *harchakos* (lit., "distances").

All the *harchakos* must be kept whether the woman is *temei'ah* as a result of a menstrual period, a *bedikah*, a *kesem*, or the like.

2. *Harchakos* must be kept even if she is in doubt whether or not she is *tehorah*. Examples include if a woman found a *mar'eh* or a *kesem* and a Rabbi must be consulted to determine if it is *tahor*, or if she immersed in the *mikvah* and a doubt arose with regard to the laws of *chatzitzah*. In such cases, all the *harchakos* are to be kept until her *taharah* is verified.

3. One may act stringently with regard to *harchakos*. To quote the *Poskim*, "One should act stringently as much as they can, and may they be blessed for doing so"; "Whoever increases in *harchakos* is praiseworthy." However, this only applies with regard to those stringencies mentioned by the *Poskim* (as will be enumerated in this chapter); one may not devise stringencies of their own.

4. All *harchakos* are binding on both the husband and

---

1. Corresponding to Chapter Fourteen in the *sefer*.

the wife, with the exception of those few instances where *halachah* clearly states that a specific *harchakah* applies to only one of the two. As such, even in those places in this chapter where the wording used is "She may not..." "He may not..." or the like, this does not imply that the given laws apply just to the husband or just to the wife; rather they apply to both spouses equally.

5. It is an accepted *halachah* with no dissenting opinion that one may not act leniently with regard to *harchakos* due to embarrassment, so that others will not realize that she is *temei'ah*. No leniency applies even if the couple feels that it is important to hide her status for reasons of modesty.

It is self understood that *harchakos* are not for one to judge with one's own understanding. Even if a couple believes that certain actions do not arouse intimate feelings, they are required to act as outlined in *Shulchan Aruch*, and G-d forbid to act in a lenient manner!

Frivolity

6. The *Shulchan Aruch* states as follows:[2] "One may not act in a frivolous or lighthearted manner with his wife [when she is *temei'ah*], **even with words,** so as not to initiate [the performing of] a transgression."

"*Words*" refers to affectionate expressions and to conversation that may arouse intimate feelings. However, a couple may converse regarding household issues and other routine matters.

6*. The prohibition to act in a frivolous manner does not

---

2. *Yoreh Dei'ah* (§195:1).

imply that they should walk about with somber expressions, G-d forbid. Rather, their conduct and conversations should reflect a more meaningful nature, as opposed to joking that borders on frivolity and lack of restrictions. (See the *sefer* [Chapter Fourteen fns. 10-11]).

Forbidden Touch

7. They may not touch each other in any manner, even by means of an extremely long object. In addition to touching her body, he may not touch the clothing she is wearing, even if they are long and extend far from her body.

A blanket has the same law as clothing, and he may not touch it if it is covering her. Accordingly, if he must place a child on her bed, he should not place him on the blanket but rather on the sheet covering the mattress (see §13).

8. Additionally, their clothing may not touch. One must therefore take caution when sitting together in a permitted fashion (see §§41ff.) that their clothing do not touch. For this reason, they should be careful not to come too close to each other when walking together or passing by one another.

However, he may touch her clothing when she is not wearing them. He may even handle a garment or sheet stained with *nidah* blood.

9. Blowing constitutes touching as well, albeit not with his body but with his breath. He may therefore not blow off lint from her clothing or cool her off by waving a hand fan.

Passing and Throwing

10. They may not pass or throw an object to each other in any manner, even one that is extremely long. One spouse

may not push a stroller to the other, rather he should let go of it and the other can then take it.

11. They may not pass a child to or take one from the other. A woman who is *temei'ah* may therefore not serve as a *kvater* together with her husband. (The *kvater* refers to the woman who brings in a child for his *bris*, and her husband accepts the child from her arms.) If they wish to accept the honor nonetheless, she should pass the child to a third person who will pass him in turn to her husband. Alternatively, she should place the child on a chair or table and her husband should take him from there.

Touching an Object She Is Holding

12. They may not touch an object that is in the hands of the other. Accordingly, the husband may not feed a baby when he is being held by the wife, as well as placing a pacifier in his mouth, clothing him, and the like. He may certainly not hug him, kiss him or play with him when he is in her hands.

One can act leniently if there is a great need, for example, if medicine must be given to the child and no one else is present to hold him. In such an instance, they should be careful not to come near one another more than necessary.

13. He may touch the bench upon which she is sitting or the bed upon which she is lying, provided that it does not move as a result. He may therefore place a child or an object on the bed upon which she is lying. It is preferable to do so in an unusual manner, such as by placing the child or object slightly far from her, using the left hand, or the like. However, he may not place anything on the blanket if it is covering her, because a blanket has the same law as her clothing (see §7).

Holding an Object Together

14. They may not hold or lift an object together, whether heavy or light, and even if others are lifting the object as well. They may also not push or pull an object together.

15. Accordingly, they may not push a stroller together or lift a child together. Additionally, they may not each hold the hand of a child who **cannot** walk properly on his own and help him walk.

However, they may each hold the hand of a child who **can** walk properly on his own and walk with him (provided they are careful not to pull or lift the child together). The reason is because in such a case, they are not moving the child's body together; rather they are each moving another hand while the child walks on his own.

16. He may not remove something from or put something into a basket, purse, or bag that she is holding.

Avoiding Touch

17. When they are doing activities that involve close proximity, they should be careful not to touch each other's body or clothing, even if the activity itself is permitted. Examples include holding an umbrella or lamp for the other and the like.

It is therefore preferable to avoid reading together from the same book. If there is an important reason to read together (for example, to say *Veyiten Lecha* together on *motza'ei Shabbos* as is customary), they should take care to keep a distance so that they will not touch each other.

Igniting a Flame

18. He may not ignite a candle, cigarette or the like from a candle, match, or lighter that she is holding. He may also not warm his hands by a flame she is holding. However, she may hold the *Havdalah* candle, and when he brings his hands close to the flame, he should take care not to touch her.

Smelling Perfume

19. He may not smell perfume found on her body, hands, or clothing. However, he may smell her perfume in its container. Preferably, she should not apply more perfume than necessary when she is *temei'ah*.

He should not smell the spices during *Havdalah* while she is holding them.

Toiletries

20. A husband and wife may use the same soap, shampoo, tube of toothpaste and the like.

Looking at Covered Areas of Her Body

21. He may not look at those areas of her body that must be covered due to reasons of modesty, including even the heel of her foot. He may not look at these areas whether directly, through a mirror, or through a thin garment by which her body can be seen.

The areas that must be covered are as follows: (1) Her arms until past her elbows. In places where women are accustomed to cover their arms from the elbow until the palm of the hand, he may not look at this area as well. (2) From the collarbone and downward, until (and including) the bottom of her feet. (3) Her hair.

22. The wife must take care not to cause her husband to see the covered areas of her body. She should not walk around the house without socks, and she should be careful to nurse in a modest fashion. She should also ensure that all her hair remains covered. Doing so is of paramount importance even when she is *tehorah*; but even more care should be taken when she is *temei'ah*.

23. He may look at those areas of her body that are allowed to remain uncovered; however, he should abstain from gazing at her in a manner that may lead to a transgression, G-d forbid.

23*. It is important to disprove a number of errors that have become prevalent by certain observant Jews:

1. Certain individuals believe that the definition of the areas of the body that are required to be covered can be decided based on the practice of current society. Since most people do not cover their feet, they believe that one can act leniently in this regard, G-d forbid. They further believe that a married woman may uncover a portion of her hair for this reason. However, this is a grave mistake!

The Tzemach Tzedek, after demonstrating that a married woman may not expose even a small portion of her hair, writes as follows:[3] "The hair of a [married] woman is *ervah* [i. e., it has the status of an area that must be covered] in every location, and no 'custom' can be applied to the contrary. Can one possibly presume that if women were to be accustomed to walk around

---

3. Novellae on Mishnah (*Berachos* Ch. 3 §4).

in the summer with an exposed *shok* [the area of the leg from the knees and below—the area of the leg from the knees and above is called *yerech*, thigh], it would no longer retain the status of *ervah*, for this has become the practice? Such a thing may never be said! No practice can offset that what is considered *ervah*. The prophet Yeshayahu (3:16) bewails the daughters of Jerusalem who were accustomed to walk with outstretched necks. [Why was he lamenting?] Wasn't this their custom?! We must say that this 'custom' is the likes of which the Shaloh writes that *minhag* [lit., custom] shares the same Hebrew letters as *gehinom* (purgatory). The same [is true regarding hair.] Since our Sages stated that the hair of a [married] woman is *ervah* and they brought proof from Scripture, it cannot be rejected due to a practice to the contrary."

2. Some individuals further believe that the laws of modesty only apply when in the presence of others, but no restrictions apply when she is in her house.

This is also a big mistake! The Alter Rebbe states clearly in his *Shulchan Aruch* (2:1), based on the words of earlier *Poskim*: "The Torah praised the attribute of modesty in many places, and the Sages have directed every person to act modestly in his every conduct, and not to act immodestly even when alone and not in the presence of others.... Even when one is alone at night in a closed room, he must act modestly and with embarrassment before the Holy One Blessed Be He.... He should therefore not expose even a small area of his body that is usually covered...." (See there for additional details.)

Listening to Her Singing

24. A husband may not hear the singing of his wife when she is *temei'ah*. She should therefore not sing the Shabbos *zemiros* audibly. He may not hear his wife sing even if others are singing as well.

She may play music for her own pleasure, but not for the pleasure of her husband.

25. A leniency can be granted under challenging circumstances such as the following: If a child is crying hysterically and the only way to calm him is by singing to him, she may do so even if the husband cannot avoid listening to the singing.

Separate Beds

26. The prohibition to sleep in the same bed is among the most stringent *harchakos*. They may not sleep in the same bed even if it is extremely wide and they are each sleeping on opposite sides, and even if they are both dressed and using separate mattresses, sheets and blankets.

27. Even if they are sleeping on separate beds, the two beds may not touch each other. This is true even if the beds are not positioned lengthwise one near the other, but rather the foot of one bed is touching the head of the other, for if the beds are touching in any manner, they are considered as one bed in this regard.

28. The beds are considered as one even if the beds themselves are not touching each other but merely share a single headboard. In such a case, one must not only move the beds away from each other but also disconnect one of them from the headboard. There are those that believe that separating

the beds is sufficient; however, this is incorrect, as the beds also may not share a single headboard. In fact, certain *Poskim* maintain that they may not both be connected to the wall as well.

Distance Between Beds

29. If the beds are positioned parallel to each other, they must be positioned far enough from each other to preclude the possibility that contact will be made unintentionally, whether between the beds themselves or between the blankets and the like.

Some authorities are of the opinion that a large distance is required between the beds, while others allow the distance of a minimum of an *amah* (a *halachic* measurement equivalent to approximately 0.5 m. or 19 in.) The best option is to position the two beds on either side of the bedroom. Some opinions maintain that a night table or the like should be placed between the beds to serve as a division. In challenging situations, one should make an effort to separate the beds with an area the size of the width of a person.

30. If the foot of one bed is positioned against the head of the other, a small separation is sufficient, provided the two beds do not touch. However, if one bed is positioned at a right angle to the other, the distance outlined in the previous paragraph is required.

30*. The accepted conduct among G-d-fearing Jews is to have a separate bed for each spouse (divided with a night table or something similar), even when she is *tehorah*.[4]

---

4. *Igros Kodesh* of the Lubavitcher Rebbe, vol. 31, p. 334.

Sitting or Lying on the Bed of a Spouse

31. The husband may not sit on his wife's bed, even when not in her presence, and he certainly may not lie on it. She, however, is only forbidden from lying on his bed in his presence, and she may sit on his bed even in his presence.

The above applies only to a bed; however, he may sit on her chair even in her presence.

32. He may not lie on her bed even after she left to go to the *mikvah*, as long as she has not actually immersed herself.

33. The above only applies to a bed that is used exclusively by one of the spouses; however, they may sleep (separately) on a bed that is used randomly by either spouse. Examples include a sofa or bed in the guestroom or a child's bed that is sometimes used by a parent.

34. The primary factor used to determine to whom the bed is associated is the use of the bed at night. Therefore, the husband may not lie on a bed that is used by his wife at night, even if it is also used by the children during the day. Under challenging circumstances, an expert rabbi should be consulted to determine if there is room to rule leniently when other factors are present.

35. He may sit on a sofa that serves as an armchair by day and as her bed at night, because it is used by the entire family by day and not exclusively by her. However, he may not lie on it.

36. The following laws apply in this scenario: A lower bed of a high riser is withdrawn at night from beneath the higher bed and returned underneath during the day. During

the day, the mattress of the lower bed is placed upon the mattress of the higher bed, and the higher bed is used exclusively by the wife during the day. In such a case, the husband may not sleep on that mattress at night (even though it is removed from the higher bed and placed on the lower bed). He may only use the mattress if it is placed on the side during the day and not on the higher bed. However, he may use the mattress if the higher bed is used during the day by other members of the family as well.

37. He may sit on her bed if she is out of town. However, he may not lie on her bed unless she is absent for a number of days. There is a basis to act stringently in the latter scenario as well.

38. The following laws apply if they decide to exchange beds, and it was decided that her bed will no longer be used exclusively by her: If the decision took place when she was *temei'ah*, he may nonetheless not use her bed. However, she may lie on his bed if it was decided that it will no longer be used exclusively by him. By contrast, if the decision took place when she was *tehorah*, and he slept on her bed at least once during that time, he may continue to use it even when she becomes *temei'ah*.

Exchanging the mattresses is insufficient; they must exchange the beds themselves as well.

39. Accessories of the bed, such as sheets, pillows, blankets and the like, share the same laws as the bed itself. He may therefore not use such items that are used exclusively by her, and she may not lie on such items that are used exclusively by him when in his presence. However, they may

use these items if they are not used exclusively by the other spouse (but rather are stored by day in a designated container, and each spouse takes the desired items when going to sleep). Similarly, they may use any sheet they desire if they are often exchanged when washed or the like.

Wearing her Clothing

40. The husband may not wear a garment used exclusively by the wife (even in a case where the prohibition against wearing clothing of the opposite gender does not apply), such as a scarf used exclusively by her and the like. However, he may wear a garment that was initially designated to be used by both of them.

Sitting on a Single Bench

41. They may not sit together on a bench or the like which **might** move while they are sitting on it. This is true even if the bench is long and they are sitting on two opposite sides. However, they may sit together if the bench is not likely to move, either due to its weight or because it is secured to the wall or floor. In such a case, they should take care not to sit too close to each other, so as to prevent touching each other by mistake with their clothing or the like.

Some opinions rule leniently with regard to Sephardim; in actual practice, however, the custom is for them to act stringently.

See note regarding the laws that apply to sitting together on a mat.[5]

---

5. A certain noteworthy authority has stated that they may not sit together on a new mat because it may move as a result. However, it ap-

42. They may not sit together on a soft sofa or seat of a car in which the body movements of one can be felt by the other. They may only sit on such a seat if they are situated far from each other and are certain that it is impossible for their movements to be felt by the other.

43. If there is a need for them to sit on the same seat, they may do so if another individual is sitting between them. He must sit between them and not merely beside them. One should act stringently and not rely on a separation of a large item or baby unless there is a great need and no other option is present.

44. They should not sit next to each other on a bus or the like unless the benches are long and they are sitting far from each other. This is true even if they take care that their clothing should not touch each other, for it is almost impossible to avoid such contact, especially when the bus makes an unexpected sharp turn or sudden brake.

Traveling for Pleasure

45. They may not travel together if the objective of the trip is not to reach a certain destination but rather to enjoy the actual excursion. Examples include traveling through gardens or orchards in order to enjoy the scenery or visiting a safari in which animals are viewed while driving. They may not go on such a trip even if other tourists are sitting between the husband and wife and even if they are sitting on separate

------

pears that this is only true with regard to a new mat, because it is rigid and doesn't lie securely on the ground. A used mat (or rug), by contrast, has become soft and lies securely on the ground, and they may therefore sit on it together.

benches. An expert rabbi should be consulted if there is an extremely great need for them to go on such a trip.

46. They may travel together if the objective of the trip is to reach a certain destination, even if that destination is one of enjoyment. Such a trip is not classified as a trip which is a source of enjoyment in itself, and it shares the laws of any other trip as outlined in the previous paragraphs (§§42-44).

47. They may travel together if the husband is traveling for personal needs and his wife is joining him for pleasure. However, they should act stringently in the opposite scenario—if the husband is traveling for pleasure, even if the wife is traveling for another purpose.

48. The law regarding traveling together by boat depends on the nature of the voyage—if the purpose of the trip is for pleasure or to reach a certain destination. There are those that rule stringently in any case if the boat is small and sways as a result of their weight.

Taking a Walk

49. One may take a walk with his wife when she is *te-mei'ah*; however, there is room to act stringently.

Harchakah Requirements During a Meal

Introduction

50. Our Sages were aware that certain circumstances can lead to intimate feelings between the spouses, and they established specific guidelines to serve as reminders so that no transgression will be committed. The guidelines and restrictions of our Sages are the only defining factors in this regard;

one cannot add new types of restrictions or new situations which one might feel require methods of restriction. One can certainly not attempt to undermine, G-d forbid, the decision of our Sages that certain situations require restrictive measures.

Employing a *Heker*

51. When the husband and wife eat or drink together, they must employ a *heker*—a "reminder," as will be elaborated upon in the following paragraphs. This is true even if they are merely eating a short meal and are eating from separate plates.

A *heker* is a difference in conduct that will remind them not to develop intimate feelings at this time. Consequently, a method of conduct that is performed during the days of *taharah* as well cannot serve as a *heker* (see, for example, §§54; 59-60).

It is preferable to employ a *heker* even if they are not eating from plates on a table but rather are each holding the food in their hand (e.g., corn on the cob, falafel pita). However, there is no need to employ a *heker* if they are not eating at a table (for example, if they are eating on benches or on the grass, unless they are using a picnic blanket as a "table").

General Laws of Employing a *Heker*

52. The *hekerim* that can be employed are as follows:

1. An item that is not usually found on the table can be placed there. The item must be somewhat high so that it will catch the eye, and it must be placed between the husband and wife (and not just anywhere on the table).

2. Each spouse can eat on a separate tablecloth.

3. If, when she is *tehorah*, they are accustomed to eat from the same plate, they can each eat from a separate plate. However, a separate plate can only serve as a *heker* if they are eating the same type of food.

4. If, when she is *tehorah*, they are accustomed to eat from the same loaf of bread, they can each eat from a separate loaf.

5. Certain authorities state that if she has a permanent place at the table, she can change her place when she is *temei'ah*. However, it is customary not to rely on a change of place as a *heker*.

53. A *heker* is only required if both spouses are eating; if one is eating and the other is just sitting at the table, no *heker* is necessary.

Elaboration on the Laws of *Hekerim*

Definition of an Item Not Usually Found on the Table

54. An item that is placed between the husband and wife to serve as a *heker* must be an item that is not usually found on the table. The objects that can be utilized therefore vary from house to house, depending on the habit in the home. An ashtray, for example, can be used as a *heker* (if it is somewhat high, see §58). However, if it is commonly found on the table, it cannot serve as a *heker*, unless it is usually removed while eating and now it is left there.

55. An item that is commonly found on the table can

serve as a *heker* if it has a permanent place on the table and they now change its place and position it between the husband and wife. For example, if a vase is usually located at the center of the table, it can be moved and placed between the husband and wife.

Food and Drink as a *Heker*

56. A bottle which is not being used or a complete loaf of bread which is not being partaken of can serve as a *heker*. Accordingly, on Shabbos and Yom Tov, some couples place the second **complete** loaf of *challah* that was used for *lechem mishneh* between them to serve as a *heker*, so as to prevent unwanted attention from the other participants. The loaf can serve as a *heker* if it will not be partaken of during the meal.

57. **A reminder:** The desire to prevent unwanted attention cannot serve as a reason to desist from employing a *heker*. A method must be found to employ a *heker* in every situation!

Height of the *Heker*

58. The *heker* must be somewhat high (in comparison to the other objects on the table) so that they will regularly take note of it; however, it does not need to be higher than a loaf of bread. Accordingly, a ring or key cannot serve as a *heker*.

Heker of a Separate Tablecloth

59. Any method by which they are not eating on the same tablecloth can serve as a *heker*:

1. They can eat on separate tablecloths.

2. One spouse can eat on the tablecloth as usual, and

the other can fold over the tablecloth and eat on the table itself.

3. One spouse can eat on the tablecloth as usual, and the other can fold over the tablecloth and eat on the folded section of the tablecloth, giving the clear impression as if he or she is eating on two tablecloths.

4. One spouse can eat on the tablecloth as usual, and the other can add an additional tablecloth under the plate. A napkin or place mat can be used as well, provided it is clearly visible.

5. Alternatively, the second spouse can place an additional, wider plate underneath his or her plate. However, this method can only be used if they are not accustomed to eat in this manner when she is *tehorah*.

60. Eating on separate tablecloths can only serve as a *heker* if they are not accustomed to eat in this manner when she is *tehorah*. However, if they are accustomed to eat on separate place mats or the like, doing so when she is *temei'ah* as well cannot serve as a *heker*.

If Others Are Present

61. A *heker* must be employed even if there are others—either guests or family members—eating at the table as well. However, some Sephardim rely on the ruling of certain *Poskim* and act leniently if others are present.

62. *Lechatchilah*, a *heker* is required even if another individual is sitting between the husband and wife. However, they may act leniently if they are in a situation where it is difficult to employ a *heker*, provided they are also sitting far

enough from each other that one cannot reach the plate of the other. They may also act leniently if they are accustomed never to take from the other's plate, provided they are sitting far from each other as described above.

This leniency can only be granted if the husband and wife are separated by adults; a separation of young children is insufficient.

63. There are those that are of the opinion that a *heker* is insufficient if the husband and wife are eating at a second table, separate from the rest of the family. The rationale is that this method of eating together is prone to a heightened measure of intimate feelings. However, the Tzemach Tzedek writes that one who acts leniently in this regard has not acted inappropriately.

Eating From the Same Plate

64. Employing a *heker* allows the husband and wife to eat together from **separate** plates; they may not eat from the **same plate** even if a *heker* has been employed. This is true even if they are careful to alternate (i.e., that each spouse continues eating only after the other has finished).

65. Accordingly, if a serving plate is brought to the table, one spouse must first take the desired amount of food and put it on his plate, and only then may the other eat directly from the serving plate. They may not both eat directly from the serving plate, as doing so constitutes eating from the same plate.

66. Common examples of the above include a bowl, plate or bag of salad, pickles, fruit, nuts, cookies, bread, or sugar cubes. When such items are brought to the table, they may

not both eat directly from the plate, rather they should place the food onto their individual plates and only then partake of it. When they finish the food on the plate, they may take once more from the serving plate in the above manner, because they are not eating **directly** from that plate but are creating an interruption by placing the food on their individual plates.

67. There are those that are of the opinion that if the item is large and is commonly eaten by holding it in one's hand and eating it gradually (such as a large piece of cake or fruit), merely holding it in the hand constitutes a sufficient interruption.

68. They may not eat from the same plate even if there are others that are eating from the plate as well.

Spreads

69. They may use the same tub of margarine, butter, or any other spread, because they are not eating directly from the tub but are first spreading it on their individual pieces of bread. Certain authorities maintain that doing so can only constitute an interruption if the bread is placed on the table while spreading.

69*. Even if they take care not to eat from the same plate, a *heker* is still required; otherwise, they may not eat at the same table in any event.

Eating or Drinking Her Leftovers

70. Even if a *heker* has been employed and they take care not to eat from the same plate, if the wife left over some of

her food or drink, the husband may not partake of the leftovers. (Under certain circumstances this is allowed, as will be elaborated upon in the following paragraphs.) However, the wife may partake of the husband's leftover food or drink (provided it is his **leftovers,** meaning that he has **finished** eating or drinking, as otherwise the prohibition of eating from the same plate would apply).

For the details of what is classified as leftover food and drink, see below (§§80ff).

General Laws of When It Is Permissible to Eat From Her Leftovers

71. The husband may partake of his wife's leftover food or drink in any one of the following circumstances:

1. If the wife is not present.

2. If the food or drink has been transferred to another plate, bowl, or cup.

3. If another individual has partaken of the food or drink after the wife and before the husband.

Elaboration on the Above-Mentioned Leniencies

72. **First leniency:** The husband may eat his wife's leftovers if she is not present in the room; however, merely turning her head in another direction is insufficient.

The husband may ask her to leave the room to enable him to partake of the leftovers.

73. The *Poskim* disagree if he may continue partaking of her leftovers if he began when she was not present and she

then entered the room. The preferred conduct in such a case is to employ one of the explicitly permissible methods stated above; however, if this is not possible, one can rely on the lenient opinions and continue eating or drinking. However, if he stopped eating or drinking after she entered the room, he may not continue once again. Needless to say, he may not partake of her leftovers if she entered the room before he began doing so.

74. **Second leniency:** One may transfer the leftovers to another plate or cup to enable him to partake of them, and he may then return them back to the original vessel if he so desires.

75. If she drank from a bottle, he may drink the leftover contents if they have been transferred to another vessel. This is true despite the fact that it is common to empty a bottle into another vessel, and doing so does not constitute a noticeable change of conduct.

76. Transferring leftovers is only effective if the food items being considered are commonly placed in a vessel. But if they are not commonly placed in a vessel, such as a slice of bread, piece of cake, or the like, he may not continue eating them even if he first puts them onto a plate or bowl.

77. **Third leniency:** The husband may partake of her leftovers if another individual partook of even a very small portion in between.

This leniency only applies if the individual partook of the food after the wife and before the husband; if he partook of it **before** the wife, the husband may not eat what she left over.

78. He may not drink from what she left over even if he first adds to the cup.

If she finished the entire cup, he is not required to rinse it out before using it; however, it is praiseworthy to do so.

79. He may not partake of her leftovers in her presence even if she had eaten or drunk when not in his presence. However, this only applies if he was aware that these were her leftovers; if he was unaware of the fact, she is not required to inform him.

If he was aware that these were her leftovers but he was unaware that she became *temei'ah*, she must inform him of her status. Furthermore, if he began partaking of her leftovers and then recalled that she was *temei'ah*, he must stop and may not continue.

Classification of Leftovers

80. The prohibition against partaking of her leftovers only applies to food and drink; however, he may use her leftover soap, toothpaste, and the like.

81. He may partake of a dish of which she merely tasted to determine if it was spiced properly or the like. However, if she actually ate or drank from the dish, he may not partake of the leftovers, even if she only ate a very small amount.

82. If she ate a portion of a dish which consisted of a single item of food or of numerous items which were combined together (as in a salad, vegetable soup, or the like), the rest is classified as her leftovers. However, the authorities disagree with regard to a dish which consists of a number of **separate items** (as in two pieces of meat, fish, fruit, or the like), one of which she partook and the rest were left over. As has been explained earlier (see §3), with re-

gard to *harchakos*, one can act stringently when in doubt.

83. If she cut a slice of bread or cake, the rest is not classified as her leftovers, because it was not initially intended to be eaten entirely by one individual. However, if she ate a portion of an item which was intended to be eaten entirely by one individual (such as a roll or cookie), the rest is classified as her leftovers.

84. Accordingly, if she took some sugar from a bowl or if she used part of a spread (such as butter, margarine, and the like), the rest is not classified as her leftovers, because it was not initially intended to be consumed entirely by her. Similarly, if she poured a glass from a bottle which was intended to be used by all those present, her husband may drink from the bottle as well. Conversely, if she left over some of the contents of a small bottle that is normally intended for one person, or if she left over part of a cup of cream or yogurt, the husband may not eat the rest.

85. If she drank from the bottle itself, the rest is classified as her leftovers even if it was not intended to be used just by her. He must therefore pour from the bottle into a cup and only then may he drink.

86. After she immersed in the *mikvah* and became *tehorah*, he may partake of food or drink that she had left over when she was still *temei'ah*.

87. Even when there is no issue of partaking of her leftovers, care must be taken not to eat from the same plate. They must also ensure that a *heker* is employed, as has been explained earlier.

Restricted Activities

88. A woman may perform most standard housework activities in the presence of her husband, such as setting the table and preparing food. However, restrictions apply to the following activities when they are done in the presence of the other spouse:

1. Pouring a drink (or preparing food on a plate) and placing it on the table.

2. Making the other spouse's bed.

3. Preparing water for washing.

4. The husband may also not send a beverage to his wife.

The details and conditions that apply to each one of these activities will be elaborated upon in the subsequent paragraphs.

Serving Food or Drink

89. Placing food or drink before each other must be done in an unusual manner (a *shinuy*), such as using the left hand if one is right-handed (or the right hand if one is left-handed). Alternatively, the food or drink can be placed in an unusual location, such as on a chair instead of on the table, or it can be placed on the table at a small distance from the other spouse, requiring it to be brought closer before partaking of it.

90. No *shinuy* is required if the other spouse turns away so that he or she will not see the food being placed, even if the spouse is aware that this is being done.

91. A *shinuy* is required when serving any type of food or

drink except for water (which *halachah* views as possessing less significance in this regard). Additionally, after reciting *Hamotzi*, the husband may place a slice of *challah* before her.

92. All the above applies whether the food or drink is consumed immediately or a while later.

Preparing Without Placing or Placing Without Preparing

93. A *shinuy* must be performed when placing the food or drink before the other spouse even if the pouring of the drink (or preparing of the food on the plate) was not viewed by the spouse or was done by another.

94. One spouse may observe the other spouse prepare food or pour a beverage into his or her plate or cup, as long as the placing on the table is done with a *shinuy*. However, it is proper to act stringently if an activity is required to prepare the beverage for consumption, such as mixing water with a concentrated juice, preparing tea or coffee, or adding sugar. Even in such a case, one may prepare the beverage for the other if the final preparation (such as adding sugar) is left for the other to perform.

95. One may not pour a beverage into a cup that is in front of the other spouse, as doing so constitutes pouring and placing simultaneously. Similarly, one may not put food onto a plate that is in front of the other spouse; rather, one should remove the plate from in front of the other, put the food onto it, and replace it with a *shinuy*.

96. A doubt exists whether one may pour into a cup that is in front of the other spouse with a *shinuy*, such as with the left hand. It is proper to act stringently in this regard.

Placing a Serving Plate on the Table

97. A *shinuy* is only required if the food or drink being served is intended exclusively for the husband or wife; however, no *shinuy* is required when placing a serving plate on the table or a pitcher that is intended for all those present, even if the other spouse will also partake of it.

98. One may not serve food from a serving plate onto the plate of the other spouse while the plate is still in front of the other, as doing so constitutes both preparing and placing, as explained earlier (§95). Instead, one must remove the plate before serving the food and then return it with a *shinuy*.

99. One may pour a beverage into a number of cups for the whole family, including the other spouse (and then each person will take a cup for himself), because the prohibition of serving food or drink applies only when done exclusively for the other spouse.

100. However, if one of the cups is intended exclusively for the other spouse, one may not pour into it even if he or she will pour into additional cups as well.

101. In the event that food or drink has already been served in a forbidden manner, it may be partaken of and there is no need for it to be removed and served a second time correctly.

Sending a Beverage to One's Wife

102. The husband may not send a glass of wine or other significant beverage (which is commonly served to guests) to his wife. However, he may send her any type of food, and the wife may send to her husband any type of beverage as well.

103. The above applies even if the beverage was poured by another individual, and even if it was not done in her presence (in another room or the like); nonetheless, the husband may not send it to her. Furthermore, the prohibition is in effect even if a *shinuy* is performed and even if she will transfer the beverage to another glass.

104. Accordingly, when the husband recites *Kiddush* and desires to give some wine to his wife to drink, he should place the *becher* in the center of the table or at his place. She should then take it on her own, without him telling her to do so.

However, he may send the *becher* to the entire family, including his wife, provided they drink before her. He may also pour the wine into a number of cups for the entire family without designating a specific cup for her, and each person will then take a cup and drink.

105. Even in the event that the husband has already sent a beverage to his wife, she may not drink from it.

Giving Presents

106. One should refrain from giving gifts to one's wife when she is *temei'ah*. If for whatever reason she is expecting a gift at this time, he should tell her that he will buy her a present shortly or the like if doing so will not cause her to take offense. An expert rabbi should be consulted if it appears that this will not be sufficient.

Certain authorities have ruled that it depends on the nature of the gift and if it will bring about intimate feelings or not.

107. One may buy flowers for Shabbos, as doing so in-

volves honoring Shabbos. One may also buy a gift for the whole family including his wife.

108. The wife may give gifts to her husband in any case.

Making a Spouse's Bed

109. One spouse may not make the bed of the other in his or her presence. However, it is permitted if the other is not present, or if the other spouse turns away so as not to see the bed being made, even if he or she is in the room and is aware that this is being done. Certain authorities rule stringently in the latter case.

110. "Making the bed" refers to the preparation of the bed for sleeping purposes (and not to the making of the bed in the morning). The Sages ascertained that such an action can arouse intimate feelings, and doing so is therefore forbidden even if done a long time before going to sleep.

111. The prohibition is limited to the preparing of the sheets and blankets; preparing the mattress and pillow is permitted, because doing so is viewed as a task and not as an intimate act. Nevertheless, it is advisable to act stringently if possible.

112. The prohibition of making a spouse's bed applies even if the beds do not belong to them, for example, if they are guests in another house. However, this is true only if it is certain that the other spouse will sleep on that bed.

113. One may not make a spouse's bed even if a *shinuy* is performed.

114. If one has already made the other spouse's bed in a

forbidden manner, the spouse may sleep on it, and there is no need to remove the bedding and make it again in a permitted manner.

Preparing Water for Washing

115. One spouse may not prepare or bring water to the other spouse for washing purposes. This is true even if the water was cold, and even if it was not intended to be used to wash the entire body but only the face, hands, or legs. This may not be done even if a *shinuy* was performed, for example, if it was done with the left hand or the like.

116. Accordingly, one spouse may not open the faucet to prepare a bath for the other. One may certainly not open the faucet to fill a vessel the other is holding or open the faucet or shower directly on the other.

117. If one spouse has already prepared water for the other, it may be used.

If one spouse opened the faucet for his or her own use, it may be left open for the other to use as well.

118. One may prepare water if the other spouse is not present, even if the other is aware that this is being done. The laws in this regard are equal to those of making a bed (see §109).

119. The prohibition against preparing water only applies to water that is intended to be used for washing. They may, however, prepare water for *netilas yadayim*, whether in the morning, before a meal, for *mayim acharonim*, or any other required washing of the hands. However, it is preferable that each spouse prepare water for him or herself or when the other is not present.

One may prepare two vessels for *netilas yadayim* if neither one is intended specifically for the other spouse, and there is no need to act stringently in this regard.

Jewelry

120. The *Shulchan Aruch* states,[6] "It was with difficulty that the Sages permitted women to don jewelry [or apply makeup] during their *nidah* period." It is therefore proper to minimize in this regard as much as possible.

As stated earlier (§19), she should also try to minimize in applying perfume as much as possible.

121. The *Shulchan Aruch* states,[7] "It is preferable to designate specific clothing [that she will wear] when she is a *nidah*, so that they will constantly remember that she is a *nidah*." Nonetheless, many *Poskim* write that this is not our custom.

Harchakos When the Husband or Wife Is Ill

The following laws apply whether the wife is *temei'ah* due to a regular period, a *kesem*, *dam besulim*, or the like.

Harchakos When the Husband Is Ill

122. If the husband is ill and his strength has weakened (see §125) to the extent that there is no concern that they will engage in marital relations, the wife may perform actions that assist in alleviating him in his illness, provided it is not possible to find another individual who can assist him (see §124). These actions include helping him stand up or

---

6. *Yoreh Dei'ah* (§195:9).
7. Ibid. (§195:8).

lie down, passing an item to him, putting on or removing his shoes, and pushing him in a wheelchair when necessary for his health.

However, she should avoid washing him if possible, rather she should place the vessel of water before him and he should wash himself on his own. Similarly, she should avoid making his bed before him, rather he should turn away so as not to see her do this. But even these actions may be performed in an outright manner if there is no other alternative (provided his strength has weakened, as stated above).

123. Even when it is permitted to assist him, she must make an effort not to touch him directly but with a garment or the like. Similarly, she should make an effort to serve him food and drink in a permitted fashion (as outlined above). As a rule, she should try to perform even those actions that are necessary for his wellbeing in the most permissible manner possible.

124. If it is possible for these actions to be performed by another, she may not perform them, even if such an arrangement is difficult to coordinate. She may certainly not perform these actions if asking another to assist involves nothing more than embarrassment. However, there is no obligation to **hire** someone for this purpose if no volunteer can be found.

125. As mentioned earlier, the above leniencies are limited to a case where the husband's strength has indeed weakened, even if the illness is not life-threatening. But if he is merely suffering from aches or pains, she must adhere to all of the *harchakos* listed above and no leniency will apply. This is true even if a great need is present; an attendant must be **hired** if there is no other alternative.

However, she may push him in a wheelchair if there is a great need to do so, even if his strength has not weakened.

126. A woman may not lead her blind husband by holding his arm; instead, she should lead him by holding one side of an object while her husband grasps the other.

Harchakos When the Wife Is Ill

127. If the husband is well, he may not perform any of the harchakos listed above to assist his ailing wife. An attendant must be hired to assist her, even if a costly expense is involved.

If an attendant cannot be found for even a large sum of money, he may perform actions that assist in alleviating her illness, whether by providing her with medication or by preventing her illness from deteriorating. However, this is only permitted if she needs the assistance greatly. Some are of the opinion that it is only permitted if the illness is life-threatening.

128. Even when permitted to assist her, he should take care not to touch her directly, only by means of another item. In any case, he may not wash her, or even spray water on her, unless withholding from doing so may pose a life-threatening danger.

129. If a circumstance suddenly arises where his assistance is needed—for example, if she fell down and needs to be lifted—there is no time to calculate the details of the situation; if no one is available to help her, he should come to her assistance immediately.

He may push her in a wheelchair if there is a great need for him to bring her to a certain location.

130. It is only permissible to wash her hands (before a meal, for the morning *netilas yadayim*, or the like) if it is impossible to find someone else.

131. If another individual is available to assist her, he may not perform any action that involves a *harchakah* even if she is adamant that her husband help her and no one else. However, he may assist her if he sees that refusing to do so causes her distress and may lead to the deterioration of her illness. It is advisable to consult an expert rabbi to determine that this is indeed the case.

132. If one's wife became injured and no one is available to be of assistance, he may do whatever first aid treatment is necessary, such as disinfecting the wound, controlling the blood, and so on. This is particularly true considering the fact that failure to apply first aid immediately can sometimes lead to later complications that may be life-threatening.

133. If drops must be inserted into her eyes or ears numerous times over the course of the day and night and it is difficult to find someone else to do it, her husband may insert the drops, provided he takes care not to touch her.

134. Under certain circumstances, a husband may treat his wife when she is a *nidah* if he is a doctor. The details of when this is permitted or forbidden have been elaborated upon in the *sefer* (§126ff.).

134*. One may not manually raise or lower the hospital bed of one's spouse. However, one may do so by pressing an electronic button.

Various Customs During *Nidah* Period

Visiting a Cemetery

135. It is customary for women to refrain from visiting a cemetery during the days of their actual menstrual period. The *Poskim* differ regarding visiting a cemetery during the *shivah nekiyim*, but it seems that one can act leniently if there is a need.

One can even act leniently during the days of her actual period if the visit is of great significance to her and being unable to go will cause her great anguish. In such a case, the best option is to stand beyond four *amos* from the graves.

There are those who permit visiting a cemetery even during the days of her actual period on the day of a *yahrtzeit* and during the days of *Selichos* until after Yom Kippur.

136. Some opinions allow visiting the gravesite of a *tzaddik*, while others do not make this distinction. Many women are accustomed to act stringently during the days of their actual period; however, it is permissible during the *shivah nekiyim*.

Blessings and Prayers

137. A woman is permitted, and indeed obligated, to recite all blessings and prayers when she is a *nidah*. The custom not to mention G-d's name or touch a *sefer* during these days is not accepted by the *Poskim*.

Entering a *Shul*

138. The *Shulchan Aruch* and its commentaries mention various restrictions regarding entering a *shul* and the method

of praying there during the days of a woman's actual period.[8] However, the Alter Rebbe and Tzemach Tzedek state that no changes need to be made in these respects when a woman is a *nidah*.

Western Wall

139. Although there is a basis to avoid visiting the Western Wall during the days of a woman's actual period, there is no definite prohibition against doing so. However, she should take care not to touch the stones of the Wall.

Passing Between Two Men

140. In addition to the Talmud's injunction that a woman should not pass between two men, particular care should be taken when she is a *nidah*.

Intimacy and *Harchakos* on Yom Kippur and Tishah B'Av

141. It is forbidden to engage in intimate relations on Yom Kippur. Additionally, all *harchakos* must be kept both at night and by day, even if she is *tehorah*. Even if it is her *mikvah* night, she must delay immersing until the next evening.

142. Since intimate relations are forbidden on Yom Kippur, a candle (or other form of lighting, such as a nightlight) should be lit before Yom Kippur in the bedroom to burn throughout the night. This will serve as a precautionary measure so the couple will not engage in intimate relations.

If the light is on in the hallway and it is shining directly into the bedroom, no additional light is required.

---

8. *Orach Chaim* (§88:1).

Some say that if relations are forbidden in any case because she is a *nidah*, it is not necessary to light a candle in the bedroom.

143. It is forbidden to engage in intimate relations on Tishah B'Av. Additionally, all *harchakos* must be kept during the night of Tishah B'Av, but not by day (provided she is *tehorah*). However, if she is dressed attractively, *harchakos* must be kept by day as well.

If it is her *mikvah* night, she must delay immersing until the next evening.

144. When the ninth of Av occurs on Shabbos, although it is permitted to eat and drink, it is forbidden to engage in intimate relations, unless it is *mikvah* night. *Harchakos* should be kept at night, but do not need to be kept by day (provided she is *tehorah*).

Sephardim who follow the rulings of R. Yosef Karo may engage in intimate relations (provided she is *tehorah*).

Additionally, in such a year relations are forbidden on the tenth of Av, when the fast of Tishah B'Av is kept.

145. When Tishah B'Av occurs during the week, relations should be avoided on the night of the tenth of Av, unless it is her *mikvah* night. However, when the ninth of Av occurs on Shabbos and the fast of Tishah B'Av is kept on the tenth of Av, one may engage in intimate relations during the night of the eleventh of Av, provided there is a significant need.

⚬ঙ৵

CHAPTER SEVEN[1]

WAITING FIVE DAYS

Introduction

Since there are numerous laws relating to the *hefsek taharah* and *shivah nekiyim*, they have been subdivided in this book into three chapters. The current chapter will deal with the obligation to wait five days before performing a *hefsek taharah*; the next chapter will discuss the laws of the actual *hefsek taharah* and the requirement to wear white garments; and the third chapter will cover the laws relating to the *shivah nekiyim*.

Waiting Five Days Before Counting *Shivah Nekiyim*

1. If a woman was *tehorah* and then became *temei'ah*, whether by means of a regular period, unclean *bedikah*, *kesem*, or medical procedure, she cannot begin the process of counting *shivah nekiyim* until **five days** have passed from the day she became *temei'ah*. In other words, the first day of the *shivah nekiyim* must be no earlier than the **sixth day** from the day she became *temei'ah*.

This requirement is based on the concern that the woman might discharge semen during the *shivah nekiyim*, in which case the day of the discharge will not be able to be counted as part of the *shivah nekiyim*. Despite the above, she must wait five days even if no marital relations had occurred

---

1. Corresponding to Chapter Fifteen in the *sefer*.

prior to her becoming *temei'ah* (and there is no concern for the discharge of semen), as will be explained further (see §3).

An example: If the tum'ah *took place on Sunday (anywhere between sunset of* motza'ei Shabbos *and sunset of Sunday evening),[2] she must wait five days (including the day of the* tum'ah*). The five days will thus conclude on Thursday evening, and she will perform a* hefsek taharah *on Thursday before sunset. This will be followed by the* shivah nekiyim*, which will begin on Friday and conclude the following Thursday evening.*

1*. In the Jewish calendar, a day begins the preceding night and concludes in the evening. For example, the first day of the week begins Saturday night and concludes Sunday evening; the second day of the week begins Sunday night and concludes Monday evening; and so on. As such, if the *tum'ah* took place on Saturday night (for example), the first of the five days will be Sunday (and not Saturday), and they will conclude Thursday evening. The same law applies in any other similar scenario.

1**. **A note for Jews from Sephardic circles:** There are various customs among Sephardic communities regarding the number of days that must be waited before beginning to count *shivah nekiyim*. Each couple should consult an expert rabbi in their community to determine how they should act.

2. A woman can only begin counting these five days once she realizes that she has become *temei'ah*. But if she was *temei'ah* from beforehand but was unaware of the fact, the previous days cannot be included as part of the five days,

---

2. One can visit chabad.org/zmanim to find out the exact time of sunset in any location.

because she had not known at that time that she was temei'ah.

An example is in a case where a woman found a kesem *on a garment she had worn, but she did not examine it to determine if she had become* temei'ah *as a result, and it was only later when she realized that she had, indeed, become* temei'ah.

Similarly, if a woman discovers that she has begun to bleed but she estimates that the bleeding had begun a while beforehand (either based on the extent of the bleeding, because she had felt wetness earlier, and so on), she can only begin counting the five days from the time she actually discovered the bleeding.

3. The duration of the bleeding is of no consequence. Hence, as mentioned above, even if she became *temei'ah* as a result of an unclean *bedikah*, external wiping, or *kesem*, she cannot begin counting *shivah nekiyim* until five days have passed from when she became *temei'ah*. This is true even if she had not engaged in marital relations with her husband for a long period of time before the *tum'ah*, and even if the possibility to do so was non-existent, for example, if one of them was out of town for a prolonged amount of time.

An expert rabbi should be consulted if the *tum'ah* was a result of a *kesem* (which is *mid'rabanan*) and her husband was out of town prior to the *tum'ah*.

4. If the bleeding ended before the fifth day, she may perform a *hefsek taharah* on that day, as long as she does not begin counting *shivah nekiyim* until the **sixth day** from when she became *temei'ah* (see also Chapter Eight §4). (See also Chapter Sixteen §47 par. 3 where it is explained whether it is preferable to perform a *hefsek taharah* before the fifth day to

determine that she has stopped bleeding.)

Waiting Five Days If a New *Tum'ah* Occurred

5. The requirement to wait five days applies only in the event where the woman was *tehorah* before the *tum'ah* occurred. But if she was *temei'ah* from beforehand for a minimum of five days and then an additional *tum'ah* occurred, there is no need to wait a second period of five days, rather she can perform a *hefsek taharah* that very day (before sunset) and begin counting *shivah nekiyim* the following day.

An example is if a woman discovered an unclean bedikah *during the* shivah nekiyim *she had begun to count as a result of an earlier* tum'ah. *Another example is if a woman was* temei'ah *due to having given birth to a child and then she menstruated. In both cases, she can perform a* hefsek taharah *as soon as the bleeding ends and begin counting* shivah nekiyim *the following day.*

(See the following paragraphs for additional examples.)

6. Furthermore, even if she had already immersed in the *mikvah* and then she became *temei'ah* before engaging in marital relations with her husband, she is not required to wait anew, rather she can perform a *hefsek taharah* as soon as she is able to do so followed by *shivah nekiyim*. (See the *sefer* [Chapter Fifteen §6 and fn. 8] for additional details regarding this law.)

7. The above is true even if the second *tum'ah* was of a more stringent nature than the first; for example, if at first she became *temei'ah* as a result of a *kesem* (which is *mid'rabanan*) and then she became *temei'ah* due to regular bleeding (which is *mid'oraysa*). Nonetheless, it is sufficient to wait

five days from the day she became *temei'ah* as a result of the *kesem*.

Waiting Five Days in Special Circumstances

8. If a woman became *temei'ah* after lighting Shabbos or Yom Tov candles or after praying *Maariv* early (as is the custom in many areas where sunset occurs at a late hour), the calculation of the five days nonetheless depends only on sunset, i.e., whether the *tum'ah* occurred before sunset or after: If it occurred before sunset, it is considered as if she became *temei'ah* during the day, and the five days can be counted from then. If, however, the *tum'ah* took place after sunset, even if it took place before *tzeis hakochavim*, it is considered as the following day and the five days should be calculated accordingly.

There might be room for leniency, after consulting with an expert rabbi, to begin counting the five days from the previous day if the *tum'ah* took place a few minutes after sunset. This leniency may be granted particularly if the *tum'ah* in question is the result of a *kesem* (which is *mid'rabanan*).

9. It must be clarified that one cannot assume a leniency during the four minutes after sunset (based on the words of the Alter Rebbe in his Siddur in the section titled *Seder Hachnasas Shabbos*), for this addition varies based on the topographical location of each country. It is of paramount importance to inform the public of the above, since lately calendars have been printed that grant this leeway anywhere and everywhere, when this is definitely not the case.

10. An expert rabbi should be consulted if she was in doubt whether the *tum'ah* began by day or at night, she

counted the five days from the day (followed by *shivah neki-yim*), and she now wants to immerse in the *mikvah* (see the *sefer* [Chapter Fifteen fn. 16]).

11. A "doubt" is defined as a case where she doesn't recall the exact time of the *tum'ah* or if she didn't pay attention to the time when it occurred. If, however, she noticed the bleeding when it was certainly the night, but she estimates that it began during the day (either based on the extent of the bleeding, because she had felt wetness earlier, or the like), it is considered as if she began bleeding at night and does not constitute a doubt whatsoever (see §2).

If Intercourse Was Forbidden for Other Reasons

12. If they were forbidden to engage in marital relations for other reasons during the day that preceded the *tum'ah*, that day can sometimes be included as one of the five days.

An example is if the tum'ah *occurred during a night which was a* veses, *and the preceding day was an* onah beinonis, *during which relations are forbidden for an entire twenty-four hour period (see Chapter Sixteen §29). In such a case, they were forbidden to engage in relations the entire day that preceded the* tum'ah *as well as the following night until the* tum'ah *occurred, and there was no period of time in the interim when relations were permitted. That day can therefore be counted as one of the five days, and she is only required to wait another four days.*

See the *sefer* (Chapter Fifteen §§14-15) for additional applications of this law.

13. If a woman did not examine herself following the day of her *veses kavua* or her *onah beinonis* to ensure that she is

tehorah, she is forbidden to engage in marital relations until she does so. If she was aware of this law and then a *tum'ah* occurred, the days of separation following the *veses* can also be included as part of the five days.

14. The above is true only if the days of separation were **mandated** by *halachah*, either as a prohibition or as a stringency which results from a law. If, however, they separated due to a stringency which **they** accepted upon themselves, the days of separation cannot be included as part of the five days, and they can only begin from when the *tum'ah* actually began. (An example of such a stringency is if they assumed that a certain discharge rendered her *temei'ah*, and after consulting a Rabbi they realized that she was actually *tehorah*.)

Special Circumstances

15. There is room for leniency—after consulting with an expert rabbi—under the following circumstances:

1. If a woman's ability to conceive is dependent on not waiting the complete five days. (See the *sefer* [Chapter Fifteen §§20-21] for additional suggestions in such a situation.)

2. If waiting five days before performing the *hefsek taharah* will cause the *tevilah* to occur on the second night of Yom Tov, on a Yom Tov night which is *motza'ei Shabbos*, or vice versa. In these situations, she would be required to rely on the *chafifah* that was performed on *erev Shabbos* or on *erev Yom Tov*, resulting in the distancing of the *chafifah* from the *tevilah* (see Chapter Ten §§29ff.), and while it is permissible to do so, it is not preferable.

3. If the husband or wife will be traveling and she will not be able to immerse before the departure if she will wait the complete five days.

4. If the night of her *tevilah* might occur on the day of her *veses*, and if she will only wait four days it will occur the night beforehand.

To emphasize once again: Whatever the situation, one may not act leniently without first consulting an expert rabbi.

If She Waited Less Than Five Days

16. If a woman erred and waited less than **five** days, counted *shivah nekiyim*, immersed in the *mikvah*, and engaged in marital relations with her husband, she is *tehorah bedi'eved*, provided that the erroneous *hefsek taharah* was performed a minimum of four days after the previous intercourse.

17. If a woman began counting *shivah nekiyim* less than **four** days after the previous intercourse, she remains *temei'ah*, even if the *tum'ah* had been due to an unclean *bedikah* and not due to a regular period. An expert rabbi should be consulted if she has already immersed in the *mikvah* and engaged in marital relations.

Error in Counting *Shivah Nekiyim*

18. A competent Rabbi should be consulted if a woman erred and counted less than seven clean days, immersed in the *mikvah*, and engaged in marital relations with her husband.

19. If a woman counted *shivah nekiyim* properly but is required to immerse a second time due to a problem with her first *tevilah*, she may do so immediately and does not need to

wait first, even if she has already engaged in marital relations.

CHAPTER EIGHT[1]

HEFSEK TAHARAH
AND WEARING WHITE GARMENTS

Introduction

The previous chapter discussed the obligation to wait five days before performing a *hefsek taharah*. This chapter will deal with the laws of the *hefsek taharah* and the obligation to wear white garments, and the following chapter will cover the laws of the actual counting of the *shivah nekiyim*, which begin the day following the *hefsek taharah*.

General Laws of *Hefsek Taharah*

1. In order to begin counting *shivah nekiyim* (after having waited five days), a woman must first verify that the bleeding has stopped. Our Sages have established that this verification is accomplished by performing a *bedikah*, as will be explained further in detail.

This *bedikah* is known as a **hefsek taharah**—lit., "stop [which leads to] purity." It is called with this name because it verifies that the bleeding has *stopped*, thus allowing for the next phase in the *taharah* process—the counting of *shivah nekiyim*, after which she will immerse in the *mikvah*.

2. As stated earlier, the only method by which a woman can verify that the blood has stopped is by performing a *bedikah* the day **before** *shivah nekiyim*. This is true even if she is

---

1. Corresponding to Chapter Sixteen in the *sefer*.

certain that the blood has stopped (either because she can tell that it has stopped or as a result of past experience). Even if her *tum'ah* was the result of a *kesem* or an unclean *bedikah* and many days have passed without any bleeding, she cannot begin counting *shivah nekiyim* until she performs a *hefsek taharah*.

3. Furthermore: Even if she has already counted *shivah nekiyim* and immersed in the *mikvah*, she remains *temei'ah* if a *hefsek taharah* had not been performed beforehand. However, in such a case, the *bedikah* that she performed on the day she assumed to be the first of the *shivah nekiyim* can take the place of the *hefsek taharah*, and the actual *shivah nekiyim* will have thus begun the next day. Accordingly, only one day is missing to complete a total of seven clean days.

An expert rabbi should be consulted if she discovered her error after engaging in marital relations with her husband.

Separation Between *Hefsek Taharah* and *Shivah Nekiyim*

4. Although the *hefsek taharah* is normally performed after five days have passed from the beginning of the *tum'ah*, it may be performed earlier (if at all practical) if there is a need, for example, if she will be unable to perform a *hefsek taharah* on the fifth day. However, she cannot begin counting *shivah nekiyim* until the **sixth** day from the beginning of her *tum'ah*.

5. In a case where an expert rabbi has approved the delay of one's immersion in the *mikvah*, it is *halachically* permissible to delay counting *shivah nekiyim* as well, even though this would constitute a separation between the *hefsek taharah* and *shivah nekiyim*. However, it is preferable to count the *shivah*

nekiyim in the proper time (directly after the *hefsek taharah*) and to delay the **immersion** until the later date.

Washing the Body Before the *Hefsek Taharah*

6. Before performing the *hefsek taharah*, she should wash her entire body, particularly between her thighs, and she should rinse her vagina thoroughly. If it is difficult for her to wash her entire body, she can suffice with washing the areas of her body where vaginal blood may have dripped (when removing her undergarments and the like), i.e., from her vagina and below. If even this is not possible, she can suffice with washing the vagina, the vaginal area, and between her thighs.

If no water is available—for example, if she is traveling or the like—she can wash these areas with any cleansing liquid, including saliva or other substances.

7. *Halachically*, one may use cold water to wash the body; however, "it is a proper custom to wash one's entire body with warm water before [performing] the *hefsek taharah*,"[2] because warm water cleanses more effectively than cold water.

7*. She should not suffice with wiping herself with baby wipes; rather she should use water (and preferably warm water, as stated above). However, if she is traveling or the like and cannot obtain even a small amount of water (to wash at least the vaginal area), it is certainly preferable to use baby wipes than to not wash at all.

8. If a woman performed a *hefsek taharah* and began counting *shivah nekiyim* without washing herself beforehand, she does not need to perform a new *hefsek taharah bedi'eved*

---

2. *Shulchan Aruch Yoreh Dei'ah* (§196:3).

(although, as is self-understood, one must *lechatchilah* fulfill this directive as laid out in *Shulchan Aruch*).

9. If a woman experienced a new discharge of blood during the *shivah nekiyim* and must perform a new *hefsek taharah* as a result, she must wash herself once again beforehand (although she had already washed herself before the initial *hefsek taharah*). However, if the need to perform a new *hefsek taharah* was due to a mere unclean *bedikah*, *kinuach*, or *kesem*, she can suffice with washing the vagina, the vaginal area, and between her thighs.

Washing the Body in Special Circumstances

10. A woman may wash her body as soon as the bleeding has stopped, even if the time to perform the *hefsek taharah* has not yet arrived. In such a case, before performing the *hefsek taharah*, she can suffice with washing the vagina and vaginal area. Moreover, she can completely rely on the original washing if not much time has passed from then until the *hefsek taharah*. Accordingly, if a woman works in the afternoon and is unable to wash herself in her place of work, she may wash herself in the morning and perform the *hefsek taharah* while at work.

11. On Shabbos, she can suffice with washing the vagina, the vaginal area, and between her thighs using water that was heated before Shabbos.

On Yom Tov, she may use water that was heated on Yom Tov itself (if no preheated water is available). Moreover, water may be heated on Yom Tov specifically for this purpose.

12. One may not open a hot water faucet (connected

to an electrical boiler or the like) on Shabbos, unless it is certain that the heat of the water is less than the *halachic* measurement of *yad soledes bo* (equivalent to 40-45°C or 104-113°F).[3]

On Yom Tov, however, one can be lenient and open such a faucet for the purpose of washing before the *hefsek taharah*. However, it is forbidden to open a hot water faucet connected to a boiler fueled by gasoline (a Junkers boiler or the like) in which a flame is ignited when the faucet is opened and extinguished when closed.

13. Additionally, one should not use conventional soap on Shabbos or Yom Tov; liquid soap, however, may be used. She also may not wash herself with a sponge, washcloth, or the like.

14. On Yom Kippur and Tishah B'Av, she may use warm water (on Yom Kippur—that was preheated) to wash her vagina, vaginal area, and between her thighs; however, she should take care to wash only as much as necessary. Needless to say, one must avoid performing forbidden types of activity on Yom Kippur, as outlined in the previous paragraphs.

15. During the nine days from Rosh Chodesh Av until Tishah B'Av she may wash herself as usual; however, she should make an effort not to wash herself more than necessary. Similarly, a woman may wash herself before performing the *hefsek taharah* when mourning, both during *shivah* and *sheloshim*.

---

3. For additional details relating to opening a hot water faucet on Shabbos, see the *sefer Shabbos Kahalachah* from the author (vol. 1, Chapter Two §§21ff.).

Manner of Performing *Hefsek Taharah* (and Other *Bedikos*)

The following laws (relating to the *bedikah* cloth and the manner of performing the *hefsek taharah*) apply equally to all the *bedikos* required to be performed during the *taharah* process (unless clearly stated otherwise).

General Laws

16. A woman may perform the *hefsek taharah* immediately after washing herself.

It is *halachically* sufficient to perform a single *bedikah* in which a *bedikah* cloth is inserted as deep as possible into the vagina **before sunset**, used to examine all the internal crevices and folds, and left there **until after *tzeis hakochavim.*** However, it is customary to perform two *bedikos*. The first *bedikah* is performed before sunset and then the cloth is removed and examined to determine that it is clean, and this is followed by a second *bedikah* (known as a *moch dachuk*) in which the cloth is inserted and left until after *tzeis hakochavim*. This custom, although not imperative, has significant advantages.

17. If it is difficult for a woman to perform *bedikos*, an expert rabbi may allow her to relinquish leaving a cloth until after *tzeis hakochavim* (the *moch dachuk*) and suffice with a regular *bedikah* performed before sunset, which will serve as the *hefsek taharah*. Similarly, if a woman performed a regular *bedikah* and did not leave a *moch dachuk*, the *hefsek taharah* is valid *bedi'eved*.

18. If the *hefsek taharah* is of a questionable color, it is advisable to insert the *moch dachuk* in consistency with the

laws of a *bedikah*—i.e., she should examine all the internal crevices and folds, as will be explained below—and then leave it until after *tzeis hakochavim*. If she does so, the *moch dachuk* will be able to replace the *hefsek taharah* in the event that it is clean and the initial *hefsek taharah* is determined as unclean. By contrast, if she merely inserted the *moch dachuk* deeply but did not examine the internal crevices and folds, she cannot rely on the *moch dachuk* in such a case, and she must perform another *hefsek taharah* the following day.

The *Bedikah* Cloth

19. Before performing the *bedikah*, she should examine the *bedikah* cloth to determine that it is completely clean. She should also ensure that her hands are clean and do not have any cuts or the like that can stain the cloth and complicate the *bedikah*.

20. It is preferable to use a white, clean, soft cotton cloth. Nowadays one can obtain ready-to-use cloths with a rabbinic authorization. (Such cloths are also available at mikvah.org, along with additional *mikvah*-related items.)

However, it is not advisable to use a knitted cloth, although such cloths are soft and easy to use. The reason is because it is difficult to determine the exact color of a *mar'eh* found on such a cloth, as the *mar'eh* gets absorbed between the stitches.

21. If a woman must use a cotton ball to perform a *bedikah*, she should ensure that it does not contain any colored fibers. She should also attempt to turn it into a sort of *bedikah* cloth by pressing it thin and wide and squeezing it together so that the fibers do not protrude. Otherwise, it can tend to

stick to a wet surface, and it may stick to the blood instead of removing it.

22. A tampon cannot be used to perform a *bedikah* because she cannot examine the internal crevices and folds with it. It can, however, be used as a *moch dachuk*, provided she uses a regular *bedikah* cloth to perform the *hefsek taharah* beforehand (which must be done as a proper *bedikah*).

23. It is advisable not to use a tissue for a *bedikah*. If no other alternative is available—for example, if she is traveling or the like—a tissue may be used, and if she sees that it did not fall apart, the *bedikah* is valid.

24. A woman who experiences difficulty performing *bedikos* due to dryness in the vagina may moisten the *bedikah* cloth with water and then squeeze the water out a bit. An expert rabbi should be consulted if this is insufficient and she must use an oily substance for lubrication. In any case, lubricating the vagina with such a substance is preferable to lubricating the cloth. If possible, she should use a transparent oil as opposed to a gel (which may affect the color of the *mar'eh*). If using oil still does not enable her to perform *bedikos*, an expert rabbi will allow her to use a transparent gel that is not oil-based (but not Vaseline and the like).

25. One may not smear gel on the cloth on Shabbos or Yom Tov. Accordingly, if one must use gel when performing a *bedikah*, she should apply the gel on her finger, insert it into the vagina without smearing it, and then examine herself with a dry cloth. If she must use a cloth with gel, she must prepare it before Shabbos (and store it in a closed plastic bag to prevent it from drying out).

26. One may not moisten the cloth on Shabbos and Yom Tov with a large amount of water, as this may lead to squeezing. One should refrain from using a small amount of water as well, although the concern that one may squeeze may not be present. In the words of the Alter Rebbe in his *Shulchan Aruch*:[4] "One who fears Heaven should act stringently, so as to avoid the possibility of [committing] a Biblical transgression." Accordingly, if there is a need, it is preferable to use an oily substance in the manner outlined above.

27. The *bedikah* cloth should preferably not be too large, as this may obstruct her from inserting it deeply and reaching the crevices and folds. It should also not be too small, as she might not examine herself properly out of concern that it will slip off her finger. Furthermore, if it indeed slips off her finger, the *bedikah* will have been done with her actual finger and not with the cloth, rendering it invalid even *bedi'eved*.

The recommended size for the cloth need not be more than 6 sq. cm. (2.34 sq. in.). Some authorities have determined the preferable size to be between 7 and 8 sq. cm. (2.75-3.15 sq. in.).

As stated above, nowadays one can obtain ready-to-use cloths with a rabbinic authorization that match the recommended size.

Performing the *Bedikah*

28. The *bedikah* cloth must cover the finger so that the *bedikah* will be performed entirely by the cloth and not partially with the finger (which could render the *bedikah* inval-

---

4. *Orach Chaim* (§302:21).

id). Some women place the center of the cloth on the tip of the finger and wrap the remainder around the finger. Others place the edge of the cloth over the finger, fold the cloth over the fingertip, and then wrap the rest of the length around the finger. (The second method has the advantage that a greater length of the cloth is wrapped around the finger.)

29. The *bedikah* must be performed as deep as she can reach. An expert rabbi should be consulted if she is unable to reach deeply due to a wound in the vagina or the like. (See also Chapter Nine §14 where suggestions are offered for dealing with such a situation.)

30. Additionally, she must examine all the internal crevices and folds by tilting her finger with the cloth in all directions. If no difficulty is involved, she should make a complete circle with the cloth so that it will reach every corner. Generally, this is done while inserting the finger and while removing it; however, it is *halachically* sufficient to do so after having already inserted the finger to the proper depth.

A woman who is subject to excessive sensitivity in the vagina should suffice with tilting her finger in all directions, as making a complete circle with the cloth may create a wound or the like.

31. The proper body position when performing a *bedikah* is as follows: She should spread out her legs and place one leg on an elevated location—a chair, bench, or the like. Alternatively, she should "sit" midair with her legs spread out. (See note for another possible position.[5]) These positions

_____

5. According to a certain noted physician, the preferred method is to stand opposite a wall and lift one leg so that the sole of her foot is pressed

enable the *bedikah* to be performed properly by allowing for a maximal, uninhibited access to the vagina. Every woman should test herself to determine which method is the most effective for her.

As a rule, one should not perform a *bedikah* while lying down (except in special situations, as per the directive of an expert rabbi).

32. If an object was inserted deeply into the vagina for medical reasons (for example, a pessary to treat uterine prolapse), an expert rabbi should be consulted to determine how the *bedikos* are to be performed.

33. It is preferable to remove vaginal rings (such as NuvaRing, used for contraceptive purposes) prior to performing the *hefsek taharah*. (The contraception is still protected if the ring was left outside for up to about three hours.)

See the following chapter (§2) whether such rings must be removed when performing *bedikos* during *shivah nekiyim*.

34. A woman being treated with suppositories inserted into the vagina should take note that the dissolving substance contained within certain suppositories is colored; accordingly, before inserting the suppository (by day), she should rinse the vagina and perform the required *bedikah*.

Correct Time of *Hefsek Taharah Lechatchilah*

35. The *hefsek taharah* should be performed before and adjacent to sunset.[6] One should take care not to delay the

---

against the wall.

6. One can visit chabad.org/zmanim to find out the exact time of sunset, *minchah ketanah*, and *tzeis hakochavim* in any location.

hefsek taharah until after sunset, for the *hefsek taharah* will then be invalid (see note[7]). It is advisable to set aside sufficient time before sunset to prevent such a situation from occurring.

An expert rabbi should be consulted if she performed the *hefsek taharah* one or two minutes after sunset.

36. *Lechatchilah*, the *moch dachuk* should be inserted before sunset as well. However, the *hefsek taharah* is valid even if the *moch dachuk* was inserted after sunset, provided the first *bedikah* was performed on time.

37. If there is a need to perform the *hefsek taharah* at an earlier time—for example, if she might need to examine herself multiple times to determine that the blood has stopped—she may perform the *hefsek taharah* from *minchah ketanah* and onward. (*Minchah ketanah* is 2½ halachic hours[8] before sunset.)

38. The following laws apply if she cannot perform the *hefsek taharah* from *minchah ketanah* until sunset—for example, if she is traveling and unable to perform a *bedikah* at that time: In those scenarios where performing a *bedikah* in the morning is valid *bedi'eved* (see §45), she may perform

---

7. However, this *bedikah* will be effective *bedi'eved* in the event that she will forget to perform a *hefsek taharah* the following day. In such a case, she will be able to rely on the *bedikah* that was performed the evening before and begin counting *shivah nekiyim* the next day (i.e., **two days** after having performed the *bedikah*), because as stated above (§§4-5), there may be a separation between the *shivah nekiyim* and the *hefsek taharah*.

8. A *halachic* hour (or *sha'ah zemanis* in Hebrew) is calculated by dividing the daylight hours into twelve equal portions. Consequently, in the summer when the days are long an hour may consist of more than sixty minutes, and in the winter it may consist of less than sixty minutes.

the *hefsek taharah* before embarking on her trip. But in those scenarios where performing a *bedikah* in the morning is invalid (see ibid.), she has no choice but to postpone the *hefsek taharah* until the following day.

39. On Shabbos or Yom Tov eve, it is preferable to perform the *hefsek taharah* before lighting candles, because lighting candles constitutes the acceptance of Shabbos and Yom Tov. The *moch dachuk* should be inserted before sunset and left until after *tzeis hakochavim*. However, the *hefsek taharah* is valid even if only a single *bedikah* was performed either before lighting candles or afterward, provided it was done before sunset.

It should be noted that unless the area is surrounded by an *eiruv*, a woman may not go out to a *reshus harabim* with a *moch dachuk* both during the *bein hashmashos* that precedes Shabbos and during the one that follows it.

40. Certain communities are accustomed to praying Maariv early (after *pelag haminchah*), especially during the summer months. A woman belonging to such a community should act as has been outlined in the previous paragraph: Lechatchilah, she should perform the *hefsek taharah* before Maariv, and then insert a *moch dachuk* before sunset until after *tzeis hakochavim*. However, the *hefsek taharah* is valid even if only a single *bedikah* was performed at either time.

Examining the Cloth After the *Bedikah*

41. After performing the *hefsek taharah*, she should examine the *bedikah* cloth to ascertain that it is indeed clean. She can then begin counting *shivah nekiyim* the next day. (See the following chapter for the laws relating to *shivah nekiyim*.)

42. If the cloth did not appear entirely clean, one should not rely on the way it appeared by electrical light; rather, the cloth should *lechatchilah* be examined the next morning by daylight. In the interim, care should be taken to keep the cloth in a clean, protected place. However, if it is certain that the cloth was clean, there is no need to examine it again during the day.

43. If the cloth was misplaced before it was examined to ascertain that it was clean, the *hefsek taharah* is invalid. In such a case, if she inserted the *moch dachuk* before sunset and **examined** all the internal crevices and folds, it can take the place of the *hefsek taharah* (see §18). But if she did not do so, she must perform a new *hefsek taharah* the following day.

44. If a woman examined herself twice (as explained in §16) and the first *bedikah* was clean, the *hefsek taharah* is valid even if the *moch dachuk* was misplaced.

Time of *Hefsek Taharah Bedi'eved*

45. The law of a *hefsek taharah* that was performed **before** *minchah ketanah* depends on the type of bleeding that necessitated the *bedikah*:

1. If the bleeding on the day of the *hefsek taharah* was a continuation of her period (as opposed to a new discharge of blood), the *Poskim* disagree if performing a *bedikah* at this time is valid. It appears that one can act leniently **(bedi'eved)**.

2. This is not the case, however, if she experienced a new discharge of blood on the day of the *hefsek taharah*. (An example is if she experienced a new discharge of blood during the *shivah nekiyim*, or if a *bedikah* was found to be unclean and she will perform a new *hefsek taharah* that very day.) In such a case, the *hefsek taharah* is invalid even *bedi'eved* if it was performed before *minchah ketanah*, and it **must** be performed afterward.[9] However, if the *moch dachuk* was not performed, the *hefsek taharah* is still valid *bedi'eved*.

3. If the *tum'ah* was a result of a *kesem*, the *hefsek taharah* is valid *bedi'eved* if performed in the morning even if it was performed the very same day as the discovery of the *kesem*.

To reiterate: Those cases where a *hefsek taharah* is valid when performed before *minchah ketanah* are only **bedi'eved.** *Lechatchilah* one should not perform a *hefsek taharah* at such a time in any case.

White Garments and Sheets

46. After performing the *hefsek taharah*, she should put on white undergarments, and when going to sleep, she should make her bed with a white sheet. Additionally, she should ensure that her pillow and blanket are clean from bloodstains. This conduct should continue throughout the *shivah nekiyim*.

Even if she is sleeping with white undergarments, her bed should still be covered with a white sheet. However, there is no need for her other night garments to be white as well.

---

9. If the new discharge took place at night and she performed a *hefsek taharah* the next day before *minchah ketanah*, one should act stringently and it is invalid. However, if the new discharge took place during *bein hashmashos*, the *hefsek taharah* is valid *bedi'eved*.

If she has no clean undergarments or bedding, she may wash them for this purpose even during the nine days from Rosh Chodesh Av until Tishah B'Av or when in a state of mourning.

47. If she does not have any white undergarments, she can suffice with ensuring that her undergarments are clean from bloodstains. Furthermore, if she continued wearing her previous clothing and did not inspect them, her counting is valid *bedi'eved*, provided they are currently found to be clean.

48. She may not wear a bloodstained garment (worn from the navel and below—see Chapter Four §15) or sleep on a bloodstained sheet during the *shivah nekiyim*, rather she must wash them thoroughly beforehand. (The *sefer* [Chapter Sixteen §§45-46] should be consulted for the law of a woman who counted *shivah nekiyim* while wearing a bloodstained garment, either mistakenly or due to lack of alternative.)

49. In unique situations—for example, if a woman is unable to become *tehorah* due to the discovery of numerous *kesamim*—an expert rabbi should be consulted to determine if she can be allowed to wear colored undergarments.

Since a *kesem* discovered on an item that is not *mekabel tum'ah* is *tahor* as well, it is preferable for a woman in such a situation to place an item which is not *mekabel tum'ah* between her body and her undergarments, rather than wearing colored undergarments. Examples include white, clean cotton balls; a white tissue; or a white pad made from plastic material (but not one made from cloth, as such a pad is *mekabel tum'ah*).

50. If a woman must begin counting *shivah nekiyim* anew

(due to an unclean *bedikah* or the like), although she must perform a new *hefsek taharah*, she is not required to put on new white undergarments and make her bed with a new white sheet. Instead, she can suffice with inspecting them to make sure they are clean.

51. If the *hefsek taharah* was performed on Shabbos, she may not make her bed before Shabbos is over, as doing so would constitute preparing on Shabbos for a weekday. However, she may do so if she is planning on lying down before the end Shabbos.

52. If the *hefsek taharah* is performed on a Yom Tov preceding Shabbos, she may make her bed on Yom Tov for Shabbos if an *eiruv tavshilin* had been prepared. If no *eiruv tavshilin* had been prepared, the *Poskim* disagree if this may be done.

53. **A reminder:** The day during which the *hefsek taharah* was performed is **not included** in the *shivah nekiyim*. If the *hefsek taharah* was performed properly, she may begin counting *shivah nekiyim* **the next day,** as explained in detail in the following chapter.

࿇

CHAPTER NINE[1]

COUNTING THE *SHIVAH NEKIYIM*

Introduction

The *shivah nekiyim* begin the day following the *hefsek taharah*. During these seven days, she is required to examine herself daily, as will be explained in detail in this chapter.

Method and Correct Time of Performing *Bedikos*

1. Before performing a *bedikah*, she should examine the *bedikah* cloth carefully to ensure that it is clean.

The *bedikos* must be performed as deep as possible and she must examine all the internal crevices and folds, as explained in the previous chapter (§§19-31).

2. If a woman has a vaginal ring (such as a NuvaRing, used for contraceptive purposes), *lechatchilah* she should remove it before performing one of the *bedikos* of either the first or seventh day. (The contraception is still protected if the ring was left outside for up to about three hours.) She does not need to remove it prior to the other *bedikos*.

3. *Lechatchilah*, she should examine herself twice daily:

The first *bedikah* should be performed in the morning when she arises, from sunrise and onward.[2] If she arose

---

1. Corresponding to Chapter Seventeen in the *sefer*.

2. One can visit chabad.org/zmanim to find out the exact time of sunrise, *alos hashachar*, sunset, and *minchah ketanah* in any location.

before sunrise, she should wait until after sunrise to perform the *bedikah*; however, it is valid *bedi'eved* if it was performed after *alos hashachar*.

The second *bedikah* should be performed adjacent to sunset, when it is still day. If it is difficult for her to perform the *bedikah* adjacent to sunset, she can perform it from *minchah ketanah* and onward. (*Minchah ketanah* is 2½ halachic hours before sunset.)

4. If she delayed performing the second *bedikah* until *bein hashmashos*, she should still examine herself. Even if it will be considered as if it was performed at night, the counting can sometimes still be valid *bedi'eved* (see §10).

See the previous chapter (§35 and fn. 7) for the law of a *bedikah* that **must** be performed (such as the *hefsek taharah*) which was performed after sunset.

5. When examining herself, she should also examine her undergarments. If she slept without tight undergarments, she should also examine her bed sheet upon arising. However, failing to do so does not hinder her ability to continue counting the *shivah nekiyim*.

6. There is no need to examine the tissues she uses to wipe herself when using the restroom; to the contrary, it is advisable not to do so. (There is no reason at all to feel that this constitutes deception or the like—see Chapter Four §4.)

7. If there is a significant need to rinse the vagina before performing *bedikos*, an expert rabbi should be consulted to determine if the need is indeed great enough to enable her to rely on the *Poskim* who permit doing so.

If she must squirt a liquid or insert a suppository into the vagina for medical reasons, she may do so during the *shivah nekiyim* as well. If possible, she should delay these activities until after the morning *bedikah*; at the least, she should make an effort to delay them on the first and seventh days. However, even if she did these activities beforehand, she may continue counting the *shivah nekiyim*. Additionally, she should rinse out the remainder of the suppository before performing *bedikos*.

Examining the Cloth After the *Bedikah*

8. If it is certain that the *mar'eh* is *tahor*, the cloth can be examined at night using electrical lighting. If its color is uncertain, it should be examined by daylight; however, if it was examined at night and appeared to be *tahor*, the *bedikah* is valid.

If a cloth must be examined at night, care should be taken not to use a type of lighting that can result in an overly white appearance, such as LED or fluorescent lighting.

9. If the *bedikah* cloth was misplaced before it was examined, it is considered as if that *bedikah* had not been performed; however, we are not concerned that the cloth contained blood and she is required to begin counting anew. Accordingly, if the *bedikah* was one of those that do not hinder her ability to continue counting—for example, the *bedikos* performed during one of the middle days of the *shivah nekiyim* (see §10)—she can continue counting as usual. Conversely, if it was one of those that must be performed even **bedi'eved**—for example, a single *bedikah* on the first or last day (see §11)—she must act as if that *bedikah* had not been performed at all. See the *sefer* (Chapter Seventeen

§23) for additional practical examples.

If She Did Not Perform All of the *Bedikos*

The laws outlined below only apply if a proper *hefsek taharah* was performed before she began counting *shivah ne-kiyim*. Furthermore, they only apply *bedi'eved*; *lechatchilah* she must examine herself twice daily, as explained above (§3).

10. If she examined herself only on the **first** and **seventh** days and not during the days in between, her counting is nonetheless valid. This is true even if she examined herself only once on each of these two days, regardless of when in the day the *bedikah* was performed (in the morning or before sunset).

11. An expert rabbi should be consulted if she examined herself less than this amount (for example, if she examined herself only on the first day or only on the seventh day). Similarly, an expert rabbi should be consulted if she examined herself only during the middle days and not on the first and seventh days.

Difficulty in Performing *Bedikos*

The following laws address situations where it is **difficult** for a woman to perform *bedikos*. However, no leniencies apply if no difficulty is involved, even if she discovers numerous unclean *bedikos*. To the contrary; the objective of performing *bedikos* is to determine the existence of such stains. An expert rabbi can be consulted in extremely challenging situations.

12. As per the directive of an expert rabbi, a woman who encounters difficulty in performing *bedikos* can suffice with

performing one *bedikah* each day of the *shivah nekiyim*. Examples include a woman who is counting during pregnancy due to bleeding or a woman with a vaginal wound. *Lechatchilah*, she should perform this *bedikah* in the morning; however, it is valid *bedi'eved* regardless of when in the day it was performed.

13. If even this proves difficult for her, an expert rabbi can determine, based on the individual case, how much more she can act leniently. See the *sefer* (§§15-18 and fns.).

Vaginal Wounds

14. If a woman has a wound at the external edge of the vagina, she should attempt to carefully perform the *bedikos*, if possible, by circumventing the wound while inserting and removing the *bedikah* cloth. If she is able to insert the cloth deeply into the vagina in the above manner and perform a proper *bedikah*, the *bedikah* is valid. Similarly, she can cover the wound during *bedikos* if possible. If neither method is effective, she should visit a *bodekes* to perform at least the *hefsek taharah* and the *bedikos* of the first and seventh days.

Separation Between *Shivah Nekiyim* and *Tevilah*

15. In a case where an expert rabbi has approved the delay of one's immersion in the *mikvah*, she may complete counting *shivah nekiyim* on time and delay the *tevilah* for the later date. There is no need to perform *bedikos* in the interim.

Discharge of Blood During *Shivah Nekiyim*

16. The *shivah nekiyim* must be counted consecutively; if she became *temei'ah* during any of the seven days, she must perform a *hefsek taharah* and count *shivah nekiyim* anew. This is true whether she became *temei'ah* as a result of a regular

vaginal bleeding, an unclean *bedikah* or *kinuach*, or a *kesem*. However, there is no need to wait five days anew; she may perform a *hefsek taharah* as soon as she can, including that very day if possible.

17. If the morning *bedikah* was discovered to be unclean and the pre-sunset *bedikah* was clean, she can begin counting *shivah nekiyim* the following day, because the second *bedikah* can take the place of a *hefsek taharah bedi'eved* (although *lechatchilah* a *moch dachuk* is required as well).

Uncertainty How Many Days Were Counted

18. If she is uncertain how many days of the *shivah nekiyim* have passed, she must act stringently and count additional days if necessary. This is true even if she is counting due to a *kesem* (which is *mid'rabanan*).

Change of Time Zone

19. If one traveled from one time zone to another, she should count based on the time in her present location. Accordingly, she can immerse in the *mikvah* the night following the seventh day even if it is still day in the location where she began counting.

20. However, if she crossed the International Date Line and lost a complete day (as is the case when traveling from the United States to Australia), she must add another day, because the missing day cannot be counted as one of the seven required days.

∽◎∾

CHAPTER TEN[1]

CORRECT TIME FOR *CHAFIFAH*

Introduction: The term *"chafifah"* includes all the preparations required to be done before the *tevilah*, such as cleaning and washing the body and hair. The details of **how** the *chafifah* is to be done will be elaborated upon in the following chapter; this chapter will deal with the correct **time** when it should be done.

1. The "proper custom" (to quote the wording of the *Shulchan Aruch*) is to begin the *chafifah* when it is still day and continue into the night. The *chafifah* is thus done both during the day and at night directly before the *tevilah*. If necessary, she may interrupt between the portion of the *chafifah* done by day and the portion done at night.

2. *Lechatchilah*, the portion of the *chafifah* done by day should include those actions that are essential to the *chafifah*, as opposed to merely washing the face or other areas that are clean anyhow.

3. One who acts in accordance with the above custom may suffice with a *chafifah* lasting **half an hour.** This time includes all the actions of which the *chafifah* is comprised, such as cleaning the teeth, cutting the nails, and washing the body and hair.

---

1. Corresponding to Chapter Eighteen in the *sefer*.

Some women presume that a complete half hour is required for the washing alone, while others even think that one should remain in the bath for this length of time. This is incorrect; as stated above, the half hour includes the entire *chafifah*.

4. A woman may perform the entire *chafifah* process at night if a significant reason is present (i.e., if she can only perform the *chafifah* at that time). In such a case, *lechatchilah* the *chafifah* should last **a full hour.**

This hour includes the entire *chafifah* process, including cleaning her mouth and cutting her nails. She does not need to remain in the bath for a full hour (to the contrary, it is not advisable to remain there for too long). Some are of the opinion that a full hour is not required if she arranges for a woman to observe her during the *chafifah* process[2] to ensure that she does it properly.

5. A woman may perform the entire *chafifah* process by day if a significant reason is present. In such a case, she should attempt to finish the *chafifah* as close as possible to nightfall. Additionally, she may not eat between the *chafifah* and the *tevilah*, even if she plans on cleaning her mouth again before the *tevilah*. However, she may drink, following which she should rinse her mouth. She must also take care not to engage in any activities that are likely to cause *chatzitzos*.

6. In addition to the *chafifah* performed by day, she

---

2. This leniency is limited to where the woman observed her during the *chafifah* process; merely inspecting her before the *tevilah* is insufficient.

must inspect her entire body and hair thoroughly before the *tevilah* to ensure that no *chatzitzos*, knots, or tangles were created in the interim. *Lechatchilah* she should also wash her body again with a hot shower, wash the hidden areas and folds of her body, and comb the hairy areas (see Chapter Eleven §19; §25 for the definition of the hidden areas, folds, and hairy areas).

7. If a woman believed that she would be unable to perform the *chafifah* at night and then it turned out that she is able to do so, she should perform another *chafifah* at night, even if she had already performed a complete *chafifah* by day.

8. If a woman must choose between performing the *chafifah* entirely by day or entirely at night, it is preferable to do it by day.

If Time Passed From the *Chafifah* Until the *Tevilah*

9. Although the *chafifah* should be performed as close as possible to the *tevilah*, she may rely on her *chafifah* the entire night if she performed the *chafifah* (also) at night. However, this is only the case if she did not engage in activities that divert her attention from the *tevilah*; otherwise, we are concerned that a *chatzitzah* was created unknowingly.

See the *sefer* (Chapter Eighteen §§34-37) for the laws that apply if a longer interruption was made between the *chafifah* and *tevilah* (for example, if she immersed in the *mikvah* the following night).

Chafifah Performed at Home

10. It may often be preferable to perform the *chafifah* at

home, because pressure and confusion can arise in the *mik-vah* due to the many women waiting to immerse, and this may affect the patience that is crucial to a proper *chafifah*. However, if the circumstances are not as described above, it is certainly preferable to perform the *chafifah* in the *mikvah* so that it will be as close to the *tevilah* as possible.

11. If a woman performed the *chafifah* at home, she must inspect her body and hair before the *tevilah* to ensure that no *chatzitzos* or tangles were created in the interim. *Lechatchilah* she should also comb the hairy areas, and if easily possible, she should wash her body again with a hot shower.

12. If a woman performed the *chafifah* at home while it is still day, she should wait to leave to the *mikvah* until nightfall. Similarly, if it is Shabbos eve, she should not leave right after lighting the Shabbos candles but should wait until nightfall. However, she may leave beforehand if the trip to the *mikvah* is long or if another significant reason is present.

Chafifah on Shabbos and Yom Tov

12*. A number of clarifications:

1. It is self-understood that even in those cases where she may perform the *chafifah* prior to the day of the *te-vilah*, she must continue counting the *shivah nekiyim* until, and including, the **seventh** day.

2. A woman immersing in the *mikvah* on *motza'ei Shabbos* or *motza'ei Yom Tov* may only begin preparing for the *tevilah* after nightfall. Preparing when it is still day would constitute preparing on Shabbos for a weekday.

3. Whenever a woman must wash the hidden areas of her body or the like on Shabbos or Yom Tov night, she should not use a washcloth or sponge. Additionally, she should use liquid soap (and not bar soap).

Tevilah on Motza'ei Shabbos

13. If a woman is to immerse in the *mikvah* on *motza'ei Shabbos*, she must perform a *chafifah* twice, once on *erev Shabbos* and a second time on *motza'ei Shabbos*, as outlined in the following paragraphs.

14. The *chafifah* on *erev Shabbos* should be done as follows:

1. A complete *chafifah* should be performed, as if she would be immersing in the *mikvah* that very evening. This includes combing the hair, cutting the nails, and cleaning her teeth, even though she will be eating on Shabbos.

2. She must also inspect her body and hair at this time.

3. If she is planning on handling items that may cause *chatzitzos*, she should try to perform the *chafifah* as close to Shabbos as possible (after having handled these items).

4. There is room to allow one who is particular to apply makeup, lipstick, nail polish and the like in honor of Shabbos to do so in this case as well. (This is despite the obligation to avoid handling items that may cause *chatzitzos* over the course of Shabbos, as will be explained in the following paragraph.) However, she should minimize in doing so as much as possible, and she should take care to remove the makeup and the like before the *tevilah* on *motza'ei Shabbos*.

15. She should avoid activities that may create a *chatzitzah* from the time of the first *chafifah* until the *tevilah*, even though another *chafifah* will be performed on *motza'ei Shabbos*. Accordingly, she should not touch sticky substances. This includes, if possible, foods that may stick to her hands. If this is not possible—for example, if no one else is available to prepare the food in her place—she may handle such food, and she should wash her hands after each time she does so to ensure that no *chatzitzah* will remain. However, there is no need to clean her teeth after each time she eats. Additionally, she should arrange her hair in such a way that it should not tangle over the course of Shabbos.

16. She may eat as usual over the course of Shabbos, including meat (although ordinarily one may not eat meat on the day of the *tevilah*).

16*. There is room to act stringently and refrain from eating on *motza'ei Shabbos* before the *tevilah*. However, she may drink a clear liquid (that does not contain pieces of fruit or the like), provided she rinses her mouth afterward.

17. The *chafifah* on *motza'ei Shabbos* should be done as follows:

In this situation, she can suffice with taking a shower (as opposed to a bath), since she has already performed a proper *chafifah* on *erev Shabbos* and was careful to avoid the creation of a *chatzitzah* over the course of Shabbos. During the summer months, she should wash herself thoroughly to remove any accumulated sweat.

She should also thoroughly comb the hairy areas of her body. Since she was allowed to eat meat on Shabbos, she should clean her teeth with more care than usual, because meat gets stuck between the teeth more than other types of food.

A reminder: She may not prepare for the *tevilah* when it is still day, as this would constitute preparing on Shabbos for a weekday.

18. The inspection of the body and hair, washing of the hidden areas and folds with hot water, and cleaning of the teeth must be done on *motza'ei Shabbos* before the *tevilah*. (See the *sefer* [Chapter Eighteen §34] for the law of one who did not do so.) However, if she cannot inspect herself properly before the *tevilah* (due to insufficient lighting or the like), she can rely *bedi'eved* on the inspection that was done on *erev Shabbos*, provided she performed a proper *chafifah* and inspection on *erev Shabbos* and was careful to avoid creating a *chatzitzah* over the course of Shabbos (as outlined above). In such a case, she can suffice with feeling all the areas of her body with her hands to ensure that no *chatzitzah* is present. The same is true if she is unable to wash the above areas before the *tevilah* (due to a lack of hot water or the like).

19. If a woman did not perform a *chafifah* on *erev Shabbos*, although she has not acted correctly, she does not need to delay her *tevilah bedi'eved*. She can perform the *chafifah* on *motza'ei Shabbos*, and the laws in this case in all their details are equivalent to those of a woman who performs the entire *chafifah* at night (see §4).

Separation of Two or Three Days Between the *Chafifah* and *Tevilah*

20. The laws of one who is to immerse in the *mikvah* **two days** after the *chafifah* are equivalent in all their details to those of one who immerses on *motza'ei Shabbos*, as outlined above. Examples include one who is to immerse in the *mikvah* the night after a two-day Yom Tov, a Shabbos following a one-day Yom Tov, or vice versa. (The two latter scenarios apply in Eretz Yisrael.)

21. Identical laws apply to one who is to immerse in the *mikvah* **three days** after the *chafifah*, such as one who immerses the night after a two-day Yom Tov following a Shabbos or vice versa. However, in this case, the *tevilah* is invalid if no *chafifah* was performed directly beforehand. Accordingly, if she is unable to perform a *chafifah* on *motza'ei Shabbos* or *motza'ei Yom Tov*, she must postpone the *tevilah* for a later date.

Tevilah on Shabbos or Yom Tov Night

22. If a woman is to immerse in the *mikvah* on Shabbos or Yom Tov night, she should perform the entire *chafifah* with all its details on *erev Shabbos* when it is still day. This includes inspecting the body and hair, cleaning the teeth, and washing the hidden areas and folds. She should try to perform the *chafifah* as close to candle lighting as possible (taking care not to violate Shabbos, G-d forbid).

23. If she is performing the *chafifah* in the *mikvah*, she should return home between the *chafifah* and *tevilah* to light the Shabbos candles. Alternatively, her husband should light in her place. If these options are not feasible, she should light before going to the *mikvah*, provided it is after *pelag hamin-*

chah (1¼ *halachic* hours before sunset).³ In such a case, she must stipulate when lighting that she is not yet accepting the sanctity of Shabbos, and her husband must accept Shabbos immediately after her lighting (i.e., within 10 minutes) so that her blessing will not have been recited in vain.⁴

24. Between the *chafifah* and *tevilah*, she must take care not to touch anything that might create a *chatzitzah*, as elaborated upon earlier (§15). She should also arrange her hair in such a way that it should not tangle or knot and lead to a *chatzitzah*.

25. She may not eat between the *chafifah* and *tevilah*. This includes the Shabbos or Yom Tov meal; she must postpone it until after the *tevilah*, and she cannot rely on cleaning her mouth again afterward. However, she may drink a clear liquid (that does not contain pieces of fruit or the like), provided she rinses her mouth afterward. In challenging situations, an expert rabbi should be consulted to determine whether she may eat between the *chafifah* and *tevilah*.

26. Before the *tevilah*, she must inspect her entire body and hair once again to ensure that they do not contain any *chatzitzos*. She must also wash the hidden areas and folds with hot water. On Yom Tov, she may use water that has been heated on Yom Tov, while on Shabbos she must use water that was heated before Shabbos. If no such water is available, she should use the *mikvah* water.

---

3. One can visit chabad.org/zmanim to find out the exact time of *p'lag haminchah* in any location.

4. The acceptance of Shabbos by another family member is insufficient; it must be accepted specifically by her husband in order for her blessing not to have been recited in vain.

Additionally, she should clean her ears and nose from mucus, and if she did eat after cleaning her teeth on *erev Shabbos*, she must clean them again in a manner permissible on Shabbos, as outlined in the following chapter (§72 par. 6).

27. She should try to immerse in the *mikvah* as close as possible to the beginning of the night (after *tzeis hakochavim*) so that the *tevilah* will be adjacent to the *chafifah*.

28. See the following chapter (§§69-72) for a lengthy elaboration of the laws that apply if a woman did not perform the *chafifah* on *erev Shabbos* or *erev Yom Tov*, or if certain details of the *chafifah* were omitted. Various restrictions apply to the way the *chafifah* should be done on Shabbos or Yom Tov so that no transgression will be committed.

Tevilah on the Second Night of Yom Tov

The following laws also apply to a *tevilah* on a Yom Tov night which is *motza'ei Shabbos* or vice versa.

29. The *chafifah* performed on *erev Shabbos* or *erev Yom Tov* should be done as per the details outlined above (§14). Similarly, she should conduct herself between the *chafifah* and *tevilah* as outlined above (§15).

She may eat the Shabbos or Yom Tov meal before the *tevilah*, because she has already eaten between the *chafifah* and *tevilah* anyhow.

30. Before the *tevilah*, she must thoroughly inspect her body and hair to ensure that they do not contain any *chatzitzos*. She should clean her teeth in a manner permissible on Shabbos and Yom Tov (see Chapter Eleven §72 par. 6), and

she should wash the hidden areas and folds with hot water. On Yom Tov, she may use water that has been heated on Yom Tov, while on Shabbos she must use water that was heated before Shabbos. If no such water is available, she should use the *mikvah* water.

It should be noted that she may only wash the above-mentioned areas with hot water; washing the rest of her body with hot water is forbidden.

31. If no other option is available, she can suffice with washing these areas with cold water. In such a case, she should take care that the water does not come into contact with the hairy areas of her body, as cold water by nature tends to cause the hair to tangle. If the water did indeed reach these areas, she should inspect them well to ensure that they did not tangle, being careful while doing so not to squeeze or pull out any hairs (which would constitute a violation of Shabbos or Yom Tov).

32. The above preparations for the *tevilah* may only be done after nightfall and not beforehand, as that would constitute preparing from the first day of Yom Tov for the second day. The only exception is with regard to washing the abovementioned areas, which may be done before nightfall as well.[5]

See the following chapter (§§69ff.) for additional important guidelines when performing a *chafifah* on Shabbos or Yom Tov so that no transgression will be committed.

---

5. A possible reason for this is because she derives pleasure from the washing that very day; hence, it is not considered to be solely a preparation for the *tevilah*.

Tevilah of a Mourner on Motza'ei Shabbos

33. If the *shivah* of a mourner concluded on Shabbos or Yom Tov and her *tevilah* is on *motza'ei Shabbos* or *motza'ei Yom Tov*, an expert rabbi should be consulted whether she should perform a *chafifah* on *erev Shabbos* (which is still during the *shivah*). In any case, the cutting of the nails should be done on *motza'ei Shabbos*.

Tevilah on Motzae'i Tishah B'Av or Motza'ei Yom Kippur

34. As is known, it is forbidden to immerse on Tishah B'Av and Yom Kippur, and if the night of the *tevilah* occurs on one of these days, the *tevilah* must be delayed to the following night.

In such a case, she should perform a *chafifah* both on **erev** *Tishah B'Av/Yom Kippur* and on **motza'ei** *Tishah B'Av/Yom Kippur*. The laws in this case are similar to those of a woman who immerses on *motza'ei Shabbos* (see §§13ff.). If she is unable to perform a *chafifah* on *erev Tishah B'Av*, she can suffice with performing a *chafifah* on *motza'ei Tishah B'Av*; in such a case, the *chafifah* should last a full hour, as has been explained above (§4).

Since she must take care to avoid the creation of a *chatzitzah* between the *chafifah* and the *tevilah*, she should not walk barefoot on Tishah B'Av or Yom Kippur; rather she should wear shoes of the type that may be worn on these days.

35. The law of one who is to immerse the night after Tishah B'Av which directly follows Shabbos (i.e., if Tishah B'Av is on a Sunday) is similar to that of a woman who

immerses the night after a two-day Yom Tov and the like (see §20).

36. See the *sefer* (Chapter Twenty-One §21) for the correct time for *chafifah* if a woman was given permission by an expert rabbi to immerse by day.

CHAPTER ELEVEN[1]

CHAFIFAH

Introduction

This chapter will discuss the preparations before the *te-vilah* which entail removing any possible *chatzitzah* (a process known as *chafifah*). The following chapter will deal with the laws of one who found a *chatzitzah* after the *tevilah*.

It is important to note that if an expert rabbi should be consulted whenever one is in doubt, all the more so is this the case regarding the laws of *chatzitzah*. These laws are of grave importance as the *tevilah* may be invalid if a *chatzitzah* is present, and it is imperative to consult an expert rabbi whenever a question arises.

Definition of *Iyun* and *Chafifah*

1. The water of the *mikvah* must reach every location of one's body and hair, and nothing may interrupt between them and the water. Such an interruption is called a *chatzitzah*.

In order to ensure that no *chatzitzah* is present, there is a Biblical obligation for a woman to inspect her body and hair thoroughly prior to the *tevilah*. This inspection is known as **iyun**.

The inspection is done by scrutinizing those parts of the body that are able to be viewed, and feeling all other parts of

---

1. Corresponding to Chapter Nineteen in the *sefer*.

the body with her hands. It is customary for the woman over-seeing the *tevilah* to inspect those areas unable to be viewed by the one immersing.

2. However, inspecting oneself is not sufficient; she must first wash and clean herself thoroughly from anything that might constitute a *chatzitzah*, including cleaning the mouth and cutting the nails. This includes removing even such sub-stances that are not *halachically* considered a *chatzitzah*. This process is known as **chafifah**.

3. If the *chafifah* was performed immediately before the *tevilah*, the *iyun* may be done at that time as well. However, if the *chafifah* was done beforehand and the previous *iyun* may not still be applicable, another *iyun* must be performed before the *tevilah*.

Water Temperature

4. It is customary to wash the entire body with hot water, as hot water is effective in removing dirt and providing a thorough cleansing. Additional care should be taken to use hot water when washing the hairy areas (as will be enumer-ated in §19), as cold water can cause the hair to tangle, ob-structing the water of the *mikvah* from entering them.

5. *Lechatchilah*, **hot** water should be used. Included in this category is water that is generally referred to as "hot." However, she has fulfilled the obligation of *chafifah* even if warm water had been used, provided she examines herself thoroughly following the *chafifah* to ensure that her hair has not tangled.

6. If there is not enough hot water to wash her entire

body, she should use hot water to wash the hairy areas (as they **must** be washed with hot water), while the rest of her body can be washed with cold water. She should first wash her body with cold water and only then wash these areas with hot water, because otherwise the hair will tangle when she will wash herself with cold water afterward. If she did indeed wash herself with cold water afterward, the law is equal to that of a woman who washed herself exclusively with cold water (see §8).

7. When she finishes showering and turns off the water, she should take care that cold water does not reach the hairy areas so that her hair will not tangle.

8. If a woman washed herself exclusively with cold water and immersed in the *mikvah*, the *tevilah* is valid *bedi'eved*, provided she examined the hairy areas before the *tevilah* to ensure that they did not tangle. However, if she has not yet immersed, she should not suffice with examining herself but should wash herself again with hot water. If it is difficult for her to do so, one can follow the lenient opinions that maintain that she does not need to wash herself again, and she can suffice with washing the hairy areas with the hot *mikvah* water.

Similarly, if no hot water is available at all (due to a power failure or the like), she should wash herself with cold water, ensure that her hair has not tangled, and wash the hairy areas with the hot *mikvah* water before immersing.

9. If a woman washed herself exclusively with cold water and did not examine herself before the *tevilah* to ensure that her hair has not tangled, the *tevilah* is invalid, and she must wash herself properly and immerse a second time.

10. If the water of the *mikvah* is cold, she should immerse immediately upon entering the water to prevent her hair from tangling before immersing.

Bathing

11. Although one has fulfilled the *halachic* obligation of *chafifah* by taking a shower, it is customary to sit in a bath as well, as doing so softens any dirt attached to the body and assists in the cleansing. However, if this is not possible, taking a hot shower is sufficient.

There is no required amount of time that one must spend in the bath; rather, every woman should determine how much time is necessary in order for her body to be cleansed properly.

12. As will be explained in Chapter Sixteen (§23), *lechatchilah* one should not wash the inside of the vagina during a *veses*. Accordingly, if a woman's *veses* occurs the day before the *tevilah*,[2] she should shower by day (while avoiding to wash the inside of the vagina) and take a bath at night to conclude the *chafifah*. If the night of her *tevilah* is Shabbos or Yom Tov when she may not wash herself (see Chapter Ten §22; §71), she may perform the entire *chafifah* by day as usual even if it coincides with her *veses*.

Alternative Methods of *Chafifah*

13. An expert rabbi should be consulted in the following scenarios (see the *sefer* [Chapter Nineteen §§12; 14-16] for additional details): (1) If one may not wash herself with

---

2. If the *veses* coincides with the **night** of the *tevilah*, she must delay her *tevilah* because they may not engage in marital relations.

water due to medical reasons. (2) Regarding the use of a wet cloth, if no water is available with which to wash herself. (3) Regarding the use of other fluids other than water. (4) Regarding the use of spring or mineral water.

Use of Soap and Shampoo

14. It is customary to wash with soap and shampoo, and this is considered the ideal way of performing a *chafifah*. However, since they may contain substances that (*halachah* recognizes as having the characteristic to) tangle the hair, she should wash herself thoroughly with hot water afterward to remove any excess of these substances, and she should comb her hair thoroughly as well.

15. Similarly, she may use conditioner to facilitate the combing, and she should then wash her hair with hot water to remove the excess. It is advisable to refrain from using conditioners of the type that do not leave the hair entirely even after washing it with hot water.

How *Chafifah* Is Performed

16. If a woman follows the "proper custom" described in the previous chapter (§1), beginning the *chafifah* by day and concluding it at night, **half an hour** is sufficient for the *chafifah* process. However, if the entire *chafifah* is performed at night, *lechatchilah* it must last an **hour** (see note[3]).

---

3. Some are of the opinion that a full hour is not required if she arranges for a woman to observe her during the *chafifah* process to ensure that she does it properly. However, this leniency is limited to where the woman observed her during the actual *chafifah* process; it is insufficient to merely inspect her before the *tevilah* (as is commonly done nowadays by the women overseeing the *tevilah*).

17. The half hour or hour includes the entire *chafifah* process, including cleaning her mouth, cutting her nails, and so on. She does not need to remain in the bath for a full hour (to the contrary, it is not advisable to remain there for too long).

What is of central importance is that she not rush, rather she should perform the details of the *chafifah* process unhurriedly, thoroughly and with care. Some women have the custom to go through each area of the body and hair three times. This does not mean that she should clean herself thoroughly three times; rather, after cleaning herself once properly, she should look herself over two more times superficially to ensure that each area is clean.

18. The most important part of the *chafifah* process is the *iyun*, i.e., to inspect each area of the body and hair to ensure that no *chatzitzah* is present. She should not suffice with water pouring over her body, rather she should simultaneously scrub herself thoroughly, especially in the hidden areas and folds where dry sweat and other *chatzitzos* may be hidden. She should also comb her hair while washing herself.

Washing the Hairy Areas

19. The *hairy areas* include the following: (1) The hair of the head. (2) The hair under the armpits. (3) The pubic hair. (4) *Lechatchilah* the eyelashes and eyebrows are included in this category as well.

The hair of the arms and legs are not included in this category.

20. One must ensure that no strand of hair is stuck to an-

other. Washing the hair alone is insufficient even *bedi'eved*; rather, the hair of the head must be combed with a comb. It is customary to comb the other hairy areas with a comb as well; however, it is *halachically* sufficient to untangle the hairs of these areas with one's fingers until it is certain that no hair is knotted or stuck to another.

21. The hair should be combed (or untangled) while she washes herself with hot water or afterwards, when the hair is still wet. She should not comb her hair when it is dry and only then wash herself.

22. If she untangled the hair of her head with her fingers (instead of using a comb), immersed in the *mikvah*, and engaged in marital relations, one can rely on the lenient opinions that hold that this is sufficient, and she is not required to immerse again. The same applies if she has not yet engaged in marital relations but it is difficult for her to immerse again.

Similarly, she can suffice with untangling the hair of her head with her fingers—provided she is careful to do so **properly**—if it is impossible for her to locate a comb, or if it is Shabbos or Yom Tov and she had not combed her hair earlier. (See §§69-69* for more details regarding one who is to immerse on Shabbos or Yom Tov and did not comb her hair properly beforehand.)

23. The *sefer* should be consulted for the laws in the following scenarios: (1) If a woman is in doubt whether or not she combed her hair (Chapter Nineteen §21-22). (2) If she combed her hair that day, but not for the sake of *chafifah* (ibid. §23). (3) If she braided her hair after combing (Chapter Twenty §18).

24. If a woman forgot to untangle the hair of the areas other than the head, but she scrubbed these areas while washing herself as usual and after the *tevilah* she examined them and no *chatzitzah* was present, an expert rabbi should be consulted to determine if she does not need to immerse again.

Washing the Hidden Areas and Folds

25. The *folds* include the following: (1) Underneath the armpits. (2) Between folds of the chin and neck. (3) Between the legs. (4) Beneath the breasts. (5) Beneath folds of excess flesh. (6) Between wrinkles.

The *hidden areas* include the following: (1) Between the toes. (2) The nostrils. (3) The ear canals. (4) The mouth and teeth. (5) The vagina and anus. (6) The folds in the navel.

26. Although the water of the *mikvah* does not need to actually **enter** each one of the above areas, they must be *halachically* **suitable** for water to enter by not containing any *chatzitzos*, and they must therefore be cleaned properly with hot water as well.

See the *sefer* (Chapter Twenty) for the *halachic* differences between a *chatzitzah* that was found in one of the above areas and one that was found elsewhere on the body.

Cleaning the Teeth

27. She must clean between her teeth properly (with dental floss, a toothpick or the like), as well as the teeth themselves, to remove any particle of food and the like. If one has holes in the teeth, it is particularly important to ensure that they are cleaned properly so that no particle will remain.

This is in addition to washing the mouth itself thoroughly to ensure that nothing remains stuck inside.

28. Accordingly, one must ensure that she will be able to clean her teeth properly, and if she has holes in her teeth that will be too painful for her to clean, they should be cleaned by a doctor in advance. After her teeth are cleaned, she should not eat anything until the *tevilah* so that no *chatzitzah* will be created. However, she may drink, provided she rinses her mouth afterwards.

29. If the night of the *tevilah* arrived and she did not do as outlined in the previous paragraph, *bedi'eved* she may suffice with cleaning as much as she can, provided it is certain that even if some residue does remain, it is found deep within the hole and does not protrude at all.

30. The laws of the *chatzitzah* status of various dental treatments have been elaborated upon in the following chapter (§§41ff.). In brief, permanent fillings and crowns are not a *chatzitzah*. If a woman has a temporary filling or crown, she must resolve to leave it in her mouth for another thirty days, beginning from that day, before replacing it. In challenging situations, she should resolve to leave it there for at least seven days.

Refraining From Eating Meat

31. Women have adopted the custom to refrain from eating meat on the day of the *tevilah*, because meat gets stuck between the teeth more than other types of food. Although the teeth will be cleaned before the *tevilah*, they are concerned that a bit of meat will remain without her realizing it. The *Shulchan Aruch* writes that this is a proper custom.

This includes poultry and meat, as well as liver and cold cuts. However, she may suck the marrow of a bone or eat a dish that was cooked together with meat. She may also eat fish.

32. A woman must refrain from eating meat even if this may cause others to realize that it is the day of her *tevilah*. However, there is room to be lenient in challenging situations, where doing so will bring her much embarrassment. In such a case, she should eat as little meat as possible, only as much as necessary to prevent embarrassment.

33. She may eat meat if the day of her *tevilah* coincides with Shabbos, Yom Tov, Chol Ha'moed, or Purim. In such an event, she should be especially meticulous when cleaning her teeth afterwards.

34. If she did eat meat (even on days other than the aforementioned), she may still immerse in the *mikvah bedi'eved*, but she should be especially meticulous when cleaning her teeth beforehand.

35. It is advisable to refrain as well from eating other foods that get stuck between the teeth and are difficult to remove. This includes oranges, corn, and the like, as well as popcorn, because the kernel may stick to the teeth or gums.

Cleaning the Eyes, Nostrils, and Ears

36. She should clean her eyes well from all dirt, mucus, and the like. She must also remove any mucus found in the nostrils, as well as clean both the inner and outer folds of the ears. She should clean these organs as much as can be reached easily; there is no obligation to clean the areas that are deep and hard to reach.

If she only cleaned the areas of the nostrils and ears that can be seen from the outside, her *tevilah* is valid *bedi'eved*.

If she is using a cotton ball to clean these areas, she should take care that no strands of cotton remain, as they can constitute a *chatzitzah*.

(Additional details pertaining to these organs and the laws in challenging situations can be found in the following chapter [§§23-27 (eyes); §§28-29 (nostrils); §§30-33 (ears)].)

Cutting the Nails

37. She should cut her fingernails and toenails until the area where they join the skin. (There is no need to cut off what is attached to the skin as well, as some women are accustomed to do.) She should then examine her nails to see if any dirt remains, and she should clean them well.

38. In principle, a woman must immerse once again if she forgot to cut even one nail; however, many details and conditions apply, as will be elaborated upon in the following chapter (§§66ff.).

39. It may often be preferable to cut the nails at home before going to the *mikvah* so that it will be done calmly and meticulously (see Chapter Ten §10).

Problems With Cutting or Cleaning the Nails

40. If a woman has a swollen finger that covers the opening of the nail, she can immerse in her present condition even if she cannot cut it or clean it properly. If she can clean a portion of the nail, she should do so, even if the rest will not

be cleaned. However, this is only true regarding dirt found underneath the nail; dirt protruding outside of the nail must be removed.

41. If a woman has a swollen finger that does not cover the opening of the nail, the nail must be cleaned before immersing. A suggested method of cleaning the nail in such a case is to soak the finger in hot water and soap to soften the area and allow the nail to be cleaned. (If this will enable her to cut the nail she should do so; but she may immerse even if she is unable to cut the nail, provided it is clean.) Soaking the finger in hydrogen peroxide can also assist in softening congealed blood. She should begin cleaning the nail early enough before the *chafifah* so that sufficient time will be left for the additional activities associated with its cleaning.

If the pain is so great that she is still unable to clean the nail, an expert rabbi should be consulted to determine if she may immerse in her present condition.

42. A treatment sometimes recommended to a person with an ingrown nail is to refrain from cutting it, and a strip of gauze is inserted beneath the nail so that it will grow properly. In such a case, the grown nail does not constitute a *chatzitzah*, because she is particular not to cut it. However, the gauze is considered a *chatzitzah* and must be removed before the *tevilah*.

43. Similarly, a doctor may direct a person with a damaged nail (for example, if a door was closed on it) to leave it untouched in order to protect the wound underneath. In such a case, the nail is not considered a *chatzitzah*. But if it has been decided to remove the nail, it constitutes a *chatzitzah*.

Laws relating to additional problems regarding cutting and cleaning the nails have been discussed in the *sefer* (Chapter Twenty §§76ff.).

44. A woman who grows her nails should consult an expert rabbi to determine if she can be allowed to immerse in the *mikvah* in her present condition. (See the *sefer* [Chapter Twenty §82].)

The same is true regarding a woman with artificial nail extensions which are attached for an extended period of time. It is self-understood that such a conduct should be avoided entirely; if, however, a woman already conducts herself in this manner and will not change her habits, an expert rabbi should be consulted regarding the possibility of immersing in her present condition. (See the *sefer* [Chapter Twenty §83].)

Makeup

45. She should remove any eye shadow on her eyes or nail polish applied to her nails. If she did not remove it before the *tevilah*, her *tevilah* is valid *bedi'eved* if the color is complete and has not begun to fade. However, if the color has begun to fade to the extent that one is usually particular to replace it, it is considered a *chatzitzah*.

If the eye shadow or nail polish has no actual substance and is merely pigmentation, it is not a *chatzitzah* if it is complete. If it has begun to fade, *lechatchilah* it should be removed; however, in challenging situations she may immerse in her present condition.

46. *Lechatchilah* she should remove any type of makeup applied to her face. *Bedi'eved*, if she has already immersed in

the *mikvah* or if she cannot remove it, her *tevilah* is valid if the color is complete. But if it has begun to fade to the extent that one is usually particular to replace it, it is considered a *chatzitzah*. See the previous paragraph for the law of makeup that has no actual substance and is merely pigmentation.

47. The law of a woman who dyed her hair with a dye that has no actual substance is the same as that of makeup that has no substance (as explained in §45). If the dye does have an actual substance, the law will depend on whether the majority of her hair has been dyed or not, and an expert rabbi should be consulted (see the *sefer* [Chapter Nineteen §47 and fns.]).

48. If a woman dyed her eyebrows or eyelashes, *lechatchilah* she should remove the dye, as some authorities consider it a *chatzitzah*. However, if there is a need one can be lenient, provided the color is complete and has not begun to fade, especially if the dye has no actual substance.

Stains

49. Stains on the body consisting of an actual substance are considered a *chatzitzah*. If she removed the actual substance and traces of color remain (for example, ink or iodine stains), she should try to remove them as well; if doing so proves difficult, she may immerse in her present condition. The same law applies to stains resulting from peeling vegetables (which are merely pigmentation to begin with).

Splinters

50. If a woman has a splinter, thorn or the like embedded **underneath** her skin (i.e., the splinter is beneath the height

of the skin), it does not constitute a *chatzitzah*, whether it is metal or wood. This is true even if the splinter is visible through the skin. However, if it protrudes from the skin, or even if it is just on the same level as the skin, it should be removed. If a layer of skin is now covering the splinter, it is not a *chatzitzah* even if it previously protruded above the skin. (See also Chapter Twelve §§109-110).

Wounds and Skin Problems

51. The following chapter (§§83-98) will deal with many details and possibilities regarding wounds, scabs, pus, and more. It will also elaborate (§§99-111) on the laws pertaining to various skin problems, such as pieces of skin that have begun to peel around the nails or on the lips; skin that has begun to peel as a result of a burn, sunburn or asthma; chapped skin; and more.

Dandruff

52. A woman suffering from dandruff should begin treating the problem a number of days prior to the *tevilah*. If the day of the *tevilah* has arrived and the problem persists, she should wash off the dandruff as much as possible so that the pieces will not remain attached to her hair, and whatever remains is not a *chatzitzah*. However, if a somewhat large piece remains attached to her hair that women are usually particular to remove, it is a *chatzitzah* and must be removed.

Lice and Nits

53. A woman suffering from lice or nits should begin treating the problem a number of days prior to the *tevilah*. If the day of the *tevilah* has arrived and the problem persists,

she should clean the lice and nits from her hair as much as possible, and if anything remains afterwards that she is unable to remove, it does not constitute a *chatzitzah bedi'eved*. (See the *sefer* [Chapter Nineteen §§66-67] for additional details.)

Flaky Skin

54. Certain authorities are of the opinion that skin that has begun to flake due to excessive time spent in a bath constitutes a *chatzitzah*; *bedi'eved*, however, one can rely on the opinions who rule leniently.

Jewelry

55. All jewelry must be removed before the *tevilah*, including rings, earrings, bracelets, eyelash extensions, and the like. Similarly, an amulet worn as a *segulah* or the like must be removed.

56. Holes pierced in the ears (for earrings) should be cleaned, as dirt and dry sweat sometimes accumulate there.

The law of one who washed her ears well but did not clean the inside of the holes will be explained in the following chapter (§32).

57. Contact lenses must be removed before the *tevilah*.

Vagina and Anus

58. The inside of these areas must be washed well to ensure they are clean, especially since pieces of tissue sometimes remain stuck there. See the following chapter (§§116ff.) for additional details regarding *chatzitzos* in these areas.

59. She should examine herself to see if she needs to use the restroom. If she used the restroom following the *chafifah*, she should wash the areas that might have become soiled once again and not suffice with wiping them alone.

60. If she walked barefoot from the room where she performed the *chafifah* to the *mikvah*, it is possible that her feet became dirty, and she should wash the soles of her feet and between her toes carefully before immersing in the *mikvah*.

Conduct on Day of *Tevilah*

61. It is customary among women to refrain from kneading dough on the day of the *tevilah*, because dough sticks to the hands and may result in a *chatzitzah*. For the same reason, women do not handle any other sticky substance on this day as well. However, if she did not follow this stringency, she should not delay her *tevilah* as a result; rather, she should wash herself thoroughly and with extra care.

If her *tevilah* is on Friday night and she is accustomed to baking *challah* on *erev Shabbos*, she may do so this week as well, and she should wash herself thoroughly as stated above.

See above (§§31ff.) regarding the custom to refrain from eating meat on the day of the *tevilah*.

Cutting Hair Before the *Tevilah*

62. One should refrain from cutting her hair three days prior to the *tevilah*, or at least on the day of the *tevilah* itself. However, she should not delay her *tevilah* even if she did cut her hair. In such a case, she should take care to wash herself thoroughly to ensure that no small hairs remain on her body.

63. If one is particular to cut her hair before the *tevilah* and only remembered to do so on the day of the *tevilah*, she should cut her hair and wash herself thoroughly when performing the *chafifah* (as stated in the previous paragraph).

See the *sefer* (Chapter Nineteen §75) for the law of such a woman who is unable to cut her hair.

64. See the following chapter (§8) for the law of a woman who is accustomed to remove her pubic hair before the *tevilah* and forgot to do so.

If Details Were Omitted From the *Chafifah*

65. The *tevilah* is invalid if a woman did not wash the hair of her head or the other hairy areas, even if she examined them before the *tevilah* to ensure that no *chatzitzah* was present. Similarly, the *tevilah* is invalid if she washed her hair but did not examine the rest of her body. This is true even if she examined herself immediately after the *tevilah* and did not discover any *chatzitzah*. In such a case, she must perform a proper *chafifah* and immerse once again with a *berachah*.

66. The *tevilah* is invalid even if she is in doubt whether she examined herself before the *tevilah* or not.

67. The *tevilah* is valid *bedi'eved* if she washed the hairy areas but did not wash the rest of her body, provided she examined her body to ensure that no *chatzitzah* was present.

68. If a woman performed a proper *chafifah* and *iyun* on her hair and body but neither washed nor examined the hidden areas and folds, she should examine these areas after the *tevilah*. If she discovers them clean from *chatzitzos*, her *tevilah* is valid *bedi'eved*.

If Details of the Chafifah Were Omitted
on *Erev Shabbos* or *Erev Yom Tov*

Introduction

The following paragraphs detail the laws that apply if a woman is to immerse in the *mikvah* on Shabbos or Yom Tov night and certain details of the *chafifah* (on *erev Shabbos* or *erev Yom Tov*) were omitted. Certain restrictions affect the manner in which the omitted details may be performed so that no desecration of Shabbos or Yom Tov will be committed.

If a woman omitted a detail which is forbidden to be performed on Shabbos and Yom Tov, the following chapter should be consulted: if the omitted detail constitutes a *chatzitzah* even *bedi'eved*, she must delay her *tevilah*; otherwise, she can immerse in her present condition.

Hair

69. If she did not comb her hair before Shabbos or Yom Tov, she can only be allowed to immerse on Friday night if she is able to use her fingers to comb her hair properly, i.e., to separate the hairs completely so that no hair remains knotted or stuck to another. She must be careful to avoid desecrating Shabbos or Yom Tov; accordingly, although the combing must be done when the hair is still damp, she should ensure that it is not wet to the extent that water might be squeezed out (which is forbidden on Shabbos and Yom Tov). She should also make sure that no hair is pulled out.

69*. If she is unable to comb hair in such a manner, she can be allowed (due to the challenging situation) to ask a non-Jewish woman to comb her hair. If her hair is extremely short and there is no concern that it is knotted or tangled, she may suffice with combing her hair with a soft-bristled brush which may be used on Shabbos and Yom Tov. In such a case, she should comb her hair carefully to ensure that every strand of hair has been separated properly.

In any event, she should take care not to part her hair in the middle, as doing so constitutes a desecration of Shabbos or Yom Tov.

70. Just as it is forbidden to braid one's hair on Shabbos and Yom Tov, so is it forbidden to undo a braid. Accordingly, if her hair is braided and she did not wash it before Shabbos or Yom Tov, it must be undone by a non-Jewish woman. If no non-Jewish woman is available, she must delay the *tevilah* to *motza'ei Shabbos/Yom Tov*.

If she washed her hair before Shabbos or Yom Tov and then braided it, it may be permissible for her to immerse in her present condition under certain circumstances—see the *sefer* (Chapter Twenty §18).

71. The way a *chafifah* may be performed on Shabbos or Yom Tov is as follows:

1. She may wash her body with cold (or lukewarm) water. She should then wash the hair of her head thoroughly with hot water, as well as the other hairy areas, the hidden areas, and the folds. On Yom Tov she may use water that was heated on Yom Tov, and on Shabbos she must use water that was heated before Shabbos.

She may not open a hot water faucet on Shabbos. See

Chapter Eight (§12) regarding the law of opening a hot water faucet on Yom Tov.

2. She may only use liquid soap (shampoo or the like, as opposed to conventional soap). It is customary to refrain from using creamy soap with a thick texture as well. One may also not use a sponge or washcloth due to the prohibition of squeezing on Shabbos or Yom Tov.

3. In addition to combing the hair of her head (as explained earlier—see §§69ff.), she must also use her fingers to separate the hairs of the other hairy areas. She must also wash her mouth and clean her teeth well in the manner that will be explained further (§72 par. 6). She must also examine her body and hair well to ensure that no *chatzitzah* is present.

72. The following paragraphs detail the manner in which various issues are to be handled when performing a *chafifah* on Shabbos or Yom Tov.

1. One may not remove pieces of skin that have begun to peel around the nails on Shabbos or Yom Tov, even if they are almost completely detached. (See Chapter Twelve §§100ff.)

2. If the majority of a nail is detached, the authorities disagree whether it constitutes a *chatzitzah* or not. If the nail causes her pain, she may remove it with her teeth or by hand, taking care that no bleeding is caused as a result.

3. If she did not cut her fingernails and no non-Jewish woman is available to remove them with her teeth or fingers, she can suffice with cleaning them extremely well, ensuring that no dirt remains stuck to them. She must take care to avoid scraping off part of the nail itself; accordingly, she should press the flesh beneath the nail downwards to allow her to remove the dirt carefully.

According to the *Mishnah Berurah*, although *lechatchilah* a non-Jewish woman should be instructed to remove the nails with her fingers, if this not possible she may cut them with a nail clipper. In such a case, she should not give her hand to the non-Jewish woman, rather the non-Jewish woman should be told to take her hand on her own. She should also not assist the non-Jewish woman (by positioning her hands and the like).

4. If she did not cut her toenails, she can suffice with cleaning them well, taking care not to scrape off part of the nail itself. She should then examine them to ensure that they are indeed completely clean.

5. The following laws apply if she has nail polish on her nails that was not removed before Shabbos or Yom Tov. If the nail polish is complete and has not begun to fade, she should immerse in her present condition and not remove it. But if the color has begun to fade to the extent that she is usually particular to replace it, she should ask a non-Jewish woman to remove it. If this is not possible, she should remove it herself with nail polish remover or the like that is located in the *mikvah* **for this purpose** (so as to avoid the issue of *muktzeh*). The same law applies if she removed the nail polish before Shabbos or Yom Tov but now noticed that a bit of polish remained.

In the above cases, she should not dip a cotton ball into the nail polish remover to remove the polish, as this may constitute squeezing on Shabbos or Yom Tov. If the nail polish is colored, she may also not pour nail polish remover on the nail and then wipe off the polish with a cotton ball or cloth, as they will be dyed as a result. If the polish is transparent or white, this latter method may be employed. It might be possible to allow this method to be used with colored polish as well if she is unable to remove it any other way.

6. The manner in which she may floss and brush her teeth on Shabbos or Yom Tov is as follows:

Flossing. She may clean between her teeth with a toothpick or with a match with a sharp end. However, the match may not be sharpened on Shabbos or Yom Tov. She may also fold a piece of paper and create a point with which to clean between her teeth. If she must use dental floss and it has not been cut to size before Shabbos or Yom Tov, she may not cut a piece from the roll, rather she should floss her teeth with the floss as it is attached to the roll.

Brushing. A **dry** toothbrush with nylon bristles may be used, provided that definite bleeding will not be caused as a result. But if her gums will definitely bleed, she may not brush her teeth.

It may be possible to allow the placing of a small amount of water in the mouth before brushing, but the toothbrush itself may not be dampened, as this may constitute squeezing. However, if each bristle is clearly separate from the others, one may dampen the toothbrush itself before using it. In any event, toothpaste may not be used.

She must also refrain from rinsing the toothbrush when she finishes using it until after Shabbos or Yom Tov.

7. Dandruff attached to the hair may be removed. However, one may not remove dandruff attached to the skull; there is no need to do so either, as such dandruff does not constitute a *chatzitzah*.

8. One may remove lice and nits from the hair, taking care not to uproot any strands of hair in the process.

9. One may remove ink or dye stains and the like with liquid soap (shampoo or the like—see §71 par. 2). If this is not effective, one may use nail polish remover or the like that is located in the *mikvah* **for this purpose** (so as to avoid the issue of *muktzeh*). She may also make use of lemon juice that was squeezed before Shabbos or Yom Tov. However, she may not use a cotton ball or cloth dipped into these substances, as this may constitute squeezing on Shabbos or Yom Tov.

10. One should not cut off or rip apart a bandage (see Chapter Twelve §98), even if it is done in a destructive manner. *Lechatchilah* one should also refrain from untying a bandage on Shabbos or Yom Tov; however, it appears that this may be done to enable her to immerse in the *mikvah* if no other option is available.

After immersing, she may replace the bandage if it will be painful to leave the wound uncovered. If a cream was spread on the bandage, she may not smear it before replacing the bandage but should replace it the way it is.

When replacing the bandage on Shabbos or Yom Tov, it may not be tied as usual (with a knot) but should be tied with a bow or fastened with a safety pin. It may also not be fastened with a band-aid or similar adhesive.

11. A band-aid (see Chapter Twelve §96) may be removed from the body on Shabbos or Yom Tov. If it is attached to a bandage, one should refrain from removing it; however, it appears that it may be removed if there is no other way to remove the bandage. If it is attached to an area with hair, *lechatchilah* it should not be removed as this may uproot the hair; rather, she should make use of substances that dilute glue, if they are located in the *mikvah* for this purpose. If this option is not available, there are those who allow it to be removed even if hair will be uprooted as a result.

12. If cream is spread over part of her body (see Chapter Twelve §97), she may wipe it off with a dry rag, cotton ball or tissue, but not with a towel (even if it is dry).

13. A splinter and the like may be removed (even with a needle or tweezers), provided that bleeding will not certainly occur as a result. (See note for the law in a case where bleeding will certainly occur.[4])

14. One may rinse blood off of a wound (see Chapter Twelve §§84ff.) if the blood is still moist. She may also wipe it off with a cotton ball or bandage that is made to absorb blood, but not with a garment or other cloth.

---

4. Although certain *Poskim* maintain that a splinter may be removed even if it will certainly cause blood to emerge, the Alter Rebbe holds that it may not be removed in such a case.

However, some authorities allow a garment to be used if no other method is available to stop the blood and no such cotton ball or the like is available. If the blood is dry and may cause bleeding if removed, she should suffice with softening it well with hot water. (See the *sefer* [Chapter Nineteen §51] for the details regarding the manner in which the blood should be softened.)

15. One may remove scabs by hand, provided care is taken that only the scab itself is removed (and not the skin), and that no bleeding will be caused as a result.

16. One may remove earrings and replace them again after the *tevilah*. This is true even if they had not been removed for a long time, because in general earrings are slightly loose and are not fastened forcefully to the ears (so as not to apply excessive pressure to the earlobes).

Cutting Nails and Hair in Special Circumstances

Nails

73. Nails may be cut before immersing on Chol Ha'moed as usual. Some authorities also permit cutting the nails on Chol Ha'moed for the sake of immersing on *motza'ei Yom Tov*; others are of the opinion that she should delay the cutting until after Yom Tov.

74. Nails may be cut before immersing during the week of Tishah B'Av as usual.

75. *Lechatchilah*, a mourner during *sheloshim* should cut her nails with her teeth. If this proves difficult, she should begin cutting each nail with scissors or the like and finish with her teeth. If she cannot cut them in this way either, they should be cut by a non-Jewish woman. If no such woman is available, she may ask another Jewish woman to cut them for her, and if this too is not possible, she may cut them herself.

Hair

76. One may cut her hair on Chol Ha'moed if she is accustomed to doing so before immersing. Some authorities also permit the cutting of hair on Chol Ha'moed for the sake of immersing on *motza'ei Yom Tov*.

77. Since such a haircut is considered as being done for the sake of a *mitzvah*, she may do so during the three weeks preceding Tishah B'Av and during the days of Sefiras Ha'omer as usual.

78. A mourner during *sheloshim* should annul her practice of cutting her hair before immersing (*hataras nedarim*— see the *sefer* [Chapter Nineteen §75] for additional details). If it is too late to do so, she may cut her hair.

If she is to immerse the night following the *shivah*, she should delay the cutting until the actual day of the *tevilah*. If possible, she should cut her hair at night before the *tevilah*.

79. The hair of a bride before her wedding does not constitute a *chatzitzah*, whether it will be cut after the wedding or on the day of the wedding before the marriage ceremony.

CHAPTER TWELVE[1]

CHATZITZAH

Introduction

While the previous chapter discussed the preparations **before** the *tevilah* (the *chafifah*), this chapter will deal with the laws of one who found a *chatzitzah* **after** the *tevilah*. This subject will be discussed in this book with relative brevity; however, it has been elaborated upon in Chapter Twenty of the *sefer*. The laws in challenging situations and in cases of *bedi'eved* are dealt with there as well.

The laws of *chatzitzah* involve many factors, each one playing an important role in determining the law. For example, the law may change if the *chatzitzah* is covering the minority or majority of the body, and there are various criteria how the minority or majority is to be calculated. Similarly, the law may change if a woman is particular or not with regard to a certain *chatzitzah*, and at times, a woman's personal position may be disregarded in view of the position of most women. Accordingly, an expert rabbi must be consulted in any case that involves precise judgment.

A number of important clarifications:

1. If one is aware of a particular *chatzitzah*-related issue, it should be dealt with in advance and not be delayed until the last moment. At times, it is difficult to

---

1. Corresponding to Chapter Twenty in the *sefer*.

contact a rabbi at that time, and an unpleasant situation may result. (It is self-understood that this is not the case if the *chatzitzah* was only created or discovered during the night of the *tevilah*.)

2. Although there are cases where certain substances do not constitute a *chatzitzah*, this only means to say that a portion of her body may remain covered by the *chatzitzah*; however, it is imperative that the **entire body** be submerged in the water of the *mikvah*. If even the smallest part of her body—be it a single strand of hair—did not enter the water, the *tevilah* is invalid **mid'oraysa**.

3. If a woman discovered a *chatzitzah* after immersing, she should not rely on her own reasoning or previous experiences, rather she must consult an expert rabbi. She should also bring the following details to the rabbi's attention (where applicable), as they may play a role, under certain circumstances, in determining whether she is required to immerse again *bedi'eved*:

(a) If she has already engaged in marital relations with her husband.

(b) If the night has already passed, even if they did not engage in marital relations (see note[2]).

---

2. The ability to rule leniently if the night has already passed is limited to a case where her husband was at home, or to a case where others are unaware that he was not at home. In these cases, were she to be required to immerse once again the following day, others will assume that she had already engaged in forbidden marital relations. However, if her husband was not at home that night and others are aware of the fact, this leniency does not apply.

(c) If she cannot immerse once again that night (because the *mikvah* is closed or the like), even if the night has not passed and they did not engage in marital relations.

4. In any case where a woman is not required to immerse once again *bedi'eved* but is required to do so *lechatchilah* (i.e., if she is only required to immerse again in cases other than those mentioned above), no *berachah* should be recited when immersing a second time.

General Laws of *Chatzitzah*

1. *Lechatchilah* one should remove **every** *chatzitzah*, even if it is only found on a minority of her body and she is not particular to remove it. However, if such a *chatzitzah* was discovered after the *tevilah*, it does not render the *tevilah* invalid *bedi'eved*.

If she herself is not particular to remove a certain *chatzitzah* but most women are particular, her position is disregarded and the *tevilah* is invalid.

2. As stated above, if part of her body, even a single strand of hair, remains outside of the water, the *tevilah* is invalid *mid'oraysa*.

3. *Lechatchilah* one should remove loose *chatzitzos* as well, even if it covers only a minority of her body or hair and she is not particular to remove it.

4. In the event that one immersed with a loose *chatzitzah* on her body or hair, the *tevilah* is valid *bedi'eved*, because the water can enter beneath the *chatzitzah*. However, various explanations have been given by the *Poskim* as to the exact

definition of "loose," and an expert rabbi must be consulted in every case.

Laws of *Chatzitzah* in Detail

Hair

5. The *hairy areas* include the following: (1) The hair of the head. (2) The hair under the armpits. (3) The pubic hair. (4) Some opinions include the eyelashes and eyebrows in this category as well, and *lechatchilah* one should follow their view.

If She Is Accustomed to Cut Her Hair Before Immersing

6. Although the hair itself does not constitute a *chatzitzah*, if one is particular to always cut the hair of her head before the *tevilah*, she is required to do so. The law of such a woman who immersed without cutting her hair is similar to that of one who immersed without cutting her nails (see §§66). However, if it is difficult for her to immerse again, one can rely on the opinions who rule leniently.

7. Even if one is accustomed to remove the hair of the legs, it does not constitute a *chatzitzah* if she and her husband are not particular that it be removed.

8. If one is accustomed to remove the pubic hair before the *tevilah* and she immersed without doing so, it does not constitute a *chatzitzah bedi'eved*, provided she washed the vaginal area well before the *tevilah* and no sweat or tangled hair remained.

Omitted Details

9. If she neither combed nor untangled the hair of her

head properly with her fingers so that the strands should not be knotted or stuck to each other, the *tevilah* is invalid even if she washed her hair well with hot water.

10. If she untangled the hair of her head properly but did not comb it, the *tevilah* is valid in the situations listed in the introduction to this chapter (par. 3) or if it is difficult for her to immerse again. In any other situation, she should immerse again without reciting a *berachah*.

11. The *tevilah* is valid if she untangled the hair of the other hairy areas properly but did not comb them. If she did not untangle the hair of these areas but she washed and scrubbed them well, and after the *tevilah* she examined them and no *chatzitzah* was present, an expert rabbi should be consulted to determine if the *tevilah* is valid.

Other Hair-Related Issues

12. A woman with dyed hair should remove the dye if possible. If she immersed without removing the dye, the *tevilah* is valid *bedi'eved* if the dye has no actual substance and is merely pigmentation. If the dye does have an actual substance, an expert rabbi should be consulted.

13. If she has lice or nits in her hair, she should avoid *halachic* issues by beginning to treat the problem a number of days prior to the *tevilah*. If the day of the *tevilah* has arrived and the problem continues to persist, she should clean the lice and nits from her hair as much as possible. If she did so and she discovered after immersing that some of them remained, it does not constitute a *chatzitzah*.

14. If she has dandruff in her hair, she should wash her

hair thoroughly and try to remove as much as possible, and whatever remains does not constitute a *chatzitzah*. It is important to avoid *halachic* issues by beginning to treat the problem in advance.

15. However, if a somewhat large piece was discovered attached to her hair that women are usually particular to remove, it constitutes a *chatzitzah*.

16. Various laws and possibilities pertaining to hair that was discovered to be knotted have been discussed by the *Shulchan Aruch* and *Poskim*; however, such cases are quite uncommon. The related laws can be found in the *sefer* (Chapter Twenty §§11ff.).

17. The following laws apply if strands of hair were discovered to be stuck to each other:

If the majority of the hair of any one of the hairy areas was stuck together, it constitutes a *chatzitzah*. If only a minority of the hair of one of these areas was stuck together, the law will differ depending on the area:

1. The hair of the head: If most women are not particular in this regard and she is not particular as well, it does not constitute a *chatzitzah*. But if most women are particular, it constitutes a *chatzitzah*.

2. The hair under the armpits: *Lechatchilah* she should immerse once again; however, in the situations listed in the introduction to this chapter (par. 3), an expert rabbi should be consulted to determine if she can act leniently. In any case, it constitutes a *chatzitzah* if she herself is particular in this regard.

3. The pubic hair: Even if only a minority of the hair is stuck together, it constitutes a *chatzitzah*, because most women are particular that it not be stuck together. Even if she and her husband are not particular, their position is disregarded.

18. If a woman sprayed the minority of her hair for aesthetic purposes, it does not constitute a *chatzitzah bedi'eved*. This is true even regarding those areas listed in the previous paragraph where a minority of hair discovered to be stuck together constitutes a *chatzitzah*. However, she must immerse again if she sprayed the majority of her hair. An expert rabbi should be consulted if she is unable to immerse again that night.

19. If a woman immersed with eyelash extensions or false eyebrows, one can rule leniently *bedi'eved* if there is a need.

20. A woman with braided hair must undo the braids before immersing, even if the braids are loose. If she immersed without undoing the braids, the *tevilah* is valid if the braids were loose. If they were braided tightly, she should immerse again; however, if it is difficult for her to do so, one can rely on the lenient opinions that she is not required to immerse again.

21. If a woman did not remove ribbons, pins, headbands or other hair accessories before immersing, the law will depend on the exact details of the scenario. See the *sefer* (Chapter Twenty §§19-21) for the relevant laws.

22. The following laws apply if soap or shampoo remained in her hair: If she washed herself well to remove the remainder of the soap and shampoo, and after immersing she discovered that some of it still remained deep in her hair, it does

not constitute a *chatzitzah*. But if she did not wash her hair to remove it and a substantial amount remained, the likes of which most women are particular to remove, an expert rabbi should be consulted (see the *sefer* [Chapter Twenty fn. 111]).

Eyes

23. The following laws apply if mucus (that was formed either naturally or as the result of an eye disease) was discovered in the eye after immersing:

> **1.** If the mucus was discovered **within** the eye, it does not constitute a *chatzitzah* if it was liquid. But if it had congealed, it constitutes a *chatzitzah*. If it has turned yellow or green, it is considered to have congealed. However, in the situations listed in the introduction to this chapter (par. 3), she should not immerse again unless she herself is particular in this regard.

> **2.** If the mucus was discovered **outside** the eye, it constitutes a *chatzitzah* whether it was liquid or had congealed, and she must immerse again even in the above situations.

24. Eye cream must be removed before immersing, and she must immerse again if it was not removed. (See the *sefer* [Chapter Twenty §25] for additional details pertaining to challenging situations.)

25. Clear eye drops do not constitute a *chatzitzah*. However, she should avoid applying them before the *tevilah* if they are of the type that spreads over the eyelashes or the like.

26. In general, eye shadow, eyelash tint, and eyebrow tint have an actual substance and must be removed. If she im-

mersed without removing it, the *tevilah* is valid *bedi'eved* if the dye is complete and has not begun to fade. (See the *sefer* [Chapter Twenty §26] for additional details.)

27. Contact lenses constitute a *chatzitzah* because most people remove them before going to sleep. Even if she herself does not do so, her position is disregarded. Another concern is that she might close her eyes tightly when immersing so that they will not fall out and get lost, and this itself constitutes a *chatzitzah* (see Chapter Fourteen §12; §15).

Nostrils

28. If mucus was discovered in her nostrils, the *tevilah* is valid *bedi'eved* if it was somewhat deep and not visible, even if she could have removed it. There are opinions that rule stringently even *bedi'eved* if it was found at the edge of the nostrils (where it is visible from the outside), because most people are particular to remove it. See note for the law of mucus that was still liquid.[3]

29. A physician may direct a woman suffering from severe migraine headaches to refrain from allowing water to enter her nostrils. In such a case, an expert rabbi should be consulted to determine how she should immerse (see the *sefer* [Chapter Twenty §32 and fn. 129]).

Ears

30. Dirt found on the exposed portion of the ear

---

3. Although it is possible that liquid mucus of the nostrils does not constitute a *chatzitzah*, the exact definition of liquid mucus versus congealed mucus still requires clarification. Accordingly, an expert rabbi should be consulted if such mucus was discovered in her nostrils.

constitutes a *chatzitzah*. If dirt was found on the concealed portion of the ear (i.e., within the ear canal) where she is able to reach and clean it, it is a matter of doubt if it constitutes a *chatzitzah*, and she should immerse again if easily possible.

31. If a woman suffers from an ear disease and was directed by a physician to refrain from allowing water to enter her ears, an expert rabbi should be consulted to determine how she should immerse. The most ideal alternative has been described in the *sefer* (Chapter Twenty fn. 131).

32. Holes pierced in the ears (for earrings) should be cleaned with a toothpick or the like. However, if she cleaned the surrounding area well, the *tevilah* is valid *bedi'eved* even if she did not clean the inside of the holes.

If dirt was discovered in the holes after the *tevilah*, there is room to act stringently in situations other than those listed in the introduction to this chapter (par. 3).

33. The following laws apply if a woman did not remove her earrings before immersing:

Earrings of the type that are fastened tightly to the ears (and do not pass through holes in the earlobes) constitute a *chatzitzah* and she must immerse again. However, earrings of the type that pass through holes in the earlobes do not constitute a *chatzitzah bedi'eved* if they are not fastened tightly to the ears.

If they are fastened tightly, *lechatchilah* she should immerse again, but if it is difficult for her to do so, one can rely on the opinions that hold that they do not constitute a *chatzitzah bedi'eved*. However, this is true only if she does not remove her earrings even when taking a shower, going to sleep and the like; but if she does remove them at these times, all agree that they constitute a *chatzitzah*.

Mouth and Teeth

34. The mouth and teeth must be washed before the *tevilah* and examined to ensure that they are completely clean (see Chapter Eleven §27). If she immersed without doing so, she should examine them immediately, and if it is discovered that everything is indeed clean, her *tevilah* is valid *bedi'eved*.

35. If something was discovered in her mouth after the *tevilah*, her *tevilah* is valid *bedi'eved* if it was able to move about freely and was not attached to the inside of the mouth at all (so that the water would have been able to reach the actual flesh of the mouth had it entered). However, if it was attached to her mouth or teeth, the *tevilah* is invalid (see the following paragraph).

36. If she cleaned her mouth and teeth as thoroughly as possible and after the *tevilah* something was discovered attached to her mouth or teeth, an expert rabbi should be consulted to determine if there is room to rule leniently in challenging situations. However, if the item that was discovered on her teeth was visible to the outside, it constitutes a *chatzitzah*, because most people are particular not to appear in public in such a manner. This is true even if she herself is not particular in this regard.

37. The following laws apply if a woman did not clean her mouth and teeth before immersing, and after immersing she ate, following which a *chatzitzah* was discovered in her

mouth: In such a case, she must immerse again, even if the *chatzitzah* can be presumed to have derived from the food she ate following the *tevilah*. However, in the situations listed in the introduction to this chapter (par. 3), she should not immerse again (see the following paragraph).

38. It is self-understood that the above is only true if there is room to believe that the *chatzitzah* derived from the food she ate following the *tevilah*. But if it certainly did **not** derive from the food, she must immerse again in any event.

39. If it is certain that the substance **did** derive from the food she ate after the *tevilah* (for example, if it derived from a type of food that she ate after the *tevilah* and not beforehand), she does not need to immerse again.

40. If a woman has a hole in her tooth and a *chatzitzah* was discovered in the hole, an expert rabbi should be consulted to determine if one can rule leniently *bedi'eved* if it is certain that the *chatzitzah* was found deep within the hole and did not protrude whatsoever. *Lechatchilah*, however, she should act as has been outlined in the previous chapter (§28).

Fillings

41. A number of clarifications:

1. As will be explained in this section, if a filling will remain in the tooth for a certain amount of time, it is considered to be a permanent filling and does not constitute a *chatzitzah*. In this regard, the decision of the woman at the time of the *tevilah* is of consequence: even if it later turns out that she is unable to leave the filling in her tooth for that amount of time (due to medical or technical reasons), the *tevilah* is nonetheless valid, because she resolved to leave it in her tooth for the prescribed amount of time before the *tevilah*.

2. Although a filling may sometimes not constitute a *chatzitzah* (as will be detailed in the following paragraphs), this is only true if it indeed fills the tooth (with plaster, lead and the like). By contrast, if the hole remains open and is merely plugged with a medically-treated cotton ball, some authorities are of the opinion that it shares the law of a piece of food found in the hole and constitutes a *chatzitzah*. (See the *sefer* [Chapter Nineteen §30 and fn. 81] for additional details.)

41*. If a woman has a tooth with a temporary filling, she should resolve to leave it there for the next thirty days (following the *tevilah*), and it will then not constitute a *chatzitzah* according to all opinions. If this is not possible, she can suffice with resolving to leave it in the tooth for thirty days from when the tooth was filled, provided she resolves to leave it there for seven days following the *tevilah*.

42. An expert rabbi should be consulted if she can only leave the filling in the tooth for seven days from when the tooth was filled (and not thirty days).

If she immersed with a filling that she was planning on removing less than seven days after the *tevilah*, she should not immerse again in the situations listed in the introduction to this chapter (par. 3). In other situations, however, she should immerse again without reciting a *berachah*.

43. The following laws apply if a woman has a temporary filling as part of a root-canal treatment, in which a substance

was placed in the tooth which may not be removed for a certain amount of time: In such a case, if she is to immerse during the time when it may not be removed, the filling does not constitute a *chatzitzah*.[4] However, if the time has come for it to be removed and it has not yet been done, it is considered a *chatzitzah* if there is an underlying reason for it to be removed (so that it should not damage the tooth or the like). If no such concern exists, the filling shares the laws of any other temporary filling, as has been outlined in the previous paragraphs.

44. A permanent filling does not constitute a *chatzitzah*. This is true even if she has fillings in most of her teeth, or even in all of them.

45. When inserting a filling, whether temporary or permanent, the physician should be requested to insert it completely within the tooth so that it does not protrude, because there are authorities that hold that only in such a case will it not constitute a *chatzitzah*. However, if the night of the *tevilah* has arrived and it is too late to resolve the matter, she may immerse, and she should try to resolve it as soon as possible.

---

4. Another possible scenario is where in addition to the root canal treatment (that may not be removed for a certain amount of time), a standard filling has been inserted into the tooth as well. The law in such a case will depend on the purpose of the filling: If it was inserted to prevent the inner filling from falling out (while eating and the like), it shares the same law as the inner filling, and it does not constitute a *chatzitzah* during the time when it may not be removed. However, if the outer filling was inserted merely for the woman's convenience (to enable her to eat comfortably and the like), it might constitute a *chatzitzah* (unless she resolves to leave it there for the prescribed amount of time). Accordingly, a woman with such a filling should ask the physician as to its purpose and should conduct herself appropriately.

46. A filling constitutes a *chatzitzah* if it bothers her (due to aesthetic reasons or discomfort) to the extent that she is planning on having it removed.

47. The following laws apply if drops of the substance from which the filling was formed got stuck to her teeth when it was being inserted: If she removed whatever she was able and a tiny drop remained that is not visible from the outside (and she can feel it with her tongue), it is considered as if she is not particular and it does not constitute a *chatzitzah*. However, if it can be noticed by others in such a way that she is particular, it constitutes a *chatzitzah* and must be removed. The same law applies if most women are particular even if she herself is not.

48. A damaged filling does not constitute a *chatzitzah* if it does not bother her and still serves its purpose (i.e., it allows her to eat; protects the tooth from infection, heat and cold; and so on).

49. However, a filling constitutes a *chatzitzah* if it is damaged to the extent that it no longer serves its purpose and it bothers her (due to aesthetic reasons or discomfort). If it no longer serves its purpose but it does not bother her, it does not constitute a *chatzitzah* if she does not plan on removing it. If she does plan on removing it, an expert rabbi should be consulted.

50. The laws of a loose filling (that has not yet fallen out) are the same as those of a damaged filling, as has been outlined in the previous paragraphs.

51. A filling she is planning on having removed due to pain in the tooth constitutes a *chatzitzah* if the pain is a result

of the filling. However, if it is certain that the pain is inherent to the tooth and is not a result of the filling (even though the filling must be removed in order to treat the tooth), one can act leniently in challenging circumstances and it does not constitute a *chatzitzah*.

52. A substance that was inserted to complete the missing section of a fractured tooth does not constitute a *chatzitzah* if it was fashioned properly and does not bother her. The same is true regarding a substance that was inserted to fill a gap between the teeth.

Crowns

53. The laws of crowns in the teeth, whether permanent or temporary, are equal in all their details to the laws of fillings, as has been elaborated upon in the previous paragraphs.

If it is possible to remove the crown (for example, a temporary crown that is not secured properly), she should do so even if it will remain in the tooth long enough to be considered permanent (see §41*). However, her *tevilah* is valid *bedi'eved* even if she did not remove it.

54. A tooth coated with gold or another material does not constitute a *chatzitzah*.

Dentures

55. Fixed dentures that cannot be removed do not constitute a *chatzitzah*. This is true no matter the type of material from which they are formed, as well as the reason they were inserted into the mouth (i.e., for medical or aesthetic purposes).

56. The following laws apply to dentures that can be re-

moved: If she only removes them in order to clean them, it is considered a *chatzitzah lechatchilah*. However, in the situations listed in the introduction to this chapter (par. 3), she should not immerse again.

If she removes them before going to sleep, they constitute a *chatzitzah* even *bedi'eved*. It is important to make note of this law, as most removable dentures in recent times are included in this category.

57. Removable dentures that are only worn when there is an aesthetic need constitute a *chatzitzah* (for example, if she only wears them when going outside so that she will not be seen with missing teeth).

58. An expert rabbi should be consulted if the dentures are inserted loosely in such a way that it is certain that the *mikvah* water can reach the area underneath (if the water were to enter her mouth).

59. Temporary dentures (that were inserted until the permanent teeth are prepared) do not constitute a *chatzitzah* if they were inserted to remain long enough to be considered permanent (see supra §§41*ff.). Nonetheless, if they are removable, they must be removed before immersing.

Various Dental Treatments and Issues

60. The laws of retainers are equal in all their details to the laws of dentures, as has been elaborated upon in the previous paragraphs.

61. A bridge does not constitute a *chatzitzah* due to its permanent nature. However, she should take care to clean it carefully from the dirt that can gather beneath and around it.

62. Braces that were inserted for medical reasons (to provide support for loose teeth until they are healed) do not
constitute a *chatzitzah* if they cannot be removed. However,
the law is more stringent with regard to braces inserted solely
for aesthetic purposes (to straighten the teeth and the like),
and an expert rabbi should be consulted to determine if it is
possible to rule leniently (see note[5]).

63. Stitches in the gums (inserted after a tooth was surgically removed) do not constitute a *chatzitzah* if they will
disintegrate by themselves (without the need for a medical
procedure). Many authorities maintain that they constitute
a *chatzitzah* if a procedure is necessary to remove them. An
expert rabbi should be consulted in challenging situations
(see the *sefer* [Chapter Twenty fn. 183]).

64. Plaque on the teeth does not constitute a *chatzitzah*,

---

5. Contemporary authorities differ whether braces inserted for aesthetic purposes constitute a *chatzitzah*. It is possible to argue that even
such braces provide health benefits, as the teeth may become damaged if
they are not straightened. However, this presumption is not all-inclusive,
and each case must be assessed individually to determine if this is indeed
so.

Another factor that must be taken into consideration is the fact that
this matter entails challenging situations of great proportions, as in modern times virtually everyone is particular to ensure that their teeth are
not crooked. Anyone who has crooked teeth deals with the problem by
way of inserting braces, notwithstanding the great expenses involved. It
is thus almost unheard of to remove them, thereby reducing the money
and effort involved to naught. As such, the expert rabbi to whom such a
question is presented must judge each particular case to determine how
much this is of importance to the individual.

It is also reasonable to state that if they are supposed to be removed
anyway in a short amount of time, she should be instructed to remove
them before immersing.

even if one is accustomed to visit a dentist every so often to remove it.

65. A tooth that will soon be removed does not constitute a *chatzitzah*, even if it is extremely loose and causes her great pain. Similarly, a fractured tooth does not constitute a *chatzitzah* in any case.

Nails

In any case where one should immerse again *lechatchilah* even though the nails were clean, she should not recite a *berachah* at the second *tevilah*.

66. The following laws apply if one forgot to cut her nails, either entirely or partially, including even a single nail: If she is certain that they were completely clean at the time of the *tevilah*—i.e., she examined them before immersing and saw that they were clean (see the following paragraph)—she should not immerse again in the situations listed in the introduction to this chapter (par. 3). In other situations, she should immerse again without reciting a *berachah*.

67. As stated in the previous paragraph, the nails must have been examined before immersing in order for them to have been considered certainly clean. Other laws apply if she did not examine them beforehand, and after immersing she examined them and saw that they were clean. In such a case, the *tevilah* is valid in the above situations only if the nails do not extend past the tips of the fingers (even though *lechatchilah* she should have cut them until where they meet the skin). However, if they extend past the tips of the fingers, she must immerse again. An expert rabbi should be consulted in extremely challenging situations.

68. In situations other than those listed in the introduction to this chapter, she should immerse again (as stated in §66) even if only a portion of a nail had not been cut. (See the *sefer* [Chapter Twenty §69] for additional relevant laws. See note for the laws that apply to Jews of Sephardic descent.[6])

69. One should immerse again if she forgot to cut her toenails; however, one can be lenient if there is a great need.

70. Wherever it was stated that she is not required to immerse again, this is only the case if the uncut nails were clean. In a case where dirt was discovered under a nail, she must immerse again in any case.

Nail-Cutting Problems

71. If a woman has a swollen finger that covers the opening of the nail, it does not constitute a *chatzitzah*, provided that any dirt present is completely covered by the nail and swelling of the finger. However, dirt protruding outside of the nail must be removed. Regardless, if she can cut or clean a portion of the nail, she should do so, even if the rest will not be cleaned.

72. If a woman has a swollen finger that does not cover the opening of the nail, the nail must be cleaned before immersing. A suggested method of cleaning the nail in such

---

6. Certain early Sephardic authorities have stated that one is not required to immerse again if dirt was discovered under the portion of the nail that is against the finger. However, it seems that this is not the case nowadays, as most women are particular not to appear in public with dirt under any portion of the nail. Accordingly, even these authorities would agree that one should immerse again in such a case.

a case is to soak the finger in hot water and soap to soften the area and allow the nail to be cleaned. Soaking the finger in hydrogen peroxide can also assist in softening congealed blood.

73. If the pain is so great that she is still unable to clean the nail, an expert rabbi should be consulted (see the *sefer* [Chapter Nineteen fn. 115]).

74. A treatment sometimes recommended to a person with an ingrown nail is to refrain from cutting it, and a strip of gauze is inserted beneath the nail to assist it in growing properly. In such a case, the grown nail does not constitute a *chatzitzah*, because she is particular not to cut it. However, the gauze is considered a *chatzitzah* and must be removed before the *tevilah*.

75. Similarly, a doctor may direct a person with a damaged nail (for example, if a door was closed on it) to leave it untouched in order to protect the wound underneath. In such a case, the nail is not considered a *chatzitzah*, even though it will eventually fall off on its own. However, if it has been decided that there is no need for it to remain any longer and it should be removed, the nail constitutes a *chatzitzah*.

76. A nail that is partially detached from the finger does not constitute a *chatzitzah* if there is space between the detached and attached portions of the nail where the water can enter. (See the *sefer* [Chapter Twenty §80] for additional laws.)

77. In any event, a nail that is partially detached from its root constitutes a *chatzitzah*.

78. If a new nail has begun to grow and is slowly replacing the old nail (as sometimes happens when a nail has been damaged due to a blow and the like), it does not constitute a *chatzitzah*, because she is unable to cut it. This is true even if there is space between the two nails.

79. A woman who grows her nails should consult an expert rabbi to determine if and how she can be allowed to immerse in the *mikvah* in her present condition. The same is true regarding a woman with artificial nail extensions which are firmly attached and cannot be removed. (See the *sefer* [Chapter Twenty §§82-83]). However, *lechatchilah* one should not wear such extensions, as it is difficult to allow one to immerse in such a state.

80. *Lechatchilah*, she should remove nail polish and the like applied to her nails. If she did not remove it before the *tevilah*, her *tevilah* is valid *bedi'eved* if the color is complete and has not begun to fade. However, if the color has begun to fade to the extent that women are usually particular to replace it, her *tevilah* is invalid, even if she herself is not particular in this regard. Similarly, her *tevilah* is invalid if she herself is particular, even if most women are not as particular as her.

81. Small drops of polish do not constitute a *chatzitzah* if women generally do not avoid going outside in such a state and she herself is not particular as well.

Makeup

82. *Lechatchilah* she should remove any type of makeup applied to her face. *Bedi'eved*, if she has already immersed in the *mikvah* or if she cannot remove it, her *tevilah* is valid if

the color is complete. But if it has begun to fade (as described earlier [§80]), it constitutes a *chatzitzah*.

Wounds

83. The following laws apply if a woman has a wound that she may not remove (for example, a wound caused by a tuberculosis vaccination that may not be removed or scratched): If she may soften it with warm water, she should do so. If this too is detrimental, an expert rabbi should be consulted to determine if she can be allowed to immerse in her present state (see the *sefer* [Chapter Nineteen fn. 170]).

Blood

84. Nowadays, most women are particular that no blood should be found on their skin, even if it is liquid. Accordingly, if a woman has a cut or the like, she must clean it well and attempt to stop the flow of blood. If, upon entering the water of the *mikvah*, she sees that the blood is being washed off of her body, her *tevilah* is valid. In any case, if she is unable to stop the flow of blood, she may immerse in her present condition and it does not constitute a *chatzitzah*.

85. The above applies to blood that is still liquid; if blood found on her body has become sticky (see §89), it is categorized as congealed blood even though it has not congealed completely, and it constitutes a *chatzitzah*.

Scabs

86. If a woman has blood on her body that is clearly visible as having congealed (a scab), it constitutes a *chatzitzah* even if it is only found on the wound itself and has not spread to the skin. Accordingly, she must remove it by softening it

with warm water and peeling it off. If she is unable to peel it off due to the great pain involved, she can suffice with softening it well with warm water.

87. In this latter case, she must soften it specifically with warm water, and it must be done thoroughly until it is certain that it has completely softened. If the scab does not soften despite her efforts, it is customary to remove it notwithstanding the great pain involved. If she cannot remove it due to the tremendous pain involved, one can rely on the opinions that allow her to immerse in her present condition.

88. Blood that has spread to the skin beyond the wound and has congealed must be removed. Removing this part of the scab generally does not pose a problem after it has been softened well. If it was not removed, the scab constitutes a *chatzitzah*.

If she is concerned that removing this part of the scab might prove detrimental to the wound itself, an expert rabbi should be consulted to determine if she can suffice with softening it (see the *sefer* [Chapter Nineteen fn. 146*]).

89. The obligation to remove blood that has spread beyond the wound applies both to congealed blood (a scab) and to blood that has become sticky, in which a strand is drawn after the finger when touched (in contrast to liquid blood, in which the flow interrupts immediately). Such blood as well constitutes a *chatzitzah* if it is not removed.

Pus

90. Pus that is found **within** the wound does not constitute a *chatzitzah* because it is liquid. The law of pus found

upon the wound (and has not yet spread to the skin beyond the wound) consists of various details and has been explained in the *sefer* (Chapter Twenty §99).

91. Pus that has spread to the skin **beyond** the wound constitutes a *chatzitzah* and must be removed by softening it with warm water (as per the details explained earlier [§88] with regard to scabs). This is true even if the pus is still liquid, because nowadays most women are particular that no such pus should be found on their body.

If, upon entering the water of the *mikvah*, she sees that the pus is being washed off of her body, her *tevilah* is valid.

92. If a woman immersed with liquid pus that spread to the skin beyond the wound, she does not need to immerse again if it is extremely difficult to do so or in the situations listed in the introduction to this chapter (par. 3). In such situations, one can rely on the opinions that hold that liquid pus does not constitute a *chatzitzah* even if she is particular. In other situations, however, she should immerse again without reciting a *berachah*.

93. Pus contained within a closed blister does not constitute a *chatzitzah*, even if the blister protrudes from the skin. However, if the blister has ruptured, she should soften the pus and remove it, even if the pus is still contained within the blister. If she cannot do so because of the great pain involved, she can suffice with softening the pus with warm water. If she immersed without doing so, she should immerse again, unless she finds herself in one of the situations listed in the introduction to this chapter (par. 3).

94. Pus of a ruptured pimple must be removed, as ex-

plained in the previous paragraph with regard to blisters. If she immersed without removing it (for example, if the pimple was on her back and she didn't discover it until after immersing), she should immerse again, unless she is in one of the situations listed in the introduction to this chapter (par. 3).

Stitches and Band-Aids

95. Stitches do not constitute a *chatzitzah* if they will disintegrate by themselves (without the need for a physician to remove them). However, stitches that must be removed by a physician constitute a *chatzitzah* if they are attached securely to the body and the water of the *mikvah* cannot reach the area underneath (as is generally the case). However, they do not constitute a *chatzitzah* if they are loose and the water can reach the area underneath. A proper assessment is required to determine that they are indeed sufficiently loose (see the *sefer* [Chapter Twenty fn. 220]).

If the stitches will remain on her body for an extended amount of time, an expert rabbi should be consulted to determine if one can act leniently in certain circumstances (a lengthy discussion on the topic can be found in the *sefer* [Chapter Twenty, *Biurim* §3]).

96. Band-aids constitute a *chatzitzah*, as do contraceptive patches. However, patches that disintegrate gradually on their own do not constitute a *chatzitzah*.

Creams

97. One should remove cream that is spread on her body, and it constitutes a *chatzitzah* if she did not do so. If removing the cream might be detrimental to the wound or result in

great pain, an expert rabbi should be consulted to determine if one may act leniently.

If she removed the actual cream, she may immerse even if her skin is still oily.

Bandages and Casts

98. Bandages and casts constitute a *chatzitzah*; however, an expert rabbi should be consulted to determine the law with regard to certain types of bandages and when found in unique situations (see the *sefer* [Chapter Twenty §§97-101; ibid., *Biurim* §3 at length]).

Skin-Related Issues

99. The following paragraphs deal exclusively with issues related to the skin. However, if one has peeling skin, she should take notice to see if any congealed blood or pus is found in the area, in which case the previous paragraphs should be consulted to determine the relevant laws.

Peeling Skin Surrounding the Nails

100. Peeling skin surrounding the nails must be cut, and the little that remains adjacent to the finger does not constitute a *chatzitzah*. If she did not cut it at all, she should immerse again if possible without reciting a *berachah*.

If she examined herself before the *tevilah* and did not notice any peeling skin and after the *tevilah* she discovered such skin, she does not need to immerse again, for we assume that the skin peeled after the *tevilah*.

101. In the situations listed in the introduction to this chapter (par. 3), she can rely on the lenient opinions that

maintain that one does not need to immerse again due to such skin in any case.

102. Although one must cut peeling skin surrounding the toenails as well, she is not required to immerse again if she immersed without cutting them, even when not found in one of the above situations.

Peeling Skin on the Body

103. A number of clarifications:

1. The reason why peeling skin does not constitute a *chatzitzah* under certain circumstances is because one is not usually particular to remove it. Consequently, if she herself is particular to remove it, it constitutes a *chatzitzah*.

2. In all the situations mentioned in the following paragraphs, the skin does not constitute a *chatzitzah* if it is closed (and contains pus or similar fluids).

104. Skin that has peeled as the result of sunburn should be removed. After she has removed as much of the skin as possible, the remaining skin does not constitute a *chatzitzah* if removing it will be painful. However, she should soak the remaining skin in warm water to loosen any skin that has reattached itself to the body, so that the water of the *mikvah* will be able to reach the area underneath. Nonetheless, she does not need to immerse again if she immersed without doing so.

105. If she did not remove the skin whose removal will not be painful, her *tevilah* is invalid and she should immerse again without reciting a *berachah*. However, she should not

immerse again in the situations listed in the introduction to this chapter (par. 3).

106. Skin that has peeled as a result of a burn, eczema, or a ruptured blister should be removed, as well as skin on the lips that has peeled. However, the skin does not constitute a *chatzitzah* if removing it will be painful or if it may not be removed due to medical reasons. In such a case, she should soak the skin in warm water to enable the water of the *mikvah* to reach the area underneath the skin that has reattached to the body.

The law of one who did not remove such skin that can be removed is the same as the law of skin that has peeled as a result of sunburn, as has been explained in the previous paragraph.

107. One should avoid spending excessive time in a bath until the skin begins to flake, as certain authorities are of the opinion that such skin constitutes a *chatzitzah*. *Bedi'eved*, however, one can rely on the opinions who rule leniently.

108. A wart (or the like) does not constitute a *chatzitzah* under normal circumstances. However, it constitutes a *chatzitzah* if it has begun to fall off and causes her pain, or if she is planning on cutting it off (even if it does not cause her pain). Nonetheless, she can be allowed to immerse in her present situation if she was unable to remove it before the *tevilah*.

Splinters

109. If a woman has a splinter, thorn, or the like embedded underneath her skin (i.e., the splinter is beneath the

height of the skin), it does not constitute a *chatzitzah*, even if it is visible. However, if she is planning on removing it, she must remove whatever she can before the *tevilah*, and it constitutes a *chatzitzah* if she did not do so. If removing it will result in pain, it does not constitute a *chatzitzah*.

110. If it protrudes from the skin, or even if it is just on the same level as the skin, and a layer of skin has not yet covered it, she must remove the embedded entity until whatever remains is found beneath the height of the skin. If she did not do so, it constitutes a *chatzitzah* even *bedi'eved*.

111. Certain sicknesses—such as severe eczema and erysipelas—necessitate that the affected area remain dry. At times, a person with such a condition may be allowed to immerse in water after applying an oil or cream over the affected area. In such a case, an expert rabbi should be consulted to determine if she may immerse in such a manner if the situation is extremely challenging (for example, if she will remain in this state for an extended period of time). In such a case, she should immerse quickly in lukewarm water so that the cream will not dissolve while immersing (see the *sefer* [Chapter Twenty, *Biurim* §4]).

Stains

112. A stain consisting of a sticky substance constitutes a *chatzitzah* (similar to scabs and pus—see above).

113. A stain constitutes a *chatzitzah* even if it is liquid, if she is particular that it should not be found on her body. If, upon entering the water of the *mikvah*, she clearly sees that the substance is being washed off of her body, her *tevilah* is valid. In the situations listed in the introduction to

this chapter (par. 3), she can rely on the opinions that rule leniently (with regard to a **liquid** stain) and she should not immerse again in any case.

114. If she removed the substance of the stain and traces of color that are difficult to remove remain, it does not constitute a *chatzitzah*. The same law applies to stains from iodine, peeling vegetables and the like, as well as to hands that are black from touching a sooty substance.

In any case, *lechatchilah* she should remove such traces of color as well, using substances that are manufactured for this purpose (and are available in many *mikva'os*).

115. The laws relating to colored substances found on a woman's body for aesthetic purposes have been explained earlier in this chapter, as indicated below:

Dyed hair—§12. Dyed eyelashes or eyebrows—§26. Nail polish—§80. Makeup—§82.

Chatzitzos in the Vagina or Anus

116. If a woman discovered particles from a cotton ball in her vagina, she must immerse again without reciting a *berachah*. The same law applies if she forgot to remove a *bedikah* cloth or if pieces of it remained in the vagina, or if she discovered remnants of toilet paper or the like. However, in the situations listed in the introduction to this chapter (par. 3), she should not immerse again.

117. If she did not wash the inside of her vagina (see Chapter Eleven §58), her *tevilah* is still valid *bedi'eved*.

118. Vaginal rings (such as NuvaRing, used for contra-

ceptive purposes) must be removed prior to immersing, as they constitute a *chatzitzah*. (The contraception is still protected if the ring was left outside for up to about three hours.)

119. An IUD does not constitute a *chatzitzah*, as it is inserted into the uterus and is not found in the vagina. A woman with an IUD should ensure that the string that hangs in the vagina is clean and is not stuck to the wall of the vagina. She should take care to wash the inside of the vagina by squirting water forcefully with a syringe or the like.

120. A woman with a pessary inserted deeply into the vagina (because of a uterine prolapse) should consult an expert rabbi to determine how she is to immerse.

121. If she did not examine herself before immersing to see if she needs to relieve herself, her *tevilah* is valid if she did not need to restrain herself strongly. But if she was forced to restrain herself strongly, she must immerse again.

122. Excrement constitutes a *chatzitzah* if it is found on any area of the body. If it is found in the opening of the anus, it constitutes a *chatzitzah* if it is in an area from where people are particular to wipe it off. But if it is deeper than this, it does not constitute a *chatzitzah*.

The *Shulchan Aruch* rules that one may not recite blessings and the like if excrement is found on an area which is exposed when sitting. It is thus self-understood that people are particular to remove excrement found in such a place.

Walking Barefoot

123. The following laws apply if she walked barefoot to the *mikvah* from the location where she performed the *chafi-*

fah and did not wash the soles of her feet before immersing: If the *mikvah* water was hot, it can be assumed that the water washed off any dirt that might have been found on her feet. But if the *mikvah* water was cold, she must immerse again if her feet indeed became soiled. (An expert rabbi should be consulted if the *mikvah* water was lukewarm.) However, if she is unsure if her feet became soiled, or if she is found in one of the situations listed in the introduction to this chapter (par. 3), her *tevilah* is valid *bedi'eved.*

In any case, if she clearly sees upon entering the *mikvah* that the dirt is being washed off of her feet, her *tevilah* is valid.

Sweat

124. Sweat that is still wet does not constitute a *chatzitzah*; but if it dried and formed a crust on her skin, it constitutes a *chatzitzah.*

Jewelry

125. Any piece of jewelry usually worn tightly on the body (such as a ring or bracelet) must be removed before immersing, even if it is loose. This is true even if it is difficult to remove it; she must visit a professional to remove it if necessary.

If she did not remove it before immersing, an expert rabbi should be consulted to determine if it can be categorized as having been loose (as explained in the *sefer* [Chapter Twenty §128]), in which case it does not constitute a *chatzitzah bedi'eved.* The same law applies if she cannot remove it and it is too late to visit a professional.

126. In any case, it is imperative to clean the skin under the ring (or other piece of jewelry). If she cannot clean the area due to the tightness of the ring, it constitutes a *chatzitzah* and she may not immerse until it is removed.

127. See above (§33) for the law of one who forgot to remove her earrings before immersing.

CHAPTER THIRTEEN[1]

CORRECT TIME FOR *TEVILAH*

Introduction

The purification of a woman from her *nidah* status can be accomplished only by means of a proper *tevilah* performed in a kosher *mikvah*, preceded by the counting of *shivah nekiyim* as prescribed by *halachah*. All of the *harchakos* with all their details must be kept until this occurs, even if an extended period of time has passed since the *tum'ah*.

1. If one's husband is in town, it is a *mitzvah* to immerse on time, i.e., as soon as it is *halachically* and practically possible. This is true even if they have already fulfilled the obligation to bear children; nonetheless, it is a *mitzvah* to immerse in order to fulfill the marital *onah* obligation. Similarly, it is a *mitzvah* to immerse even if it is impossible for her to conceive, for example, when she is pregnant and the like. Indeed, our Sages have emphasized the reward of those who immerse as soon as (*halachically* and practically) possible.

Traveling on the Day of the *Tevilah*

2. The husband may not depart on a journey on the day when his wife is to immerse; rather he must first wait until she immerses and he fulfills his marital obligations.

The above is the *halachic* **requirement;** if possible, he

---

1. Corresponding to Chapter Twenty-One in the *sefer*.

should try to wait even beyond this length of time (i.e., even if she is to immerse at a later date).

3. The husband may depart if the journey is of great importance (and cannot wait until after the *tevilah*), and certainly if it is for the sake of a *mitzvah*. A business trip is generally classified as an ordinary trip and may not be undertaken on the day of the *tevilah*.

4. In any event where the husband must depart, he must first ensure that his wife consents to the trip and will not take offense for delaying her *onah*. He should make sure that she indeed agrees with a full heart (and not just because she doesn't want to delay his trip, because she is afraid of his reaction if she will not agree (!), or the like).

Tevilah That Will Not Be Followed by Marital Relations

5. *Lechatchilah* one should not immerse if no marital relations will follow that night, and the *tevilah* should be delayed accordingly. This is true whether the cause is *halachic*—if that night is a *veses* during which they must separate (see Chapter Sixteen §16), or if she is in a state of mourning—or practical—for example, if her husband is out of town or if one of them is not feeling well. The reason for this admonition is because there is concern for spiritual harm if the *tevilah* is not followed by marital relations.

6. At times, a significant reason is present to immerse at a time when no marital relations will follow, for example, if delaying the *tevilah* will result in further delays.

An example is if the night of her tevilah *[which will not be followed by marital relations] is on Thursday, and the* mikvah *will be closed on Friday night. In such a case, refraining from immersing on Thursday night will result in delaying the* tevilah *until* motza'ei Shabbos.

The law in such a circumstance will depend on the reason why marital relations cannot occur following the *tevilah*: If such relations are forbidden due to a mourning status (of the husband), she may not immerse until marital relations may be resumed. However, if they are forbidden because that night is a *veses*, she may immerse, and *segulos* for protection should be performed (as listed in §9). The same law applies if relations are not forbidden *halachically* but cannot occur for practical reasons.

Even though she has immersed, relations are forbidden during a *veses*, and affectionate touch should be avoided as well (see Chapter Sixteen §16).

7. If her husband is out of town and she does not know when he will return (and he may return at any time), she should immerse in the correct time so that she will be *tehorah* when he arrives, and *segulos* for protection should be performed (as listed in §9). However, if she knows when he is due to return and she will be able to immerse at that time, she should delay her *tevilah* until then.

8. If her husband is ill and she must assist him in ways that are forbidden when she is *temei'ah* (see Chapter Six §§122ff.), she may immerse, although the *tevilah* is not for the purpose of engaging in marital relations. She should recite a *berachah* over this *tevilah* as well. (Doing so is preferable to assisting him while remaining in a state of *tum'ah*. See

the following paragraphs for precautions to be followed when found in such a situation.)

9. The following are *segulos* (as a protection from spiritual harm) to be performed by one who immerses when marital relations will not follow: (1) She should place a knife under her pillow when she goes to bed. (2) She should cover herself with a garment of her husband when she goes to bed.

She should continue performing these *segulos* until relations can occur.

10. In a case where a woman may immerse although her husband is home and no relations will follow, care should be taken to avoid affectionate touch, as this may produce in negative results (such as the wasteful release of semen or the like). See note.[2]

---

2. The following are a number of quotes from the *Poskim* concerning affectionate touch during a *veses* or at any other time when they are not engaging in marital relations:

"Anyone who fears the word of G-d should refrain from engaging in kissing, hugging, and similar affectionate touch which will lead to erection [of the organ] if he does not want to engage in marital relations [at that time]" (*Mekor Chaim* §240).

"Anyone who guards his soul should distance himself from [hugging and kissing during a *veses*], as this may result in the wasteful release of semen" (Pardes Rimonim §184).

"One must refrain from engaging in hugging and kissing [during a *veses*]. Since it is forbidden for him to engage in marital relations, how can he engage in hugging and kissing, thereby provoking the passions of his evil inclination?!" (*Ben Ish Chai, Shanah Sheniyah,* Tzav §2)

"If one will engage in hugging and kissing and take care not to engage in relations, there is concern that this may result in the wasteful release of semen...which is a grave sin...as explained in Zohar and in Sefer Yerei'im. It appears to me that even those who allow hugging and kissing during a *veses* permit this only for one who is not that passionate [by

11. Even if one plans to delay her *tevilah* for any of the above-mentioned reasons, a *hefsek taharah* should be performed in the correct time followed by the counting of *shivah nekiyim*. Once this has been done, there is no need to perform additional *bedikos*, even if several days will pass from the end of the *shivah nekiyim* until the *tevilah*. Rather, she should pay heed to her *taharah* status (and to any unexpected bleeding that might occur), and when the appropriate time arrives, she can perform a *chafifah* and immerse in the *mikvah* immediately.

One should certainly act in the above manner if one follows the opinion of the Alter Rebbe with regard to the *haflagah* calculations (i.e., that they are calculated from the *hefsek taharah* until the subsequent discharge of blood—see Chapter Sixteen §47). For such a woman, performing a *hefsek taharah* to determine when the bleeding has ended will allow her *haflagah* calculations to be accurate. Accordingly, she should perform a *hefsek taharah* even if she will not be counting *shivah nekiyim* (for example, if she will not be able to immerse until after her next period).

---

nature] and is certain that no erection of the organ or wasteful release of semen will result.... It appears to me that if one is not certain that no erection of the organ or wasteful release of semen will result, it is forbidden to engage in hugging and kissing even if she is *tehorah* and it is not during a *veses*, if they are not engaging in marital relations at that time, for this will result in the erection of the organ, G-d forbid" (*Taharas Yisrael* §184—see there for more on the severity of the issue).

"One should be aware that the words of the *Poskim* who permit hugging and kissing [during a *veses*]...are dealing solely with the *nidah* prohibition. One must certainly exercise caution [in this regard] due to the concern of immoral thoughts and the wasteful release of semen" (*K'nei Bosem* §184).

Immersing on Shabbos When No Marital Relations Will Follow

12. If marital relations cannot occur because her husband is out of town or due to a similar reason, it is *halachically* forbidden to immerse on Shabbos night. However, one can act leniently if delaying the *tevilah* will result in further delays.

If her husband will arrive on *motza'ei Shabbos*, an expert rabbi should be consulted to determine if she may immerse on Shabbos night if possible (see the *sefer* [Chapter Twenty-One fn. 18*]).

13. It is *halachically* permissible to immerse on *motza'ei Shabbos* or *motza'ei Yom Tov* even if her husband is out of town; however, it should be avoided if there is no need to do so (see §§5ff.).

14. One may immerse on the night of *nittel*, and they should try to delay marital relations until after midnight.

Scheduling a *Tevilah* for Shabbos Night, *Motza'ei Shabbos*, or *Motza'ei Yom Tov*

15. If her husband is in town and they are able to engage in marital relations, she may immerse at any time, including Shabbos night, Yom Tov night, *motza'ei Shabbos*, or *motza'ei Yom Tov*. (The only exceptions are on Tishah B'Av, Yom Kippur, or when found in a state of mourning.) However, this is only if the night of her *tevilah* coincided with one of these nights; but if she is able to complete the *shivah nekiyim* and immerse at an earlier time, she may not schedule her *tevilah* to occur on Shabbos night, *motza'ei Shabbos*, or *motza'ei Yom*

Tov (by delaying to count the *shivah nekiyim* or by postponing the *tevilah*). However, she may schedule her *tevilah* to occur on Yom Tov night if there is a need.

16. An expert rabbi should be consulted when found in challenging situations in which there appears to be a justified reason to postpone the *tevilah* to one of these nights (see the *sefer* [Chapter Twenty-One fn. 25]).

17. As stated above (§5), if the night of her *tevilah* coincides with a *veses*, the *tevilah* should be delayed so that it will be followed by marital relations. However, if her *tevilah* coincides with a *veses* on **Thursday night,** she should immerse despite the fact that no marital relations will follow, and they should take care to avoid any affectionate touch. (The *segulos* listed above [§9] should be performed as well.) This is preferable to delaying the *tevilah* until Shabbos night. However, if she did not immerse on Thursday night, she may immerse on Shabbos night.

18. The following laws apply if she scheduled her *tevilah* to occur on Shabbos night, *motza'ei Shabbos,* or *motza'ei Yom Tov*:

1. If she did **not** have any reason at all for scheduling her *tevilah* for that night, she may not immerse on that night, and she must postpone her *tevilah* to Sunday night or to the night after Isru Chag. An expert rabbi should be consulted in extremely challenging situations. In any case, her *tevilah* is valid if she has already immersed.

2. If she **had** an underlying rationale for scheduling her *tevilah* for that night, she may immerse, even if the reason would not have been sufficient to allow her to schedule her *tevilah* for that night *lechatchilah*. Similarly, if one must immerse a second time due to a *chatzitzah* in her first *tevilah*, she may immerse on one of these nights.

19. There are times when a woman cannot perform the *chafifah* adjacent to the *tevilah*, for example, if the *tevilah* occurs on a Yom Tov night which is *motza'ei Shabbos* or vice versa, or if it occurs on the second night of a two-day Yom Tov. In these cases, the *chafifah* must be performed on *erev Shabbos* or *erev Yom Tov*, resulting in an interruption between the *chafifah* and the *tevilah* (see Chapter Ten §§29ff.).

Even if there seems to be a need to do so, a woman should not schedule her *tevilah* to occur on such a night; rather, she must postpone the *tevilah* to a night when she will be able to perform the *chafifah* adjacent to the *tevilah*. An expert rabbi should be consulted if there is an extremely great need.

Tevilah by Day

20. It is forbidden to immerse by day, even if the *tevilah* is because of a *tum'ah* which is *mid'rabanan*, for example, a *kesem* or *dam besulim*; rather, the *tevilah* must take place during the actual night (i.e., after *tzeis hakochavim*).[3] The

---

3. One can visit chabad.org/zmanim to find out the exact time of *tzeis hakochavim* in any location.

A number of related points:

(1) Even those who are usually stringent to follow the calculation of Rabbeinu Tam with regard to *tzeis hakochavim* can be lenient (with regard to *tevilah*) and follow the calculation of the *Geonim*. On the other hand, there are women who follow the calculation of Rabbeinu Tam with regard to *tevilah* as well.

(2) The requirement to immerse after *tzeis hakochavim* applies to Friday night as well.

prohibition to immerse by day applies even if she will only return home from the *mikvah* after nightfall.

21. The prohibition to immerse by day applies even if one is immersing again due to a problem with the first *tevilah*.

22. The following laws apply if one immersed by day *be-di'eved*: If she immersed on the **eighth** day of her counting and onwards, her *tevilah* is valid; however, she must refrain from returning home until nightfall. But if she immersed on the **seventh** day, she should immerse again at night if possible, albeit without reciting a *berachah* on the second *tevilah*. If she immersed during *bein hashmashos*, she is not required to immerse again.

23. An expert rabbi should be consulted if one has no choice and is compelled to immerse by day. It should be noted that immersing during *bein hashmashos* is always preferable to immersing by day. As such, even in those cases where a Rabbi has ruled that she may immerse during the day, if she is able to immerse during *bein hashmashos*, she should do so.

Modesty on the Night of the *Tevilah*

24. The *Shulchan Aruch* states, "A woman should behave modestly on the night of her *tevilah*. Accordingly, women are accustomed to conceal the night of their *tevilah* by avoiding to go to the *mikvah* publicly or in the presence of others, so that people will not realize [that they are on their way to immerse]." A woman who behaves modestly when immersing is guaranteed to give birth to virtuous children.

Caution should be taken to conceal the *tevilah* (not only

from men but) from women as well. However, one may ask another woman to accompany her to the *mikvah* if necessary.

25. In places where husbands wait outside the *mikvah* to bring their wives home, they should avoid waiting or parking the car near the entrance of the *mikvah*, as this (and similar conduct) can result in a lack of the proper modesty required by the *tevilah* (as stated above).

CHAPTER FOURTEEN[1]

TEVILAH

Introduction

1. The *Shulchan Aruch* states, "A woman does not leave her state of *tum'ah* by washing in a bathhouse. Even if all of the water in the world is poured over her, she still remains in her state of *tum'ah*, and [engaging in marital relations with her] is forbidden until she immerses her entire body in the water of a *mikvah*."

2. One should be particular to immerse in a *mikvah* that is managed properly and is under the constant supervision of a rabbi who is competent in the laws of *mikva'os* and can assure that it retains its kosher state. As is known, effort is exercised with regard to *mikva'os* to follow all of the relevant opinions. The *hiddurim* of Rabbi Shalom Dovber of Lubavitch are particularly well-known.[2] Rabbi Shalom Dovber was an unparalleled expert in the laws of *mikva'os* in his generation, and

---

1. Corresponding to Chapter Twenty-Two in the *sefer*.

2. Those that follow the directives of the Rebbeim of Lubavitch must make as much of an effort as possible to immerse in such a *mikvah*. In the words of the Lubavitcher Rebbe: "The *mikvah* must be built according to the directives of Rabbi Sholom Dovber, as he is our *posek*. It is also known [the rule] in *halachah* that in the location where [the Amoraic sage] Rav [served as rabbi], one must follow his directives" (*Sha'arei Halachah Uminhag, Yoreh Dei'ah* §49).

Nonetheless, one can immerse in a regular *mikvah*—provided it is supervised properly—if she is unable to immerse in such a *mikvah*, for example, if the night of her *tevilah* is Shabbos or Yom Tov and the closest *mikvah* built in such a manner is far and difficult to visit.

the *mikva'os* built according to his directives comply with all of the relevant opinions and *hiddurim*.[3]

A list of *mikva'os* worldwide is available at mikvah.org, where one can also find the closest *mikvah* to one's present location.

Immersing in a River or Sea

3. If there is absolutely no way to visit a proper *mikvah* and she must immerse in a river, sea, or the like, one must consult an expert rabbi and discuss the matter with him, because there are various details that can render immersing in such a place invalid (sometimes even *bedi'eved*), and it is extremely difficult to immerse there properly.

Depth of the Water

4. The water of the *mikvah* must extend 20-26.5 cm. (7.87-10.43 in.) higher than her navel. The rationale for this requirement is because if the water is too low, she will be forced to bend down while immersing, and this will

---

3. See the Alter Rebbe's *Shulchan Aruch* (addenda to vol. 5-6, pp. 78ff. [1910ff.]) for the details relating to this method of constructing a *mikvah*.

The advantage of using such a *mikvah* is evident from the words of the Lubavitcher Rebbe, "Anyone that is familiar with [the laws of] *mikva'os* will recognize the numerous advantages present in a *mikvah* constructed over a cistern [i.e., a *mikvah* constructed according to the directives of Rabbi Sholom Dovber]" (*Sha'arei Halachah Uminhag*, ibid.).

Rabbi Yeremiyahu Katz, in his *sefer Mikveh Mayim* (Jerusalem 2002), discusses the advantages of such a *mikvah* at length. He explains how it complies with all the relevant opinions, responds to the questions that were raised against it, and refutes the opinions of those who disagreed with it. See also the booklets *Mikvah Al Gabei Mikvah* (Montreal, 1987) and *Yisbareru Veyislabnu Hadevarim* (Jerusalem, 1989).

result in the creation of folds in her skin that will prevent the water from reaching those areas. (See below [§§22-23] for additional relevant laws.)

5. Similarly, the water of the *mikvah* should not be too deep, as she might be frightened as a result and will not be able to focus properly on standing in the correct position (as will be explained further [§§11ff.]).

6. If one is of a short height, the *mikvah* may be too deep for her, and she may be frightened to enter. This can result in problems regarding the validity of her *tevilah*. As such, she should stand on the steps of the *mikvah* and immerse there.

Avoiding Distractions While Immersing

7. Due to the above concern—that she will not focus properly on standing in the correct position—any potential distraction should be avoided while immersing. Accordingly, the water should be neither too cold nor too hot, and any factor that might cause her to be frightened or distracted should be eliminated.

8. For this reason, one may not stand on a box or similar object while immersing, as she may be frightened that she may fall.

9. If such distractions were not avoided, the *tevilah* is valid if she is certain that she immersed properly despite the distraction. We are not concerned that she did not immerse properly but didn't realize due to the distraction.

Standing on an Object That is *Mekabel Tum'ah*

10. One may not stand on an object that is *mekabel tum'ah*

while immersing, and her *tevilah* is invalid even *bedi'eved* if she immersed in such a manner.

Accordingly, one should not stand on a plastic or rubber mat while immersing, as certain opinions hold that such a mat is *mekabel tum'ah*. However, if she immersed while standing on such a mat and cannot immerse again that night, one can rely on the opinions that hold that these materials are not *mekabel tum'ah* and her *tevilah* is valid.

Body Position While Immersing

11. The water of the *mikvah* must reach every area of her body that is sometimes exposed. Accordingly, over the course of the *tevilah* she must bring her body to such a position that will cause every such area to be exposed to the water. Similarly, she must avoid body movements that can cause these areas to become concealed.

12. The following guidelines should therefore be followed while immersing:

One should not immerse while standing upright, as certain areas are concealed when standing in such a manner. She should also not bend over exceedingly for the same reason.

She should not close her mouth tightly, rather her lips should touch each other gently. She should also not clench her teeth tightly.

She should not close her eyes tightly or open them wide, rather she should close them gently. She may keep her eyes open if she desires, provided they are only open slightly. However, it is preferable to close them gently as stated above.

13. Her legs should be separated slightly from each other, similar to their position when walking. Her body should lean forward slightly, so that the areas near her anus and vaginal area are slightly elevated and exposed. This position will also allow her breasts to lean forward (as opposed to them lying on her chest).

Her arms should be raised slightly and positioned somewhat to the side, allowing the water to reach under and around her armpits. She should part her fingers somewhat and not press them against each other. She should not bend her arms at the elbow excessively, as this can prevent water from reaching the folded area.

14. If possible, she should attempt to perform at least one *tevilah* by stretching out her entire body horizontally. Although this is not obligatory, the Tzemach Tzedek conveyed to his wife that this is the primary method of immersing. (See also §22.)

However, it is important to note that this may only be done by someone who can immerse in such a manner without holding on to the railing or the like. But if she must hold on to something or if she is frightened to immerse in this way, she may not do so. In such a case, immersing in such a manner will be counterproductive, as she will close her fists tightly and perform movements that create folds in the skin, preventing water from reaching these areas.

If She Immersed in an Incorrect Position

15. If one immersed without positioning her body in the manner described above, she should immerse again. However, in the following three scenarios, she should not

immerse again (unless she performed one of the actions detailed in the following paragraphs): (1) If she is unable to immerse again (because the *mikvah* is already closed or the like). (2) If she has already engaged in marital relations with her husband, even if she is able to immerse again. (3) If the night has already passed, even if they have not yet engaged in marital relations.

The following paragraphs list actions that, if performed, require her to immerse a second time even in the above three scenarios:

16. If she closed her fist tightly in such a way that the water was unable to enter, her *tevilah* is invalid even *bedi'eved* and even in challenging situations (see note[4]). Similarly, her *tevilah* is invalid if her hands or another limb were pressed tightly against her body in such a way that the water was unable to reach that area.

17. If she pressed her lips together tightly, her *tevilah* is invalid even *bedi'eved* and even in challenging situations.

18. The *Poskim* differ with regard to one who clenched her teeth tightly, and an expert rabbi should be consulted if there is a need.

Avoiding Unnecessary Stringencies

19. The Ramban writes as follows: "One should not act in an exceedingly stringent manner—i.e., searching for doubts to render her *tevilah* invalid due to a minor issue—

---

4. However, the *tevilah* is valid if she closed her fists when her hands were already in the water (and they remained in this state until after the *tevilah*). See the *sefer* (Chapter Twenty-Two fn. 36).

for if [one will act in such a manner,] there will be no end [to the amount of times she will immerse]. Rather, once she has washed [the hair of] her head, combed [her hair] with a comb, washed her entire body, was careful to avoid touching substances that can result in a *chatzitzah*, and immersed by stretching out her limbs and entire body, she should not occupy herself with doubts and stringencies that have no end. For example, [one should not worry to no end] whether she closed her eyes or shut her lips too tightly or [entertain] similar doubts, for who can differentiate between one who closed [her eyes or the like] too tightly or not?!"

Washing the Eyes, Lips, and Hidden Areas Before Immersing

20. *Lechatchilah*, before the actual immersion, one should enter the water until her neck and then wash her eyes, lips, and hidden areas (see Chapter Eleven §25) with the water of the *mikvah*. Doing so alleviates the concern that a portion of her body remained concealed and was unable to be reached by the water. Of particular concern are wrinkles and folds of excess flesh, as they can be partially concealed during the *tevilah*. For this reason, women are accustomed to immerse several times (see §27), so that if the water did not reach a certain area the first time, it will reach there during the subsequent immersions.

21. As stated, washing the hidden areas and immersing several times merely alleviates the concern that water was unable to reach a certain area of the body. However, if a concrete concern is present that a certain area was concealed during the *tevilah* (see §§16ff.), these actions will not validate the immersion.

22. If the *mikvah* water is lower than the height described above (§4), she **must** act as outlined in §20. In such a case, it is preferable—and according to some opinions, it is **mandatory**—to immerse by stretching out her body horizontally if she is able to do so (see §14). If it is possible to find another *mikvah* with the correct water height, she must immerse there and may not rely on performing the above actions.

23. If she immersed in a *mikvah* without the correct water height and did not wash herself before immersing as described in §20, her *tevilah* is valid *bedi'eved*, provided she is certain that she did not bend over in a way that concealed an area of her body from being reached by the water.

Overseeing the *Tevilah*

24. The *Shulchan Aruch* states: "One must [appoint] an adult Jewish woman over twelve years of age to stand near her when she immerses and ensure that no part of her hair remains floating above the water. If she does not have someone to stand near her [see note[5]] or if it is at night [i.e., if the *mikvah* is in a dark place and one cannot tell if her hair is floating above the water], she should wrap her hair over her head."

In this latter case, she should take care to wrap her hair in a way that will not result in knots or tangles. She should also make sure that the string or band with which she wraps her hair is loose so that the water can reach her hair.

---

5. If a couple lives alone in an area where it is impossible to locate a Jewish woman who follows the laws of *taharas hamishpachah* to oversee the *tevilah*, an expert rabbi should be consulted regarding the possibility for the husband to do so.

If no one stood near her and she did not wrap her hair over her head, her *tevilah* is invalid even *bedi'eved* and she must immerse again.

Reciting the *Berachah*

25. The following *berachah* is recited when immersing: *Boruch atah adonai eloheinu melech ha'olam asher kideshanu bemitzvosav vetzivanu al hatevilah* ("Blessed are You, Lord our G-d, King of the universe, who has sanctified us with His commandments and commanded us concerning immersion"). This *berachah* should be recited whether she is immersing due to a *tum'ah* which is *mid'oraysa* or a *tum'ah* which is *mid'rabanan* such as a *kesem* or *dam besulim*. In fact, even if she is immersing because an expert rabbi instructed her to do so **out of doubt,** the *berachah* should be recited, including G-d's name. However, if the rabbi ruled leniently but she and her husband decided to act stringently (see note[6]), the *berachah* should not be recited.

In certain scenarios (see Chapter Twelve), one should

---

6. Such a decision may only be made with the consent of her husband; otherwise, she may not act stringently and immerse again, as this will affect her marital obligations toward her spouse. Similarly, her husband should not instruct her to act stringently if there is no *halachic* basis to do so. This is all that more applicable if she has already immersed and a question arose regarding the *tevilah*; if an expert rabbi has ruled leniently, he may not instruct her to act stringently.

Furthermore: It is frowned upon to act stringently (once an expert rabbi has ruled leniently) even if **both** the husband and wife agree to do so. Our sages have employed an important rule regarding such conduct: "Is it not enough what Torah forbade upon you that you desire to forbid other things upon yourself as well?!" (See also the quotes cited in the introduction to the *sefer*.)

not immerse again if she has already engaged in marital relations or if the night has already passed, but in regular circumstances she must immerse again. In such scenarios, a *berachah* should not be recited on the second *tevilah*.

26. Regarding the exact time when the *berachah* should be recited, the custom based on the conclusion of the *Poskim* is as follows: She should immerse once before reciting the *berachah*. She should then (cover her head,[7]) submerge her body until her neck, embrace herself beneath her heart (in such a way that her hands will serve as an interruption between her heart and pubic area), and recite the *berachah*. She should not look at the water while reciting the *berachah*, rather she should look upward. She should then immerse a second time, positioning her body as described above (§§11ff.) by the first *tevilah*.

Number of Immersions

27. In addition to the two immersions required by *halachah* (once before the *berachah* and once after), women are accustomed to immerse additional times as well. Certain women immerse three times, while others immerse nine times or other numbers. Every woman should conduct herself according to the custom of her family or community, or as per the instructions of her community's rabbi. (See also §§20-21.)

Objective of Immersion

28. If a woman immersed with the intent of enabling her to assist her ill husband and not for the purpose of engaging

---

7. Although certain *Poskim* mention this custom, others do not make reference to it, and it has therefore been placed in parentheses.

in marital relations (although *lechatchilah* one should not immerse if marital relations will not follow—see Chapter Thirteen §5; §8), her intent is valid for the purpose of marital relations as well. Accordingly, she is not required to immerse again before engaging in marital relations.

Additional Recitations While Immersing

29. Certain women are accustomed to recite between immersions: *Yehi ratzon milfanecha adonai eloheinu veilohei avoseinu sheyibaneh Beis Hamikdash bimheirah veyameinu vesein chelkeinu besorasecha* ("May it be Your will, L-rd our G-d and G-d of our fathers, that the Beis Hamikdash be speedily rebuilt in our days, and grant us a portion in Your Torah"). She should embrace herself while reciting this prayer as described above (§26).

30. After immersing, the woman appointed to oversee the *tevilah* should declare, "[She has immersed properly,[8]] *kasher*." By doing this, a similar declaration is proclaimed simultaneously in heaven, and she will merit to give birth to upright children who will serve G-d wholeheartedly.

Leaving the *Mikvah*

31. The *Shulchan Aruch* states: "Women should be careful to meet a friend upon leaving the *mikvah* before meeting a non-kosher animal or non-Jew. If she did meet a non-kosher animal or non-Jew first, she should immerse again if she is G-d-fearing." It is self-understood that a *berachah* is not recited on this second *tevilah*.

---

8. Certain sources mention these words as well; however, the prevalent custom is to only state "*kasher*," and they have therefore been placed in brackets.

32. *Poskim* add that her friend should walk towards her and touch her as well. Certain places have adopted the custom that the woman appointed to oversee the *tevilah* walks toward the woman immersing and touches her as she emerges from the water.

However, there is no need to immerse again even if she did not act in the above manner, as long as a friend met her before she saw a non-kosher animal or non-Jew (see note[9]).

33. If she met a non-kosher animal or non-Jew and did not return immediately to immerse again, she should not immerse again if the *mikvah* is already closed, if the night has already passed, or if she has already engaged in marital relations (even if the *mikvah* is still open).

Washing Herself After the *Tevilah*

34. After the *tevilah*, *lechatchilah* one should not wash the head and the majority of the body simultaneously by taking a bath or shower. Certain authorities extend this directive to the following day as well, while others limit it to the actual night of the *tevilah*. In any case, if one does take a shower or bath, the *tevilah* is not invalidated as a result, and there is no need to immerse again whatsoever.

35. Individual portions of the body may be washed. If she

---

9. Some later *Poskim* posit that according to those *Poskim* who state that her friend should touch her as well, the same is true with regard to the (spiritual) damage resulting from meeting a non-kosher animal or non-Jew, and it is only detrimental if they actually **touched** her. However, from the wording of the Lubavitcher Rebbe when mentioning this directive it is clear that one should immerse again even if she merely **met** a non-kosher animal or non-Jew, even if they did not touch her (see *Likkutei Sichos*, vol. 25, p. 311).

must wash her entire body—for example, if the *mikvah* water was unclean, if she is sweating (during the summer), or the like—she should take a shower in such a way that the water will not fall on her head and body simultaneously. As such, she should bend her head when washing it so that the water will not fall on her body at the same time, and conversely, when she washes her body, she should direct the shower so that the water will fall on her body from the side and not from above.

36. One authority is of the opinion that the directive to refrain from washing oneself is limited to taking a shower or bath in the *mikvah*; upon coming home, however, she may take a shower or bath if there is a need to do so. In any case, it is preferable to act as has been outlined in the previous paragraph, which is permissible according to all opinions.

Telling Her Husband That She Has Immersed

37. When one returns from immersing, she must state verbally that she has immersed, either by saying "I have immersed" or by answering "Yes" or the like to her husband's question whether she has immersed. Any form of contact, including touch, is forbidden as long as she does not state this **clearly.** One should not suffice with hints, touching, or the like; she must **state** clearly that she has immersed and is *tehorah*. This is true whether she immersed due to a *tum'ah* which was *mid'oraysa* or one that was *mid'rabanan*.

Certain authorities state that using a prearranged hint is sufficient. However, it is preferable to act in a manner which is permissible according to all opinions (i.e., to state clearly that she has immersed), especially since this is easy to do.

The custom among Sephardic Jews is to rely on a pre-arranged hint.

38. In order to avoid misunderstandings, one should ensure that his wife is aware that he will be asking her afterwards whether she has immersed. One should realize that this question is not due to a lack of trust, G-d forbid; rather it is an additional step in the *taharah* process, in continuation to the counting of *shivah nekiyim, chafifah,* and *tevilah.*

CHAPTER FIFTEEN[1]

BEDIKOS BEFORE AND AFTER MARITAL RELATIONS

General Laws

1. Our Sages have obligated a married woman to create a *chazakah* (*halachic* assertion) that marital relations do not cause her to menstruate. This *chazakah* is created by performing a *bedikah* with a *bedikah* cloth both before marital relations and immediately afterward to ensure that she is clean. Additionally, the husband must wipe his organ after marital relations with a clean, white cloth (that he has prepared for this purpose). After this procedure has been done before and after **three** marital relations, *halachah* asserts that marital relations do not cause her to bleed.

This chapter will explain the details of these *bedikos* and the exact time when they are to be performed.

2. After she has examined herself three times and has determined that marital relations do not cause her to menstruate, there is no requirement to perform further *bedikos* before or after subsequent marital relations.

2*. A woman who has remarried must perform these *bedikos* as well, even though she had already done so while married to her first husband.

---

1. Corresponding to Chapter Twenty-Three in the *sefer*.

When These *Bedikos* Should Be Performed

3. As long as it is possible that blood being discharged is *dam besulim*, one cannot begin the process of determining whether the blood is a result of marital relations. Accordingly, these *bedikos* can only be performed once the blood is no longer assumed to be *dam besulim* (see Chapter Eighteen §§20ff.).

An expert rabbi should be consulted if one is unsure if the time to begin performing these *bedikos* has arrived.

4. Following a woman's *taharah*, there are typically a certain amount of days when she is certain her period will not arrive, following which are days when the next period may begin. We will refer to these two categories as "certain days" and "uncertain days" respectively, because it is certain that the days in the former category will be clean from blood, while her period may begin during one of the days in the latter category.

5. A woman is not required to perform *bedikos* before and after marital relations during the "certain days." Furthermore: since the purpose of performing *bedikos* is to determine that marital relations do not cause her to menstruate, and there is no concern that she will menstruate during the "certain days," the *bedikos* must be performed specifically during the "uncertain days" when such a concern exists.[2]

6. The "certain days" are calculated as follows: The three most recent *haflagos* (the amount of days between her peri-

---

2. Similarly, a woman who has a *veses kavua* must wait until the *veses* has been uprooted before performing these *bedikos*. (For details on how a *veses kavua* is uprooted, see Chapter Sixteen §§38ff.; §§49ff.; §§62ff.)

ods) are calculated, and the shortest *haflagah* of the three is selected. The amount of days of which the shortest *haflagah* was comprised is what will constitute the "certain days." Once these days have passed, the subsequent days are considered "uncertain days," and she will then be required to perform *bedikos* before and after marital relations.

7. If one is unaware of the duration of her three most recent *haflagos* (as is common by newlyweds), the most recent *haflagah* is taken into account to determine the length of the "certain days." Once an equal amount of days has passed and she has not yet begun to menstruate, she is required to perform these *bedikos*.

8. Nonetheless, if they performed *bedikos* during the "certain days," the *bedikos* are valid *bedi'eved* to create a *chazakah*.

9. In light of the above, it is possible for a lengthy period of time to pass after the wedding without having performed these *bedikos*, because the couple has not yet had a chance to engage in marital relations during the "uncertain days." However, this is of no consequence, as there is no need for the three rounds of *bedikos* to be performed at three **consecutive** marital relations. Accordingly, if they were only able to engage in marital relations once during the "uncertain days" before her next period arrived, the remaining rounds of *bedikos* can be performed during the subsequent months (whenever an opportunity arises), until all three rounds of *bedikos* are performed.

Bedikah Before Marital Relations

10. This *bedikah* does not need to be performed immediately prior to marital relations, rather it can be performed a

while beforehand, provided she has already begun focusing on relations and is not preoccupied with anything else. Following the bedikah, the bedikah cloth must be examined to determine that it is clean. Bedi'eved, the bedikah is valid even if it was performed before the above time; however, if they have not yet engaged in marital relations, it is advisable to perform another bedikah during the correct time.

11. If there is a need, one can be lenient with regard to the bedikah performed before marital relations and suffice with wiping herself (a kinuach, instead of examining the internal crevices and folds). In such a case, she should leave the cloth in her vagina for a while (and not remove it right away). It should be noted that a bedikah performed in this manner cannot be performed while lying on her back, because a kinuach done in such a position is invalid even bedi'eved.

Bedikah After Marital Relations

12. This bedikah must be performed by examining the internal crevices and folds, similar to the bedikos performed during shivah nekiyim and the like (see Chapter Eight §30). This bedikah must also be performed immediately following relations (i.e., as soon as the organ has completely finished discharging the semen). Lechatchilah this bedikah should also not be performed while lying on her back; however, it is valid bedi'eved if it was performed in this position, and similarly, she is not required to turn over if it involves great difficulty. Following the bedikah, the bedikah cloth must be examined to determine that it is clean.

13. The bedikah performed by the husband following

marital relations must be performed by wiping the organ with a clean, white cloth.

Women Exempt From These *Bedikos*

14. A woman classified as a *mesulekes damim* is not required to perform *bedikos* before and after marital relations, because *halachah* establishes that such a woman is not expected to menstruate (similar to the "certain days" described above).

Each of the following women is classified as a *mesulekes damim*:

1. A pregnant woman, beginning from the fourth month of her pregnancy.

2. A nursing woman, for a period of 24 months following the birth. Even a woman who is presently not nursing, and even one who has not begun to nurse at all, is included in this category.

3. A woman who suffered from a miscarriage. (See Chapter Two §9 and fns. ad loc.)

15. A pregnant woman is required to perform these *bedikos* during the first three months of her pregnancy (if she has not yet completed all three rounds), even if it is certain that she is pregnant. If there is concern that doing so will harm the fetus, one can rely on the opinions that suffice with a *kinuach* both before and after marital relations. In such a case, she should take care not to perform the *bedikah* while lying on her back, as stated above (§11).

If They Engaged in Marital Relations Without Performing *Bedikos*

16. If they engaged in marital relations three times during the "uncertain days" and inadvertently did not perform *bedikos*, they are not required to perform further *bedikos bedi'eved*. Although they did not fulfill the obligation of our Sages to create a *chazakah* by performing *bedikos*, no further *bedikos* are required, because ultimately it has been determined that marital relations do not cause her to menstruate.

Performing *Bedikos* Beyond the Halachic Requirements

17. If one wishes to continue performing *bedikos* **before** marital relations (after the *halachic* requirement of performing *bedikos* three times has been fulfilled), there is room for this stringency if it is certain that no complications will arise due to the additional *bedikos*. However, nowadays it is not advisable to do so, because it is common for complications to arise as a result of frequent *bedikos*. If one nonetheless wishes to conduct herself according to this stringency, she may do so only if her husband instructed her to perform a *bedikah*; she may not perform a *bedikah* on her own accord.

However, she should not perform a *bedikah* **after** marital relations in any case. Similarly, her husband should not examine himself at all. Accordingly, he should wipe himself after marital relations with a cloth upon which blood will not be noticeable at all. Alternatively, he should wipe himself with a tissue and immediately dispose of it (without glancing at it first).

18. She should also not perform *bedikos* at all during the

"certain days," and certainly not if she has a *veses kavua*[3] or if she is classified as a *mesulekes damim* (see §14).

Performing *Bedikos* When Not Engaging in Marital Relations

19. The *Shulchan Aruch* states that it is praiseworthy to increase in performing *bedikos* when she is *tehorah*, even when not engaging in marital relations. However, the *Poskim* explain that nowadays one should not perform *bedikos* that are not *halachically* required, because it is common for complications to arise as a result of frequent *bedikos*.

20. See Chapter Two (§§24ff.) for the laws of a woman who began to menstruate as a result of engaging in marital relations.

---

3. The *Poskim* explain that a woman who has a *veses kavua* for stringent purposes alone should also not perform *bedikos* before and after marital relations. (See Chapter Sixteen for a number of scenarios where a woman is categorized as having such a *veses*.)

CHAPTER SIXTEEN[1]

VESTOS

Introduction

1. The Torah states, *And you shall separate the children of Israel from their tum'ah* (*Vayikra* 15:31). Our Sages interpreted this verse as a directive to separate from one's wife adjacent to the time when her menstrual period is expected to arrive. In other words, even before her period actually arrives, the husband and wife must separate from each other during the time when it is likely to arrive (based on the calculations that will be elaborated upon in this chapter). For this reason, our Sages have obligated the wife to perform a *bedikah* during this time as well.

2. A number of clarifications:

1. The *veses*-related calculations elaborated upon in this chapter are based solely on the **Hebrew** date. The secular date is of no relevance in this regard.

2. This chapter will deal with *veses* calculations that are time-related, i.e., when the concern that her period will arrive is based on the **date** of the prior discharge of blood or on the **duration of time** between such discharges (as will be explained further). The *Shulchan Aruch* (*Yoreh Dei'ah* §189) enumerates additional *vestos* associated with physical sensations, but since they are

---

1. Corresponding to Chapter Twenty-Four in the *sefer*.

presently uncommon, they will not be dealt with in this book.

3. It is important to gain proficiency in *veses* calculations, including those calculations that appear to be highly unlikely. The reason for this is because the majority of women presently do not have a set time when their periods arrive, and the lack of systematic dates can sometimes create a seemingly random combination that will constitute a *veses kavua*. If one is not proficient in the various *veses* calculations, one might not imagine that these discharges carry significance, when in reality they share the laws of a full-fledged *veses kavua*.

Another important point: Due to the lack of systematic *vestos* in our time, even if a *veses kavua* is created, it will not usually persist. It is therefore vital to acquire proficiency in the numerous laws of how a *veses kavua* is uprooted, as will be explained further.

One should not be deterred from the many calculations that may appear (at first glance) difficult and complicated. If one experiences difficulty in understanding the calculations, a friend or the like should be approached who will explain them until they are clear.

4. An important note related to Hebrew dates mentioned in this chapter: In the Jewish calendar, a day begins the preceding night and concludes in the evening. For example, if a calendar indicates May 3 as equivalent to Iyar 23, the Hebrew date will begin the previous night (the night of May 2) and conclude in the evening. The following night (the night of May 3) will mark the beginning of Iyar 24, which will conclude the following eve-ning (of May 4), and so on.

Keeping a Calendar

3. The leading *Poskim* have emphasized the importance of constantly recording the days of the *veses*, allowing one to calculate the *vestos* properly. Indeed, experience has shown that keeping a detailed calendar—in which are recorded the days when blood has been discharged and the days of the *veses*—ensures that one will keep the *vestos* accurately.

4. It is very important to record not only the **day** when blood has been discharged but also the **onah** in which it occurred, i.e., whether it occurred by day or at night. One should also record the **time** when the discharge occurred. The reason for this is because the separation is usually re-quired during the *onah* identical to the one in which the dis-charge occurred, while the *bedikah* that must be performed during this *onah* should be performed from the time when the discharge occurred and onward, as will be explained fur-ther in this chapter.

4*. Recently, an online *veses* calendar has become avail-able, allowing those who may encounter difficulty in calcu-lating *vestos* to make use of this convenient service. Howev-er, it is recommended to calculate one's *vestos* separately as well and not rely on an online calendar alone.

The online calendar is available at mikvah.org. Two-year print calendars are available there as well.

Types of Discharges With Regard to *Vestos*

5. With regard to the laws of *vestos*, only discharges of

blood that render her *temei'ah mid'oraysa* are taken into account. These include a regular menstrual period and blood discovered when performing a *bedikah*.

The latter scenario refers to a case where the *bedikah* cloth was examined beforehand and was clean, following which she performed an internal *bedikah*, and a *mar'eh* was discovered that was certainly *tamei*. But if she discovered blood as a result of an external *kinuach*, it is not taken into account with regard to *vestos* (although it renders her *temei'ah*). The same applies to blood that was discharged as a result of a medical procedure.

6. Discharges of blood that render her *temei'ah mid'rabanan* are not taken into account with regard to *vestos*. These include hymenal blood (*dam besulim*); *kesamim*, even if discovered on the day of a *veses*; and blood that was discharged while urinating. This is true even though these discharges share the laws of a *tum'ah mid'oraysa* with regard to *harchakos, shivah nekiyim, tevilah,* and so on.

7. Blood discharged at childbirth (*dam leidah*) is not taken into account with regard to *vestos*, although she is *temei'ah mid'oraysa*. The same law applies to blood discharged during a miscarriage that occurred after 40 days from the beginning of the pregnancy.

Blood discharged after birth is considered to be *dam leidah* if it has not yet stopped since the birth. In order to determine whether blood discharged after birth is to be accounted for with regard to *vestos* or not, it is preferable to perform a *bedikah* once the blood has stopped, even if she will not be counting *shivah nekiyim* at this point (due to post-partum weakness or the like). This will allow her to know with certainty that any future discharge is not *dam leidah*.

8. A woman's actual period is often preceded by *kesamim*, sometimes for a number of days and at times for only a few hours. In any case, these *kesamim* are not taken into account with regard to *vestos*, although they may appear as an indication that the period will soon follow. What is reckoned with is only the period itself, or blood discovered while performing a *bedikah* (for whatever reason it was performed). (It is self-understood that *harchakos* begin as soon as impure *kesamim* are discovered. Similarly, she can begin counting the five days [see Chapter Seven] as soon as impure *kesamim* are discovered. See Chapter Four for the related laws.)

Duration of Separation

9. The obligation to separate applies to a single **onah** on the day of the *veses*, i.e., either the day or the night: if the blood was discharged by day, they will be obligated to separate on the day of the *veses* by day, and if the blood was discharged at night, they will be obligated to separate at night. The *veses* known as *onah beinonis* is an exception to this rule; such a *veses* requires separation for a full **twenty-four hours** (see §28).

10. According to many *Poskim*, there is no need to separate longer than the above-mentioned duration of time. Indeed, this is the actual practice of those who follow the opinion of the Alter Rebbe. However, there are those who act stringently and separate during an additional *onah* preceding the obligatory *onah*. Additional laws regarding this additional *onah* (known as "the *onah* of the *Ohr Zarua*," after

the medieval authority to whom this stringency is attributed) can be found in the *sefer* (Chapter Twenty-Four §8).

Definition of "Day" and "Night"

11. With regard to *vestos*, "day" begins at sunrise and concludes at sunset, and "night" begins at sunset and concludes at sunrise.[2] Accordingly, if blood was discharged early in the morning before sunrise, the *vestos* that will result will be kept at **night** (although it was already somewhat light outside when the blood was discharged). Similarly, if blood was discharged in the evening after sunset, the *vestos* that will result will be kept at night.

12. If one is in doubt if her period began by day or at night, both *onos* should be kept. For example, if blood was discharged in the morning and she does not know if it was before or after sunrise, they should separate on the day of the *veses* both at night and by day. Similarly, if blood was discharged in the evening and she does not know if it was before or after sunset, they should separate both by day and at night.

13. The above is true only if the time when the blood was **discovered** is in doubt. However, if she is certain of the time when the blood was discovered but she believes that her period began during the previous *onah*, the *veses* calculations are counted from the present *onah*. For example, if she discovered upon awakening in the morning that her period had begun and she believes that it began at night, she does not take this assumption into account, and all the calculations are counted based on the time when the blood was actually discovered.

---

2. One can visit chabad.org/zmanim to find out the exact time of sunrise and sunset in any location.

14. Different laws apply if the discharge of blood began before sunrise and extended only a few hours into the day, or if it began before sunset and extended only a few hours into the night. The laws in these scenarios have been explained in the *sefer* (Chapter Twenty-Four §12; §40*).

15. Although a woman's period will usually last a number of days, only the *onah* when it began is taken into account with regard to these laws (i.e., separating and performing a *bedikah*). Once the corresponding *onah* has passed (and a *bedikah* has been performed), they are permitted to engage in relations immediately, and there is no need for them to continue separating or perform further *bedikos* during the days that correspond to the continuation of the bleeding.

Nature of Separation

16. The husband and wife may not engage in marital relations during the *onah* of the *veses* (or during the twenty-four hour period of separation required by an *onah beinonis*). One should also act stringently and separate from affectionate touch, such as hugging, kissing, caressing, and the like, and certainly from sleeping in the same bed. In fact, the *Poskim* write that doing so is **halachically forbidden** when marital relations cannot be performed (see Chapter Thirteen fn. 2). However, it is not necessary to keep the *harchakos* that are kept when she is *temei'ah* (see Chapter Six).

Performing a *Bedikah*

17. The wife must perform a single *bedikah*[3] during the

---

3. Certain contemporary authorities state that one should perform two *bedikos*, similar to what is done during the *shivah nekiyim* (see the *sefer* [Chapter Twenty-Four fn. 33]).

onah of the *veses*, whether the *veses* is a *veses kavua* or a *veses she'eino kavua*. The manner in which the *bedikah* should be performed is identical to the way it is performed during *shivah nekiyim* (see Chapter Eight §§19-34). (See ibid. [§§24-26] for how one should conduct herself if she experiences difficulty performing the *bedikah* due to dryness in the vagina.)

18. This *bedikah* can be performed at the time of day when the discharge of blood (that resulted in this *veses*) took place or later, but not beforehand.

If one has a *veses kavua*, the *veses* is a result of three separate discharges of blood which may have occurred at different times of the day or night (see §36; §52). In such a case, the *bedikah* on the *onah* of the *veses* should be performed after the latest time from within the three discharges that created the *veses*.

18*. The following laws apply if she does not recall the time of day when the discharge took place: If the *onah* of the *veses* is by day, she should perform a *bedikah* at the end of the day before sunset. If the *onah* of the *veses* is at night, she should perform a *bedikah* before going to sleep, and if the *veses* is a *veses kavua*, she should perform a second *bedikah* when she gets up in the morning.

19. During an *onah beinonis* (kept by a woman without a *veses kavua* on the thirtieth day from the previous discharge of blood—see §27), the *bedikah* should be performed at the end of day before sunset. *Lechatchilah* (if doing so will not result in complications), she should perform a second *bedikah* after *tzeis hakochavim*.

Certain authorities state that she should also wear tight white undergarments.

20. If she did not perform a *bedikah* on the *onah* of a *veses she'eino kavua*, relations may nonetheless be resumed *bedi'eved*. However, if she did not perform a *bedikah* on a *veses kavua* or *onah beinonis*, they must continue to separate (as explained in §16) until she performs a proper *bedikah*. Once she performs a *bedikah* and is found to be *tehorah*, relations may be resumed even if the *bedikah* was performed a long time after the *veses* (see note[4]), and even if she washed her vagina in the interim (even though *lechatchilah* she may not do so—see §23).

21. After an *onah beinonis* has passed, relations may not be resumed until the wife states clearly to her husband that she has performed a *bedikah* and is *tehorah*. The same law applies if one has a *veses kavua*. However, after a *veses hachodesh* or *veses hahaflagah* that is not *kavua*, the husband is not required to ask his wife if she has performed a *bedikah*.

22. If the *bedikah* cloth was misplaced before it was examined to see if it was clean, it is considered as if she has not performed the *bedikah*. Accordingly, if the *onah* has not yet passed, she should perform another *bedikah*. If she only remembered after the *onah* had already passed, the law will depend on whether or not the *bedikah* is compulsory in order for relations to resume, as explained earlier (§20).

---

4. According to one *posek*, although the *bedikah* is valid even if it was performed a long time after the *veses*, a *bedikah* performed before engaging in marital relations cannot suffice for this purpose. However, the other *Poskim* who discuss this topic do not mention this restriction, and this may possibly lead us to imply that they disagree (although their underlying rationale is uncertain).

Washing on Day of Veses

23. *Lechatchilah*, one should not wash the vagina during the *onah* of the *veses*. She should therefore not take a bath, go swimming, and the like. Similarly, if she did not perform the required *bedikah* during a *veses kavua* or *onah beinonis*, she should not wash her vagina *lechatchilah* until she does so even once the *veses* has passed (see §20).

If the night following the *onah* of the *veses* is the night of her *tevilah*, she should perform the section of the *chafifah* done by day while taking a shower and delay washing her vagina and taking a bath until the evening. However, if the following night is Shabbos or Yom Tov, she may perform the entire *chafifah* process on Friday or *erev Yom Tov* as usual.

Veses She'eino Kavua

General Guidelines

24. Nowadays, the majority of women do not have a *veses kavua*, i.e., they do not have a set time when their periods arrive. Three *vestos* are therefore kept as a result of each discharge of blood (see note[5]): (1) *onah beinonis*, (2) *veses hachodesh*, and (3) *veses hahaflagah*. Each *veses* will be discussed in detail in this chapter.

---

5. Certain noteworthy *Poskim* have stated that the *veses* calculations of each particular woman are to be determined based on all the days when she sometimes experiences discharges of blood. However, the consensus of most authorities is that they are determined based on the days when blood was **actually** discharged, and not on the days when it was **possible** for blood to be discharged (see the *sefer* [Chapter Twenty-Four fn. 47]).

25. A *veses she'eino kavua* is uprooted when the day of the *veses* arrives **once** and no blood was discharged (known as an *akirah*). Even if a discharge of blood was experienced twice on the same day, the *veses* is uprooted when it arrives once and no blood was discharged, and there is no need to continue keeping the *vestos* resulting from these discharges.

26. Additionally, if a woman establishes a *veses kavua* (as will be explained further in the chapter), all the *vestos she'einam kevu'im* that resulted from her previous discharges are automatically uprooted, even if they did not yet arrive.

Onah Beinonis

27. Our Sages have established that any woman who does not have a *veses kavua* must keep the **thirtieth** day from the discharge of blood as a *veses*, known as an *onah beinonis*. The day when the discharge began is counted as the first day, and the thirtieth day from that point should be marked down as the *onah beinonis*.

28. On an *onah beinonis*, the husband and wife must separate from each other for an entire twenty-four hour period, beginning with sunset of the thirtieth day until sunset of the following day. This is true whether the discharge of blood (which resulted in the *onah beinonis*) took place by day or at night.

Certain individuals follow the opinion of the *Poskim* who require separation during an additional *onah* preceding the thirtieth day, known as the *onah* of the *Ohr Zarua* (see §10). Some follow the opinion of those who also require separation during the **thirty-first** day. However, in certain situations one can act leniently as per the instructions of an expert rabbi (see the *sefer* [Chapter Twenty-Four §29] for further details).

29. In addition to separating from each other, the wife must perform a *bedikah* to ensure that no blood has been discharged. The details regarding the separation and *bedikah* have been explained earlier (§§16ff.).

30. The *onah beinonis* can never be totally uprooted. Even if she has kept the *onah beinonis* numerous times and blood was never discharged on that day, she must continue to keep the thirtieth day from each discharge as an *onah beinonis*, unless she has established a *veses kavua*.

31. If, before the *onah beinonis* arrived, she experienced a discharge of blood which renders her *temei'ah mid'oraysa* (i.e., a regular period or blood discovered after performing an internal *bedikah*), she is not required to keep the thirtieth day from the **original** discharge. Rather, she should transfer the date of the *onah beinonis* to the thirtieth day from the **new** discharge.

32. However, the above is true only if the new discharge took place after seven days from the beginning of the first discharge. If the new discharge took place **within** the first seven days, it is considered (in this regard) as a continuation of the previous discharge, and the original date of the *onah beinonis* should be kept.

32*. If the day of the *onah beinonis* passed and no blood was discharged, she should not keep the thirtieth day from the first *onah beinonis* as her next *onah beinonis*; rather, she should wait until she actually experiences a discharge of blood and keep the thirtieth day from the new discharge.

33. If a woman has established a *veses kavua*, she is not required to keep the *onah beinonis* (see note[6]). This is true even if she then experiences a discharge of blood on a different day (i.e., a day that is inconsistent with her *veses kavua*). Although the law in such a case is that she must keep both her *veses kavua* and the *vestos* that result from the new discharge (see §64), she is not required to keep the *onah beinonis* until the *veses kavua* is **uprooted** (by the day of the *veses* arriving three times and no blood being discharged).

Veses Hachodesh

Calculating the *Veses Hachodesh*

34. Our Sages were concerned that the day of the Hebrew month when the blood was discharged is what triggers the onset of one's period, and they therefore obligated the equivalent day of the next month to be kept as a *veses*, known as a *veses hachodesh*. The amount of days of the previous month (twenty-nine or thirty) is of no consequence; in either case, the equivalent day of the next month should be kept.

---

6. Certain early *Poskim* are of the opinion that a woman with a *veses kavua* that is less than thirty days must keep the *onah beinonis* if the day of her *veses* arrived and no blood was discharged. However, although certain later *Poskim* maintain that one should follow this view, the wording of both the *Shulchan Aruch* and the Alter Rebbe clearly indicates that there is no need to do so (see the *sefer* [Chapter Twenty-Four, *Biurim* §5]).

*For example: If blood was discharged on Nissan 23, Iyar 23 should be marked down as the veses hachodesh. When this day arrives, they must separate and she must perform a be-*dikah *(during the* onah *corresponding to when the blood was discharged), as explained above (§§16ff.).*

35. The authorities differ regarding the law of a woman who experienced a discharge of blood on the **thirtieth** day of the month if the next month consists of only **twenty-nine** days. The Tzemach Tzedek and others are of the opinion that she is not required to keep a *veses hachodesh* at all in such a case. She is also not required to keep the thirtieth day of the subsequent month (i.e., the third month from the discharge). Conversely, others hold that she is required to keep the first day of the subsequent month. (See the *sefer* [Chapter Twenty-Four §35] for additional opinions.)

Establishing a *Veses Kavua Lechodesh*

36. A *veses hachodesh* can only become established as a *veses kavua* if she experienced three discharges of blood during three consecutive months on the same **day** of the month as well as during the same *onah*. Accordingly, if she experienced a discharge of blood on the same day for three consecutive months and they either all took place by day or they all took place at night, she has established a *veses kavua lechodesh*.

37. If one has indeed established a *veses kavua* in such a manner, all her previous *vestos she'einam kevu'im* are auto-matically uprooted, even if they have not yet arrived. Accordingly, from then on she is only required to keep her *veses kavua* (until she experiences a discharge on a different day, as will be explained in the following paragraph).

Uprooting a *Veses Hachodesh*

38. If a *veses hachodesh* has not been established as a *veses kavua*, it is uprooted when the corresponding day of the next month arrives **once** and no blood was discharged. This is true even if she experienced a discharge of blood twice on the same day of the month.

However, if the *veses hachodesh* has been established as a *veses kavua*, it is only uprooted when the corresponding day of the month arrives **three** times and no blood was discharged. But if she experienced a discharge of blood **once** or **twice** on other days of the month, she must continue to keep her *veses kavua* as well as keeping the *vestos* that result from the new discharge (see §§64ff.).

39. The *veses hachodesh* is not uprooted if she experienced a discharge of blood **before** the day of the *veses*.

An example is if she experienced a discharge on Nissan 23 and Iyar 23 was marked down as the veses hachodesh. *If she then experienced an additional discharge on Iyar 9, she must still keep Iyar 23 as a* veses, *in addition to keeping the* veses hachodesh *that results from the new discharge—i.e., Sivan 9.*

40. If a woman's period began prior to the *veses hachodesh* and continued until the actual day of the *veses*, the *veses* is still uprooted.

An example is if she experienced a discharge on Nissan 23 and Iyar 23 was marked down as the veses hachodesh. *If her next period began on Iyar 21 and continued until Iyar 23, the* veses *is uprooted, since the blood discharged on that day was merely a continuation of her period and not the beginning of a new discharge. She is therefore only required to keep Sivan 21 as a veses hachodesh (and not Sivan 23).*

41. The above is true with regard to uprooting a *veses kavua* as well: if a woman has a *veses kavua* for the twenty-third of the month (for example) and her period began before the twenty-third and continued until the twenty-third, it is considered as one of the three *akiros* necessary to uproot a *veses kavua*.

42. The laws that apply in the following scenarios can be found in Chapter Twenty-Four of the *sefer* (due to their irregularity, they will not be dealt with here): (1) If the discharge of blood began before the day of the *veses* and extended only a few hours into the *veses* (§40*). (2) If her period began prior to the *veses* and then stopped, following which it began again on the day of the *veses* (§41). (3) The possibility to establish two *vestos kevu'im lechodesh* (§42).

43. As stated above (§36), a *veses kavua* can only be established if all three discharges of blood took place on the same day of the month **consecutively.** Accordingly, if she experienced **two** consecutive discharges of blood on the same day of the month and on the third month she did not experience a discharge on that day, a *veses kavua* has not been established, even if she then experienced a discharge on the same day of the **fourth** month. This is true even if she did not perform a *bedikah* on the equivalent day of the third month (although she was obligated to do so, as this day is a *veses hachodesh*); nonetheless, the previous *veses* is uprooted, since it was not *kavua* at that point. The discharge of the fourth month is thus viewed as the **first time** she experienced a discharge on that day.

44. The above is true even if she performed a *bedikah* the next day and was found to be *temei'ah*; nonetheless, since she was assumed to be *tehorah* on the day of the *veses*, the *veses hachodesh* (*she'eino kavua*) is uprooted.

Veses Hahaflagah

General Laws

45. Our Sages were concerned that the amount of time that passes between one period and the next is what triggers the onset of one's period. They therefore instructed that one should calculate this interval (known as a *haflagah*), and when an equal interval passes after the subsequent discharge of blood, they must separate and she must perform a *bedikah* as explained above (§§16ff.). This *veses* is known as a *veses hahaflagah*.

46. If a woman experienced three consecutive discharges of blood following three equal *haflagos*, she has established a *veses kavua lehaflagah* (see also §52). By virtue of establishing a *veses kavua* alone, all the *vestos she'einam kevu'im* that resulted from her previous discharges are automatically uprooted, and she is only required to keep her *veses kavua*. This remains the case until she experiences a discharge at a different *haflagah*. When this occurs, she must continue to keep her *veses kavua* as well as keeping the *vestos* that result from the new discharge. She must continue keeping her *veses kavua* until it is uprooted by means of three *akiros* (see §§49ff.).

Calculating the Veses Hahaflagah

47. There are two methods how the *haflagah* separating one period and the next can be calculated:

1. One method is to calculate the amount of days in which her uterus was **sealed** and no blood was discharged, and to take note of the day and *onah* when the next period began. After the next period has ended and her uterus is sealed once again, an equal amount of time is counted, after which the *veses hahaflagah* is kept.

2. An alternative method is to calculate the amount of days that passed from the **beginning** of one period until the **beginning** of the next, and when an equal amount of days has passed once again, the *veses hahaflagah* is kept.

This issue is a matter of dispute among the *Poskim*.

47*. The opinion of the the Alter Rebbe's *Shulchan Aruch* (and others):

1. The *haflagah* is to be calculated according to the first method described above, i.e., to calculate the amount of days in which her uterus was sealed. Certain noteworthy *Poskim* have praised the Alter Rebbe's opinion, writing that it is much more logical than the opposing view.

An example: A woman experienced a discharge of blood on Nissan 1, performed a hefsek taharah *on Nissan 5 before sunset, and experienced a second discharge on Nissan 25. It thus follows that her uterus was sealed from the night of Nissan 6 until the day of Nissan 25, i.e., it was sealed for a total of 19.5 days (equaling 39 onos). Consequently, after she performs a* hefsek taharah *following the second discharge (for example, on Nissan 29), she should count another 19.5 days (39 onos) from the* hefsek taharah, *and she should mark down the fortieth* onah *as her* veses hahaflagah.

2. Her uterus can only be considered to be sealed if it is certain that this is the case. Hence, this must be determined by performing a *bedikah*, and a presumption that the bleeding has stopped is insufficient.

Such a *bedikah* is typically performed as the *hefsek taharah* on the fifth day from the beginning of her period (see Chapter Seven). However, if she performed a *bedikah* beforehand (for whatever reason), although it is not advisable to do so, the *haflagah* is calculated from that point. For although she cannot begin counting *shivah nekiyim* until the sixth day from the beginning of her period, the early *bedikah* has nonetheless established that the bleeding has stopped.

3. If five days have passed from the beginning of her period and it appears that the bleeding has stopped, it is preferable (although not obligatory) to perform a *bedikah* even if she will not yet begin counting *shivah nekiyim* (for example, if her husband is out of town), allowing her to calculate her *haflagos* accurately.

4. If it appeared that the bleeding had stopped but she did not perform a *bedikah* to determine this, *bedi'eved* it is considered as if she performed a *bedikah* on the seventh day from the beginning of her period, and the *haflagah* is calculated from that point. If the bleeding continued for more than seven days, *bedi'eved* it is considered as if she performed a *bedikah* on the day it appeared that the bleeding had stopped.

If she is uncertain if the day the bleeding stopped was the seventh day or onward (in which case the *haflagah* can be calculated from that point) or beforehand (in which case the *haflagah* cannot yet begin to be calculated), the law is equal to that of one who is uncertain regarding the date of her *veses* (see §101).

47**. Other *Poskim* hold as follows:

A *haflagah* is to be calculated from the **beginning** of one period until the **beginning** of the next (the second method described above).

Certain authorities have stated that although this is the view that should be followed (according to their opinion), a person of exemplary character should follow the view of the Alter Rebbe as well. However, very few individuals act in this manner.

Days Versus *Onos*

48. Additionally, the *Poskim* differ whether the *haflagos* should be calculated based on the amount of *onos* that passed between periods or based on the amount of complete **days.**

48*. The opinion of the Alter Rebbe's *Shulchan Aruch* (and others):

The *haflagos* should be calculated based on the amount of *onos* that passed between periods.

An example is if a woman performed a hefsek taharah before sunset and experienced another discharge of blood twenty days later at night. In such a case, she should mark down that she experienced a discharge on the thirty-ninth onah. Alternatively, if she experienced a discharge twenty days later by day, she should mark down that she experienced a discharge on the fortieth onah. According-ly, after she performs a hefsek taharah *following the second discharge, she should count 39 or 40* **onos**, *and that will be her veses* hahaflagah.

This applies to establishing a *veses kavua* as well: a *veses kavua* for *haflagos* can only be established if all three *haflagos* consisted of an equal amount of **onos**.

Other *Poskim* hold as follows:

The *haflagos* should be calculated based on the amount of **days** that passed between periods; how-ever, when the day of the *veses* arrives, the obliga-tion to separate and perform a *bedikah* will only apply during the **onah** equivalent to when the discharge took place.

An example is if 28 days passed between one period and the next, and the second discharge took place at night. In such a case, her veses will be kept 28 **days** *later at night. Similarly, if the second discharge took place by day, her veses will be 28 days later by day.*

According to this opinion, a *veses kavua* for *hafla-gos* can only be established if all three *haflagos* con-sisted of an equal amount of **days** and were followed by a discharge that took place on the same *onah* (ei-ther all by day or all at night).

Uprooting a *Veses Hahaflagah*

49. An *akirah* consists of the passing of the *veses* without any discharge of blood taking place. If the *veses* is a *veses she'eino kavua* (including if she experienced a discharge twice at equal *haflagos*), **one** *akirah* suffices for it to be uprooted; and if it is a *veses kavua*, **three** *akiros* are necessary.

50. However, a *veses* can only be uprooted if the actual day of the *veses* passed without a discharge taking place. But if she experienced a discharge **before** the arrival of the *veses*, it has not been uprooted. In such a case, she must now keep two *vestos hahaflagah*: the previous one (that has not yet been uprooted) as well as the new one (based on the *haflagah* of the new discharge).

An example is if a woman has a veses *consisting of a 33-day* haflagah, *and she then experienced a discharge of blood at a 24-day* haflagah. *In such a case, she was unable to determine if blood would have been discharged after 33 days, because she experienced a discharge before that day arrived. She must therefore now keep two* vestos hahaflagah: *one after 24 days (her most recent* haflagah), *and another after 33 days (her previous* veses hahaflagah *which has not yet been uprooted). (The way these two* vestos *should be kept will be explained in the following paragraph.)*

51. The definition of a *haflagah* is the interval **between two periods.** It thus follows that in the case described in the previous paragraph, although she must continue to keep her previous 33-day *veses*, she must erase it from its present spot on the calendar, because the previous *haflagah* has been interrupted by the new discharge (on the twenty-fourth

day). She must therefore transfer the 33-day *veses* to the new discharge, and calculate all of her *vestos hahaflagah*—the new one, as well as the old one which has not yet been up-rooted—based on this later date. Accordingly, 24 days should be counted from the new discharge, following which she should keep her **new** *veses hahaflagah*. If she then contin-ues to stay clean until the thirty-third day, she should keep the next day as her **previous** *veses hahaflagah*.

52. It is possible for a long *haflagah* to remain for an ex-tended amount of time without being uprooted, because her periods continue to begin at shorter *haflagos*. Nonetheless, she must continue to mark down both *haflagos*—the longer and shorter one—after each period.

If, after some time has passed, she experienced a discharge at a *haflagah* equivalent to this long *haflagah*, she should mark down that she has experienced a discharge **twice** at an equal *haflagah*. If she experiences a **third** discharge at an equal *ha-flagah*—even if this, too, was separated from the second by a number of shorter *haflagos*—all three discharges join togeth-er and she has established a *veses kavua* for this *haflagah*.

53. A *veses hahaflagah* can become uprooted even if she did not perform a *bedikah* on the day of the *veses* to deter-mine that she is clean (see §§43-44 for additional relevant details).

Calculating *Vestos* If a New Discharge Occurred During the *Shivah Nekiyim*

54. If a woman experienced a new discharge of blood **with-in seven days** from the beginning of her previous period, the new discharge is considered to be a continuation of the pre-

vious discharge, and it is not taken into account with regard to calculating *vestos*. However, if she experienced a new discharge on the **eighth day** or onward, it is considered to be a new discharge, and she must take it into account as well. (See the following paragraph for a practical example of this case.)

55. If a woman performed a *bedikah* during the *shivah nekiyim* and it was discovered to be *temei'ah*, the law will depend on the day when the *bedikah* was performed. If it was performed **within seven days** from the previous discharge—for example, if she performed a *hefsek taharah* on the fifth day and discovered an unclean *bedikah* on the first or second day of the *shivah nekiyim*—the unclean *bedikah* is not taken into account with regard to calculating *vestos*, and no new *vestos* must be marked down as a result. However, if it was performed on the **eighth day** or onward—in the previous example, on the third day of the *shivah nekiyim* or onward—the unclean *bedikah* must be taken into account as well. She must therefore mark down the *veses hachodesh* that results from the *bedikah*, in addition to keeping the *veses hachodesh* that resulted from the previous discharge.

56. Additionally, the unclean *bedikah* interrupts her present *haflagah*. She must therefore erase her *veses* (or *vestos*) *hahaflagah* from where they had been marked down (as calculated based on her previous discharge) and transfer them to the new discharge (i.e., the unclean *bedikah*). Similarly, she must erase the *onah beinonis* from where it had been marked down and transfer it to the thirtieth day from the present discharge (i.e., the *bedikah*).

57. The above is only true with regard to a *bedikah* that is certainly *temei'ah*. But if it was merely determined that they

should act stringently out of doubt, it is not taken into account with regard to calculating *vestos*.

57*. If she performed an unclean *bedikah* during *shivah nekiyim* following a *tum'ah mid'rabanan*, it is taken into account even if it was performed within seven days from the *tum'ah*. The rationale is because as stated above (§6), a *tum'ah mid'rabanan* is not taken into account with regard to calculating *vestos*.

58. Additional laws apply with regard to establishing a *veses kavua* when blood was discharged within seven days from the beginning of the previous discharge. Since such cases are uncommon, they will not be dealt with here, and they can be found in the *sefer* (Chapter Twenty-Four §§53-57).

Veses Kavua

How a Veses Kavua is Kept

59. The method in which a *veses kavua lehaflagah* is kept is different than that of a *veses kavua lechodesh*:

If a woman has established a *veses kavua lechodesh*, she must keep the day of the *veses* during the next three **consecutive** months. Even if the day of the *veses* passed during the first month and no blood was discharged, she must still keep the equivalent day during the following two months.

However, different laws apply if a woman has established a *veses kavua lehaflagah*. In such a case, if the day of the *veses*—for example, the twentieth day—passed and no blood was discharged, she should not count another twenty days and keep the fortieth day as her second *veses*. Rather, she must wait until another discharge of blood actually occurs, count 20 days, and keep the twentieth day from the second discharge as a *veses*. (This in addition to keeping the new *veses hahaflagah* that results from the new *haflagah*—see §64.)

60. As explained in the previous paragraph, a woman with a *veses kavua lehaflagah* does not keep the fortieth and sixtieth days (for example) from the original discharge as a *veses*. However, despite the above, the *veses kavua* is uprooted if a period of time **three times** the length of the *haflagah* passes uninterruptedly without blood being discharged (60 uninterrupted days in the above example). When she then experiences a new discharge of blood (on the sixty-third day, for example), she is only required to keep the *veses hachodesh* and *veses hahaflagah* that result from the new discharge. Furthermore, because her *veses kavua* has already been uprooted, she must keep the *onah beinonis* as well (see §§64-65).

61. The method by which an *onah beinonis* is kept (if a woman does not have a *veses kavua*) is similar to the way a *veses kavua lehaflagah* is kept, as described above: if the day of the *onah beinonis* passed and no blood was discharged, she should not keep the thirtieth day from the first *onah beinonis* as her next *onah beinonis*; rather, she should wait until she actually experiences a discharge of blood and keep the thirtieth day from the new discharge (see §32*).

Uprooting a *Veses Kavua*

62. As mentioned earlier several times, a *veses kavua* is uprooted when the day of the *veses* passes **three times** and no blood is discharged. As will be explained further (§67; §70),

at times the *veses kavua* is considered to be uprooted temporarily, and at times it is considered to be uprooted entirely.

(See above [§60] for an additional way how a *veses kavua lehaflagah* can be uprooted.)

63. A *veses kavua* can only be uprooted if *bedikos* were performed on the days of the *veses* and she was found to be *tehorah* (unlike a *veses she'eino kavua*—see §§43-44). *Bedi'eved*, a *bedikah* performed after the day of the *veses* can serve as an *akirah* as well.

64. The following laws apply if a woman has not yet uprooted her *veses kavua* but she experienced a discharge of blood once or twice on other days. In such a case, in addition to keeping her *veses kavua* (because it has not yet been uprooted), she must also keep the *vestos* that result from the new discharge(s). However, she is only required to keep the *veses hachodesh* and *veses hahaflagah* and not the *onah beinonis* (beacuse she still has a *veses kavua*).

65. However, once her *veses kavua* has been uprooted, she must keep all the *vestos* that result from each new discharge, including the *onah beinonis* (see the following paragraph), just like any other woman without a *veses kavua*.

66. If the third *veses* of a *veses kavua* arrived and no blood was discharged (thereby uprooting the *veses kavua*) and the *onah beinonis* immediately followed, it must be kept even though she has not yet experienced a new discharge of blood (see note[7]).

---

7. Attention must be given to this law, because a woman in such a situation will not have marked down the *onah beinonis* after the previous discharge, since she still had a *veses kavua* at that point. But now that the

An example: A woman has a veses kavua lehaflagah *for 20 days. If she experienced a discharge once after 21 days (counting as one* akirah) *and then again after 23 days (equaling two* akiros), *she will mark down both the* veses hachodesh (*resulting from the last discharge), her* veses kavua lehaflagah (*as it has not yet been uprooted), and the* veses hahaflagah *resulting from the new* haflagah. *However, she will not mark down the* onah beinonis, *because she still has a* veses kavua. *But if a 20-day* haflagah *then passes once again without blood being discharged (equaling a third* akirah), *she will be required to keep the* onah beinonis *a few days later (on the thirtieth day from the beginning of the last discharge).*

Renewing a *Veses Kavua* After It Was Uprooted

67. The following laws apply if a woman had a *veses kavua*, and after it was uprooted she once again experienced a discharge on the day of her previous *veses kavua*. In such a case, if she has not established another *veses kavua* in the interim, her *veses kavua* returns to its previous state by means of this single discharge (even if a long time has passed since it was uprooted). All the laws that apply to a *veses kavua* will thus apply: she must keep the day of the *veses* until it is uprooted three times; if she did not perform a *bedikah* on the day of the *veses* they may not resume relations until she does so (see §20); and so on.

68. In the case described in the previous paragraph, by virtue of returning to her previous *veses kavua* alone, all the *vestos she'einam kevu'im* that resulted from her previous dis-

---

day of the *veses* has passed a third time and no blood was discharged, the *veses kavua* has been uprooted, and she must keep the *onah beinonis* (just like any other woman without a *veses kavua*).

charges are automatically uprooted, even if they have not yet arrived.

An example: A woman has a veses kavua lehaflagah *for 20 days. If she experienced a discharge once after 23 days, a second time after 25 days, and a third time after 29 days, her* veses kavua *has been uprooted, and she will mark down the* veses ha-haflagah, *the* veses hachodesh, *and the* onah beinonis *resulting from the last discharge. If she then experienced a discharge after 20 days once again, all the previous* vestos she'einam kevu'im *(including the* onah beinonis) *are automatically uprooted, and she is only required to keep her recurrent* veses kavua lehaflagah *of 20 days.*

This will remain the case until she experiences a discharge at a different *haflagah*. When this occurs, she will keep both her *veses kavua* and the *vestos* that result from the new discharge (see §§64ff.), until it is uprooted once again.

69. The fact that it is possible for a *veses kavua* to recur necessitates an extra degree of caution. Although nowadays *vestos kevu'im* do not persist and are uprooted before long, one must continue to keep note of the *veses kavua* even once it has been uprooted, not in order to actually keep it, but in order to constantly remember it. This will enable it to be kept as a full-fledged *veses kavua* in the event that it recurs even once and even a long time later.

70. The laws described in the previous paragraphs apply only if she has not established another *veses kavua* in the interim. But if she has established a second *veses kavua* in the interim, the previous *veses kavua* is uprooted entirely. Accordingly, if she experiences a discharge of blood on the day

of her first *veses kavua*, it is considered a *veses she'eino kavua* (which can be uprooted with one *akirah* and so on).

Different laws apply if a longer *veses kavua lehaflagah* is followed by a shorter *veses kavua lehaflagah*—see the *sefer* (Chapter Twenty-Four §51).

71. It is possible for a single discharge to indicate that both a *veses kavua lechodesh* and a *veses kavua lehaflagah* have been established. In such a case, only a *veses kavua lehaflagah* has been established, as a *veses kavua lehaflagah* is considered to be more common than other *vestos kevu'im*.

72. *An example: A woman experienced discharges of blood on Tishrei 2, Cheshvan 1, Kislev 1, and Teves 1, and the intervals between the discharges consisted of an equal amount of time. It thus follows that the discharge that took place on Teves 1 seemingly established both a* veses kavua lechodesh *for the first day of the month as well as a* veses kavua lehaflagah *(see note[8]). However, she will only mark down the* vestos *that result from the*

---

8. The method in which a *veses hachodesh* can turn into a *veses haflagah* depends on the two opinions described earlier (§§47ff.). According to the opinion that a *haflagah* is calculated from the **beginning** of one period until the beginning of the next, this can happen quite simply, as in the example given in the text. But according to the opinion that a *haflagah* is calculated from the **end** of one period until the beginning of the next, all three *haflagos* must consist of an equal amount of *onos* from the *hefsek taharah* until the beginning of the next period.

On the other hand, however, according to this opinion it is possible for such a scenario to occur during any time of the year (and not necessarily when the months are arranged so that the intervals between one Rosh Chodesh and the next are identical), because one period may extend longer than another, resulting in an equal amount of *onos* between the end of one period and the beginning of the next, while each period will begin on the same day of the month.

veses kavua lehaflagah, *and she will ignore the fact that a* veses kavua lechodesh *seems to have been established as well.*

See the sefer *(Chapter Twenty-Four §§72; 78-79; 94) for additional examples where a* veses kavua lehaflagah *overrides other* vestos kevu'im.

73. The law described in the previous paragraph (in which one *veses kavua* overrides another) only applies with regard to a *veses kavua lehaflagah* in relation to other *vestos kevu'im*. However, it is possible for a woman to establish two *vestos kevu'im*, as explained in the *sefer* (Chapter Twenty-Four §42; §69; §79; §94).

Veses Hasirug and Veses Hadilug

Introduction

74. The *vestos* described in the following paragraphs appear to be uncommon. However, particularly because the majority of women presently do not have a set time when their periods arrive, it is possible for a seemingly random combination of discharges to occur that will constitute such a *veses*. If one is not proficient in or does not pay attention to these *veses* calculations, one might not imagine that these discharges carry significance, when in reality they share the laws of a full-fledged *veses kavua*.

It is important to note that many details and laws apply to these *vestos*. While this *sefer* will only outline the basic relevant laws, one can study the numerous details in the *sefer* (Chapter Twenty-Four §§72ff.).

75. It is advisable to mark down the dates when one ex-

periences a discharge of blood as well as the duration of one's *haflagos* on a separate sheet in an orderly fashion, allowing one to immediately notice any combination of discharges that might carry significance. An example of a sheet formatted in the above manner can be found at the end of the chapter.

76. Unlike other *vestos*, these *vestos* are only kept if they have been established as a *veses kavua*. As long as they have not been established as such, one is only required to keep the usual *vestos*—namely, the *veses hachodesh*, *veses hahaflagah*, and *onah beinonis*.

Weekly *Veses Hasirug*

77. The definition of a weekly *veses hasirug* (lit., an alternating *veses*) is as follows: If a woman experienced a discharge of blood on the same day (and *onah*) of the week three consecutive times at equal intervals, she has established a *veses kavua* **lechumra** (for stringent purposes). If she then experiences a discharge in such a way a fourth time, she has established an **absolute** *veses kavua*.

78. *An example: A woman experienced a discharge of blood on Tuesday. She then experienced a second discharge three weeks later on Tuesday and then again three weeks later on Tuesday. She has now established a* veses kavua lechumra *for every third Tuesday, and she must keep every third Tuesday as a* veses *(until it is uprooted). But since this* veses kavua *is only* lechumra, *she must also keep the usual* vestos *that result from each discharge, namely, the* veses hachodesh, veses hahaflagah, *and* onah beinonis.

If she then experienced a fourth discharge of blood three weeks later on Tuesday, she has established an absolute veses kavua *for every third Tuesday, and she is only required to keep this* veses *(until she experiences a discharge on another day—see §§64ff.).*

Monthly *Veses Hasirug*

79. The definition of a monthly *veses hasirug* is if a woman experiences a discharge of blood on the same day (and *onah*) of the month every two months (or the like), for example, if she experienced three consecutive discharges, once on Nissan 15, a second time on Sivan 15, and a third time on Av 15. In such a case, she has established a *veses kavua* **lechumra** for the fifteenth day of every two months, and she must keep (in this example) Tishrei 15 as a *veses*, and so on. But since this *veses kavua* is only *lechumra*, she must also keep the usual *vestos* that result from each discharge, namely, the *veses hachodesh* (the same day of the **following** month—in the above example, Elul 15), the *veses hahaflagah*, and the *onah beinonis*.

If she then experienced a fourth discharge on the same day of the month two months later (in the above example, Tishrei 15), she has established an **absolute** *veses kavua* for this day every two months, and she is only required to keep this *veses* (until she experiences a discharge on another day—see §§64ff.).

As stated above (§74), many additional details apply (for example, if she experienced a discharge of blood on the same day every month but on alternating *onos*), and they have been explained in the *sefer*.

Veses Hasirug That Turned Into a *Veses Hahaflagah*

80. If a woman established a weekly or monthly *veses ha-*

sirug by experiencing four discharges of blood and the *hafla-gos* between the discharges are equal, the *veses* has turned into a *veses kavua lehaflagah*, and the *vestos* required to be kept are those resulting from such a *veses* (and not those resulting from a *veses hasirug*).

Veses Hadilug

81. The definition of a *veses hadilug* (lit., a *veses* that "skips") is a *veses hachodesh* or *veses hahaflagah* in which the subsequent consecutive discharges of blood "skip," i.e., they occur at later dates or at longer intervals than the previous discharges, but in equal increments (as will be explained in the following paragraphs). In such a case, a *veses kavua* has been established to continue experiencing discharges in such a manner.

82. The following is the definition of a *veses hadilug* with regard to the **dates of the month:** If a woman experienced four discharges of blood, and each subsequent one occurred on a later date of the month than the previous one in equal increments, a *veses kavua* has been established to continue experiencing discharges in such a manner.

An example is if a woman experienced a discharge of blood on Nissan 15, Iyar 16, Sivan 17, and Tamuz 18. In such a case, she has established a veses kavua *to continue experiencing discharges in such a manner, and she must keep Av 19 as a* veses, *followed by Elul 20 and so on. (More details regarding how such a* veses *should be kept can be found in the* sefer *[Chapter Twenty-Four §92].)*

83. A similar law applies if the increments consisted of more than one day, as long as each increment is equal to the previous one.

An example is if a woman experienced a discharge of blood on Nissan 15, Iyar 17, Sivan 19, and Tamuz 21. In such a case, each increment is two days long, and the vestos of the following months should be kept accordingly.

84. The following is the definition of a *veses hadilug* with regard to **haflagos**: If a woman experienced four discharges of blood at four different *haflagos*, and each subsequent *haflagah* was greater than the previous one in equal increments of days or *onos*, a *veses kavua* has been established to continue experiencing discharges in such a manner.

An example is if a woman experienced four discharges of blood, the first following a 20-day haflagah, the second following a 21-day haflagah, the third following a 22-day haflagah, and the fourth following a 23-day haflagah. In such a case, she has established a veses kavua to continue experiencing discharges in such a manner, and she must keep a veses 24 days after the next discharge, and so on. (More details regarding how such a veses should be kept can be found in the sefer [Chapter Twenty-Four §§92ff.].)

85. As stated in the previous paragraphs, a *veses hadilug* is created by experiencing **four** discharges on four different dates of the month or following four different *haflagos*. However, if a woman experienced **three** discharges in a manner that creates a *dilug* system—for example, if she experienced a discharge of blood on Nissan 15, Iyar 16, and Sivan 17— she has only established a *veses kavua lechumra* (for stringent purposes).

The same applies to a *veses hadilug* with regard to *haflagos*: if a woman experienced three discharges of blood, the first following a 20-day *haflagah*, the second following a 21-day *haflagah*, and the third following a 22-day *haflagah*, she has only established a *veses kavua lechumra*.

86. In the above cases (where she has only established a *veses kavua lechumra*), she must keep the *vestos* that result from the *veses hadilug* as well as the usual *vestos* that result from each discharge (namely, the *veses hachodesh* and *veses hahaflagah* of the most recent discharge and the *onah beinonis*).

86*. A *veses hadilug* can only be established if the increments are equal; if they are not so, no *veses* has been established, even if a system seems to be present. (An example is if the second discharge occurred one day later than the first, the third occurred two days later than the second, and the fourth occurred three days later than the third.) In such a case, the discharges are to be viewed as a *veses she'eino kavua*.

Dilug of Earlier Dates or Shorter Intervals

87. A *veses hadilug* can be established if the subsequent discharges occurred **earlier** than the previous ones as well.

An example is if a woman experienced a discharge of blood on Nissan 15, Iyar 14, and Sivan 13. In such a case, she has established a veses kavua lechumra, *and she must keep Tamuz 12 as a* veses. *If she experienced a discharge on Tamuz 12 as well, an absolute* veses kavua *has been established, and she must keep Av 11 as a* veses, *followed by Elul 10 and so on.*

88. The same applies to a *veses hadilug* with regard to *haflagos*: If a woman experienced three discharges of blood, the first following a 23-day *haflagah*, the second following a 22-day *haflagah*, and the third following a 21-day *haflagah*,

she has established a *veses kavua lechumra*, and she must keep a *veses* 20 days after the next discharge. If she then experienced a discharge following a 20-day *haflagah*, an absolute *veses kavua* has been established, and she must keep the appropriate *vestos* until it is uprooted.

All the laws and details mentioned above regarding a regular *veses hadilug*—for example, if the increments consisted of more than one day—apply to such a *veses hadilug* as well.

Vestos of a *Mesulekes Damim*

Pregnant Woman

89. A pregnant woman is considered a *mesulekes damim* from the fourth month of her pregnancy and onward, i.e., once 90 days have passed from when she immersed in the *mikvah* after her last period before the pregnancy. During the first three months, however, she does not share the laws of a *mesulekes damim* even it is certain that she is pregnant and is not receiving periods.

90. The laws of a pregnant woman with regard to *vestos* are as follows: During the first three months of her pregnancy, she must keep any *vestos* that were created before her pregnancy and have not yet been uprooted. However, she is not required to keep a *veses* created before her pregnancy if it occurs during the fourth month and onward.

A number of examples:

1. A woman experienced a discharge of blood following a long haflagah *and then she became pregnant. In such a case, she must keep the resulting* veses haflagah *if it occurs during the first three months of her pregnancy. But if it occurs during the fourth month of her pregnancy or afterward, she is not required to keep it.*

2. *A woman had a* veses kavua lechodesh *before she became pregnant, which requires* vestos *to be kept over the course of the next three months (or longer, if it is a* veses ha-sirug—*see* §79*). In such a case, she must keep the resulting* vestos *that will occur during the first three months of her pregnancy. (Consequently, lacking to experience a discharge on the day of the* veses *will constitute an* akirah.*) But* vestos *that will occur during the fourth month of her pregnancy or afterward are not required to be kept.*

91. If a pregnant woman experienced a discharge of blood (in a manner that requires *vestos* to be kept—see §5), the days of the *vestos* must be kept if they will occur during the first three months. But if the discharge occurred during the third month and the days of the *veses* will occur during the fourth month or afterward, they are not required to be kept.

92. If the discharge occurred during the fourth month of her pregnancy or afterward, the resulting *vestos* must be kept, following the laws of a *veses she'eino kavua*.

(See §§97*ff. for additional laws concerning a pregnant woman.)

Nursing Woman

93. A nursing woman is defined as a *mesulekes damim* for a period of 24 months following the birth. Even a woman who is presently not nursing, and even one who has not begun to nurse at all, is included in this category. Even though nurs-

ing women frequently experience regular periods during this time—a woman who is not nursing will certainly experience periods within the 24 months following the birth!—they still share the laws of a *mesulekes damim* with regard to *vestos*.

94. A miscarriage that occurred after 40 days from the beginning of the pregnancy carries the status of a birth, and the mother is considered as a nursing woman for the next 24 months. The 40 days are calculated from when she immersed in the *mikvah* after her last period before the pregnancy.

95. Although one can possibly infer from the *Poskim* that a woman who gave birth through a caesarean section is considered a *mesulekes damim* (just like one who gave birth naturally), the matter still requires clarification, and an expert rabbi should be consulted. (For a discussion of the matter, see the *sefer* [Chapter One, *Biurim* §3].)

96. The laws of a nursing woman with regard to *vestos* are as follows: If she experienced a discharge of blood, the standard *vestos* must be kept accordingly. However, she cannot establish a *veses kavua*; even if she experienced discharges in a way that would usually create a *veses kavua*, the discharges are viewed as a *veses she'eino kavua*.

97. If a nursing woman experienced a discharge of blood, the resulting *vestos* must be kept (as a *veses she'eino kavua*) even if they occur after the 24 months have concluded.

97*. To note:

1. There are those who are accustomed to separate both on the thirtieth and thirty-first day for the *onah beinonis* (see the *sefer* [Chapter Twenty-Four §29]). However, even such a woman may suffice with separating on the thirtieth day alone if she is a *mesulekes damim*.

2. As mentioned above (§10), there are those who separate during an additional *onah* preceding the obligatory *onah* (known as "the *onah* of the *Ohr Zarua*"). However, even such a woman may suffice with separating during the *onah* of the *veses* alone if she is a *mesulekes damim*.

98. It is possible for one or two of the three discharges of blood that are required to create a *veses kavua* to be discharged at a time when she is not a *mesulekes damim*, and the remainder to be discharged at a time when she is in this category. In such a case, the discharges do not join together to create a *veses kavua*.

An example: A woman experienced a discharge of blood three times on the fifteenth day of the month, but while the first two discharges occurred during the first three months of her pregnancy, the third discharge occurred during the fourth month. Alternatively, a nursing woman experienced two discharges on the same day of the month prior to the conclusion of the 24 months, while the third discharge occurred afterward. In these cases, a veses kavua *has not been established, because all three discharges creating the* veses *must occur at a time when she is not a* mesulekes damim.

99. If a woman had a *veses kavua* before becoming pregnant and it was not uprooted during the first three months of the pregnancy, she must continue to keep the relevant *vestos* after the conclusion of the 24 months following the birth. However, if she had a *veses she'eino kavua* beforehand

and it was not uprooted, she is not required to keep the *veses* afterward.

Medications That Affect the Menstrual Cycle

100. If a woman takes pills or other medications that affect her menstrual cycle (by delaying her period, advancing it, regulating it, or the like), the laws of *vestos* may be affected as well. Various details apply in such a case, and an expert rabbi should be consulted to determine how she should act.

One Who is Unsure of the Date of Her *Veses*

101. There are various opinions in the *Poskim* regarding the law of one who is unsure of the date of her *veses*. The accepted practice is to allow relations during all the days that are under doubt (see also the discussion in the *sefer* [Chapter Twenty-Four fn. 170]). Certain authorities have suggested that during the days that are under doubt, her husband should ask her to perform a *bedikah* before engaging in marital relations. (She may not, however, perform a *bedikah* on her own accord.) However, this is just a precautionary measure and is not mandated *halachically*.

In any case, if the *veses* is an *onah beinonis* or a *veses kavua*, she must perform a *bedikah* as soon as the day of the *veses* has certainly passed in order to allow relations to resume (see §20).

102. One must be extremely careful to avoid such situations, as certain noteworthy *Poskim* have ruled stringently, and there may be circumstances where one should act stringently in practice as well.

103. If one is unsure of the date of her *veses* and she be-

gins to feel premenstrual symptoms, it is proper to abstain from engaging in marital relations until her status is clarified (i.e., until the symptoms recede or her menstruation indeed begins).

Traveling On the *Onah* of a *Veses*

104. One should try as much as possible to refrain from traveling on the *onah* of a *veses*. The reason for this is because departing on a journey normally requires the husband to fulfill his marital obligations toward his wife before leaving.[9] Thus, when one departs during the *onah* of a *veses* (when relations are generally forbidden), a *halachic* question arises whether the husband may engage in marital relations (and is indeed required to do so) or not.

If he must depart during such a time, he should appease his wife in other ways so that she will forgo her conjugal rights.

However, he may travel for the sake of a *mitzvah*, as there is no *onah* obligation in such a case (see note[10]).

---

9. The *Poskim* differ regarding the length of the journey that requires a husband to fulfill his *onah* obligation. From the wording of certain authorities it can be implied that the journey must be at least three days long. Others state that the journey must extend beyond that particular husband's minimum *onah* obligation (see *Shulchan Aruch Orach Chaim* §240). Yet others explain that this obligation stems from the fact that departing on a journey arouses the wife's feelings for marital relations; hence, each case must be assessed individually to ascertain whether the trip will arouse such feelings or not.

10. It is unclear if one is required to fulfill one's *onah* obligation if the departure for the *mitzvah* will occur (not that night but) the following day.

See the *sefer* (Chapter Twenty-Four fn. 175) for a discussion whether

Tevilah On the *Onah* of a *Veses*

105. Marital relations are forbidden during the *onah* of a *veses* even if it is the night of her *tevilah*. In such a case, she must delay her *tevilah* to the following day. In a situation where the *tevilah* cannot be delayed—for example, if delaying the *tevilah* will result in additional delays—she should immerse, and she should perform the *segulos* that serve as protection when immersion is not followed by marital relations (namely, covering herself with a garment of her husband and placing a knife under her pillow when going to bed—see Chapter Thirteen §9).

(See Chapter Thirteen §10 and fn. 1 for another important concern in such a case.)

105*. To note:

1. As mentioned above (§10), there are those who separate during an additional *onah* preceding the obligatory *onah* (known as "the *onah* of the *Ohr Zarua*"). If the night of her *tevilah* coincides with this *onah*, marital relations are permitted. In such a case, she should perform a *bedikah* beforehand and make sure that she does not feel any symptoms associated with her menstruation.

2. The same laws apply to those who are accustomed to separate both on the thirtieth and thirty-first day for the *onah beinonis* (see the *sefer* [Chapter Twenty-Four §29]) if the night of the *tevilah* coincides with the thirty-first day.

---

or not traveling for business purposes is considered as traveling for the sake of a *mitzvah*. As explained there, it seems that this is not the case.

Marriage During the *Onah* of a *Veses*

106. If the marriage of a couple will take place during the *onah* of a *veses*, an expert rabbi should be consulted to determine whether the *be'ilas mitzvah* (the first intercourse to take place after the wedding—see Chapter Eighteen §1) may be performed that night. In any case, even if the *be'ilas mitzvah* will not be performed, they may seclude themselves (*yichud*) without the need for a *shomer*.[11] Additionally, there may be room to rule leniently if the marriage will take place during an *onah beinonis*, provided she performs a *bedikah* before engaging in marital relations.

Accurate and Orderly Recording of the *Vestos*

107. As stated in the beginning of the chapter (§3), the importance of keeping a detailed calendar in which the days of the *veses* are recorded cannot be underestimated. In order to prevent doubts from arising, it is extremely important to mark down the relevant details accurately and immediately. In addition to marking down these details in a calendar, it is advisable to prepare a separate sheet where the days of the *veses* will be listed in an orderly fashion. This will allow one to take note of unusual combinations that might constitute the creation of a *veses kavua* (such as a *veses hasirug* or *veses hadilug*), which might otherwise be difficult to notice if the days are only marked down in a calendar over the course of a number of pages. An example of such a sheet has been provided here.

One who tries their best to calculate and keep the *vestos*

---

11. In contrast to a case where the *kallah* is a *nidah*, where *yichud* is forbidden (see Chapter Seventeen §16).

properly is assured from G-d of success, as our Sages have stated: "One who comes [with the intent] to become purified will find themselves assisted [from Above]" (Talmud, *Yoma* 38a).

ADDENDUM

As noted in this chapter (§75; §107), in addition to marking down the details of the *vestos* in a calendar, it is advisable to mark down these details on a separate sheet as well. This will allow one to immediately notice any combination of discharges that may carry significance, especially unusual combinations (such as a *veses hasirug* or *veses hadilug*) that might be difficult to notice in a calendar. An example of a sheet that can be used for this purpose has been provided following this Addendum.

How to Use This Chart

The following instructions can be of assistance in using this chart:

First column. In this column one should mark down the onah and time when the menstrual period began (see §§11ff.). For example, if she began bleeding at 9:00 p.m. (after sunset), one should write "9:00" in the left side of the column, and if it took place at 7:30 a.m. (after sunrise), one should write "7:30" in the right side of the column.

The reason it is important to note the **onah** when the *tum'ah* took place is because the separation and *bedikah* of the resulting *vestos* apply during the same *onah* as the one in which the period began—see §9. (An exception is the *onah beinonis* which must be kept for a full twenty-four hours—see §28.) Additionally, a *veses kavua* can only be established if all periods began during the same *onah* (see §36).

The reason it is important to note the **time** when the period began is because the *bedikah* of the resulting *vestos* should be performed at the time of day when the period began or later (see §18).

Second column. In this column one should mark down the day of the week when the period began. (Reminder: A period that began after sunset belongs to the following day—see §2 par. 4.)

Marking down the day of the week will assist one in identifying a pattern that may create a weekly *veses hasirug* (see §§77–78).

Third column. In this column one should mark down the day of the Hebrew month when the period began. (For example, if the period began on 23 Nissan, one should write "23" in the left side of the column and "Nissan" in the right side.)

Marking down the day of the month will enable one to calculate the *veses hachodesh* (see §34). Additionally, it will assist one in identifying patterns that may create a *veses kavua lechodesh* (see §36), a monthly *veses hasirug* (see §79), or a *veses hadilug* with regard to the dates of the month (see §§82–83; §§85–87).

Fourth column. In this column one should mark down the Hebrew date when the *hefsek taharah* was performed. This will enable one to calculate the next *haflagah* accurately—see the following paragraph. (It should be noted that this is not necessary for those that follow the opinion of the other *Poskim*—see ibid.).

Fifth column. In this column one should mark down the *haflagah* between the previous and current discharges of blood. Those that follow the opinion of the Alter Rebbe (and others) should note the amount of *onos* that passed from the previous *hefsek taharah*[12] until the beginning of the current period, while those that follow the opinion of the other *Poskim* should note the amount of **days** that passed from the **beginning of the previous period** until the beginning of the current one (see §§48).

Marking down the *haflagah* will enable one to calculate the *veses hahaflagah* (see §45). Additionally, it will assist one in identifying patterns that may create a *veses kavua lehaflagah* (see §46) or a *veses hadilug* with regard to *haflagos* (see §§84–86; §88).

Sixth column. In this column one should mark down the Hebrew dates when the *vestos* resulting from the current discharge will be kept. The *onah* that will be kept should be noted as well, except by an *onah beinonis*, when a full twenty-four hour period is kept.

Additionally, one should mark down any other *veses* that will be kept during the following month, for example, a *veses hahaflagah* for a longer *haflagah* that has not yet been uprooted (see §52) or a *veses kavua* that has not yet been uprooted (see §64).

For example, one might write in this column: "21 Iyar (night)—*veses hahaflagah* for current *haflagah*. 22 Iyar—*onah beinonis*. 23 Iyar (night)—*veses hachodesh*. 27 Iyar (day)—*veses hahaflagah* for previous *haflagah*."

---

12. Under certain circumstances, it may be possible for the *haflagah* to begin before the *hefsek taharah* was performed—see §47* par. 2.

Seventh column. In this column one should note any relevant information of significance.

A number of examples:

1. One should mark down longer *haflagos* that have not yet been uprooted.

2. One should mark down a *veses kavua* that has not yet been uprooted and must still be kept.

3. One should continue to mark down a *veses kavua* even once it has become uprooted. The reason for this is because the *veses kavua* can return to its previous state by means of a single discharge on the day of the *veses*, even if a long time has passed since it was uprooted (see §67; §69). This is the case until a new *veses kavua* is established (see §70).

4. One should make note if a *veses kavua* is only *kavua lechumra* (see §§77–79; §§85–88).

Onah and Time		Day of the Week	Day of the Month		Hefsek Taharah	Haflagah	Times of Separation	Notes
Night	Day		Day	Month				

CHAPTER SEVENTEEN[1]

A *KALLAH*
BEFORE AND DURING HER MARRIAGE

Scheduling the Wedding Date

1. One should try to schedule the wedding date so that
the *kallah* will be *tehorah* at the time of the wedding. This
will avoid the *halachic* complications that result when she is
temei'ah at that time (as will be enumerated in this chapter),
as well as the accompanying tension and heartache.

Taharah Process Before the Wedding

2. Every *kallah* must count *shivah nekiyim* and immerse
in the *mikvah* before her marriage. This applies even if she
was *tehorah* from beforehand, and even if she is a *mesulekes
damim* (for example, an elderly woman who has not experienced periods for an extended length of time). The reason for this is because our Sages were concerned that the
pre-wedding emotions may have initiated minimal uterine
bleeding (known as *dam chimud*).

However, if she is not actually a *nidah* and the *taharah*
process is being performed solely due to *dam chimud*, some leniencies apply in certain situations, as explained in the *sefer*
(Chapter Nine §2).

---

1. Corresponding to Chapter Nine in the *sefer*.

Bedikos

3. A *kallah* is required to perform the entire *taharah* process, including the *hefsek taharah*, counting *shivah nekiyim* (along with the accompanying *bedikos*), *chafifah*, and *tevilah*. Although a *besulah* cannot perform *bedikos* as deeply as one who is not a *besulah*, she cannot suffice with a *kinuach* either. Rather, she must perform a *bedikah* as deep as she can and tilt the *bedikah* cloth so that it will reach every corner, as explained in Chapter Eight (§§28ff.). She should perform the *bedikah* carefully and gently, taking care not to hurt herself. She may moisten the *bedikah* cloth if it is difficult for her to perform *bedikos* when it is dry.

Hefsek Taharah

4. A *kallah* before her wedding may perform a *hefsek taharah* as soon as her menstrual period has ended, and she is not required to wait five days (see Chapter Seven). Additional relevant details have been explained in the *sefer* (Chapter Nine §§5-6), and one should consult a *kallah* teacher regarding this issue.

Correct Time of Tevilah

5. A *kallah* should immerse in the *mikvah* as close to the day of the wedding as possible. The accepted custom is to allow her to immerse up to four nights before the wedding; for example, if the wedding will take place on Thursday night, she may immerse as early as Sunday night, but not beforehand. However, her *tevilah* is valid *bedi'eved* even if she immersed at an earlier time, and she may do so *lechatchilah* if a great need is present (for example, if there is no *mikvah* in the location where the wedding will take place and she will

be traveling there more than four days before the wedding).

6. Although generally one may not schedule the *tevilah* to occur on *motza'ei Shabbos* or *motza'ei Yom Tov* (see Chapter Thirteen §§15ff.), a *kallah* before her wedding may do so.

Chafifah

7. The *chafifah* of a *kallah* before her wedding may begin at night (unlike after the wedding, when the *chafifah* must begin by day and continue into the night—see Chapter Ten §1).

Bedikos After the Tevilah

8. Even after immersing, she must continue to perform two daily *bedikos* until the wedding (see the following paragraph).

9. *Lechatchilah* she should continue performing *bedikos* until the *be'ilas mitzvah* (the first marital relations to take place after the wedding), even if it took place at a later night (and not on the night of the wedding). However, there is a *halachic* basis for one who performs *bedikos* only until the actual wedding.

10. If she did not perform *bedikos* from the *tevilah* until the wedding, she is *tehorah bedi'eved* if she performed *bedikos* during the *shivah nekiyim* as required. However, if seven days passed by without a single *bedikah*, she must count *shivah nekiyim* and immerse again. See the *sefer* (Chapter Nine §§11-12) for a number of laws that apply if one must count again.

Immersing on the Day of the Wedding

11. The following laws apply if the seventh day of the *shivah nekiyim* is the actual day of the wedding:

1. If the days are short and the marriage ceremony can be delayed until after nightfall, she should immerse at night before the marriage ceremony.

2. If the marriage ceremony cannot be delayed to such an extent, she may immerse by day, provided that the marriage ceremony will take place at night.

3. If the marriage ceremony must take place by day as well (for example, in those times and places where the night begins at an extremely late hour), the *chasan* and *kallah* may not seclude themselves (*yichud*) until night-fall.

Special Circumstances

12. If one remarries his divorcee, she must count *shivah nekiyim* and immerse just like any other *kallah*, even if she is *tehorah* and is a *mesulekes damim* (i.e., if she is pregnant, nursing, or is elderly).

13. Similarly, if a couple has engaged in marital relations prior to the wedding (G-d forbid), she must count *shivah nekiyim* and immerse just like any other *kallah*, even if she is *tehorah* and is a *mesulekes damim*.

14. If a couple converted to Judaism, they must separate for three months. However, under certain circumstances, she is not required to count *shivah nekiyim* if she is *tehorah* before resuming marital life together (see the *sefer* [Chapter Nine §14*]). However, she is required to do so if she is a *nidah*.

15. If the wedding has been postponed to a later date, an expert rabbi should be consulted to determine if she is required to count *shivah nekiyim* and immerse again.

If the *Kallah* Is a *Nidah* at the Wedding

16. If the *kallah* is a *nidah* at the time of the wedding, all the standard *harchakos* must be kept (see Chapter Six). Additionally, the couple may not seclude themselves (*yichud*) without a *shomer*, as will be explained below (§19). Although *yichud* is normally allowed between a husband and wife even when she is a *nidah*, our Sages were concerned that in this case a transgression may take place, because they have never yet engaged in marital relations.

Even if she was *tehorah* at the wedding, *yichud* is forbidden if she became *temei'ah* before they had a chance to engage in marital relations. The definition of marital relations in this regard will be explained in Chapter Eighteen (§32).

17. If a man remarried his divorcee and she was unable to complete counting *shivah nekiyim* before the wedding (see §12), *yichud* is permitted. However, this is only true if she is *tehorah* and the counting of *shivah nekiyim* was only due to *dam chimud* (and not because she was a *nidah*—see the *sefer* [Chapter Nine fn. 29]).

18. If a couple has engaged in marital relations prior to the wedding (G-d forbid) and she is a *nidah* at the wedding, an expert rabbi should be consulted to determine if they may be allowed to seclude themselves.

19. The laws of *yichud* in this case differ in certain details from the standard laws of *yichud* (as will be explained in Chapter Twenty):

1. At night, two *shomrim* are necessary, a male for the *chasan* and a female for the *kallah*. It is customary to use a boy to act as the *shomer* for the *chasan* and a girl to act as the *shomer* for the *kallah*. The children should be no younger than five and no older than nine. If it is difficult to find children of this age, one can use children up to (and including) the age of eleven. If it is difficult to find children at all, one may rely on the opinions who allow the use of adults to act as *shomrim* for this purpose.

2. *Shomrim* are sometimes necessary even if the *chasan* and *kallah* are sleeping in two separate rooms and each one locks the room from the inside. They are necessary in such a case if both rooms are in the same house and it is possible to pass from one room to the next without exiting to the street, a public staircase, or the like.

3. In extremely challenging situations where two *shomrim* cannot be found, one *shomer* can suffice in the following manner: The room of either the *chasan* or the *kallah* should be locked, and the key should be given to the *shomer*. The *shomer* should keep the key near him so that it will be impossible to take it without his knowledge. (This possibility is only an option if the *chasan* or *kallah* cannot unlock the door from the inside without the key.)

4. By day one *shomer* is sufficient (as per the criteria outlined in par. 1). However, if it is difficult to find children and an adult is acting as a *shomer*, a single adult woman is insufficient, and two such women are required (see Chapter Twenty fn. 8).

If the room where the *chasan* and *kallah* are found is open to the street, the courtyard, or a stairwell where passersby are present, no *shomer* is required (see ibid. §§9ff. for the conditions that apply in this case).

20. A suggestion:

The most suitable arrangement in such a case is for the couple to stay in the home of their parents, **married** friends, or the like until she becomes *tehorah*. They should sleep in separate rooms, the *chasan* with the husband or father and the *kallah* with the wife or mother. Although one may possibly be embarrassed to do so, experience has shown that this arrangement is far simpler and easier than any other option.

Additional Concerns When the *Kallah* Is a *Nidah*

21. The *Poskim* differ how—if at all—the *chasan* may place the ring on the *kallah's* finger if she is a *nidah*. The custom is to place the ring on her finger as usual, and he should try to only touch the ring and not the actual finger.

22. The *chasan* may drink the wine following the recital of the *sheva berachos* even though the *kallah* drank from the very same glass earlier (after the *birchas eirusin*), something usually forbidden when she is a *nidah* (see Chapter Six §§70ff.).

23. According to a custom followed by certain individuals, the *chasan* steps gently on the *kallah's* foot under the *chupah* or in the *yichud* room. This custom may not be followed if she is a *nidah*, as their clothing—and in our case, their shoes—may not touch (see Chapter Six §8).

24. It is important to exercise vigilance when posing for pictures to ensure that the *chasan* and *kallah* do not touch each other.

Marriage During the *Onah* of a *Veses*

25. If a couple's marriage will take place during the *onah* of her *veses*, an expert rabbi should be consulted to determine whether the *be'ilas mitzvah* may be performed that night (see Chapter Sixteen §106 for additional details).

CHAPTER EIGHTEEN[1]

DAM BESULIM (HYMENAL BLEEDING)

Be'ilas Mitzvah

1. The first marital act to take place after the wedding is known as the *be'ilas mitzvah* (the *mitzvah* intercourse). Various explanations have been given for this name.

Tum'ah Following the First Intercourse

2. A woman becomes *temei'ah* following the first intercourse even if no blood was discovered (if she is a *besulah*). Even so, she should perform a *bedikah* afterward, and the husband should wipe his organ with a clean, white cloth. If no blood is discovered, the sheet should be examined to determine if blood has been discharged.

(If a woman is not a *besulah*, she does not become *temei'ah* following the *be'ilas mitzvah*, and no *bedikos* are required [unless the wedding occurred during the "uncertain days"—see Chapter Fifteen §2*; §5].)

3. The above (that she always becomes *temei'ah* following the first intercourse) only applies if the intercourse was **completed,** i.e., if the entire organ entered the vagina. If, however, only a portion of the organ entered the vagina and no blood was discovered, the *Poskim* differ whether she is *temei'ah* or *tehorah*, and an expert rabbi should be consulted (see the *sefer* [Chapter Ten §2 and fns.]).

---

1. Corresponding to Chapter Ten in the *sefer*.

4. If the organ slipped out of the vagina before semen was released, the law will depend on how much of the organ entered the vagina: If the entire organ entered the vagina, she is *temei'ah* and they must separate immediately. But if part of the organ did not enter the vagina—even if the majority entered—and no blood was discovered, she is *tehorah*. (This is true even according to the *Poskim* [mentioned in §3] who rule stringently in a case where semen was released.)

5. If semen was released or if erection ceased while the organ was still in the vagina and before it entered completely, he may wait in his present position until erection reoccurs and continue with the intercourse. However, this applies only if the **entire** corona (*atarah*) is still in the vagina; but if the organ slipped out of the vagina—as usually occurs in such a case—he may only continue with the intercourse if she is *tehorah* (as per the guidelines outlined in the previous paragraphs).

6. Although in certain situations she is *tehorah* and they may continue to engage in marital relations, this is only true if she performed a *bedikah* and was found to be *tehorah*. But if even the smallest drop of blood was discovered, they must separate immediately.

7. It is common for no *dam besulim* to be discovered following the first intercourse. Indeed, the Talmud states that from the age of twelve-and-a-half and on, it is possible for the *besulim* (hymen) to disintegrate on their own. Nonetheless, as stated above, it is possible to become *temei'ah* following the first intercourse regardless.

Words of Caution for the *Chasan*

8. The *chasan* should do his best to complete the inter-course on the night of the wedding. This is in contrast to those who, for whatever reason, delay this important *mitzvah* until a later point. In addition to not fulfilling the above directive, severe transgressions may occur as a result (such as the wasteful release of semen). If he was unable to complete the intercourse due to excitement, exhaustion, or the like, it is imperative to discuss the matter **as soon as possible** with an expert *chasan* teacher or rabbi who will provide him with the necessary assistance.

9. Additional important words of caution can be found in §37.

Words of Caution for the *Kallah*

10. The *kallah* should assist the *chasan* in completing the intercourse, and the *kallah* teacher should teach her how to do so. Additionally, the *kallah* should visit the *kallah* teacher after the wedding to learn the details relating to marital relations that were not taught beforehand (see §37).

Words of Caution for the *Chasan* Teacher

11. The *chasan* teacher must explain as clearly as possible how to differentiate between an incomplete intercourse and a complete one, until he is certain that the *chasan* has understood it properly. He must also explain the delicate manner in which the first intercourse should be performed, as well as additional practical directives that will enable him to fulfill the *mitzvah* as calmly and completely as possible. Embarrassment to supply the necessary information in the clearest

possible manner may result, G-d forbid, in transgressions and unnecessary complications, the responsibility of which lies entirely on the *chasan* teacher.

12. Additionally, he should tell the *chasan* that he should not be embarrassed, and if he has any question, he should feel free to call either him or an expert rabbi (whomever he is more comfortable speaking to), and they will answer any question that may arise. He should also supply the *chasan* with the relevant telephone numbers so that he will be able to contact him or the rabbi even in the middle of the night if necessary.

Words of Caution for the *Kallah* Teacher

13. The words of caution outlined in the previous paragraphs—regarding the importance of clarifying all the relevant details and ensuring that they are understood properly—apply to the *kallah* teacher as well. As stated above (§10), the *kallah* teacher must explain all the details necessary for the *mitzvah* to be fulfilled properly.

14. A shocking phenomena which has unfortunately occurred in the past is that the *kallah* did not perform the *bedikos* in the proper place, and as a result she assumed that she was *tehorah* when in reality she was a **full-fledged *nidah*.** Despite the awkwardness involved, a tremendous responsibility lies on the *kallah* teacher to ensure that the *kallah* understands how to perform *bedikos* properly. Indeed, many teachers will send *kallos* to an expert *bodekes* (if neccesary) to demonstrate how a *bedikah* is actually done.

Conduct Following the First Intercourse

15. After the semen has been released, the organ generally slips out of the vagina. They must then separate immediately and he must exit her bed. From that point and on, all the *harchakos* enumerated in Chapter Six must be kept.

Tum'ah Following the Subsequent Intercourses

16. As stated above (§§2-3), the *kallah* becomes *temei'ah* following the first intercourse even if no blood was discharged. However, she remains *tehorah* following the subsequent intercourses (after she counted *shivah nekiyim* and immersed) if no blood was discovered. This is true even if pain was felt during the intercourse.

See below (§19) for the law if the first intercourse was incomplete.

17. Certain authorities maintain that as long as pain is still being felt, it must be determined that no blood was discharged at the subsequent intercourses. Accordingly, the bed should be covered with a white sheet, and she should perform a *bedikah* and examine the sheet after the intercourse.

By contrast, many authorities are of the opinion that if blood had been discovered following the first intercourse or if the first intercourse had been completed (see §3), there is no need to perform a *bedikah* or examine the sheet following the subsequent intercourses.[2] However, if blood was

---

2. As explained in the *sefer* (Chapter Ten fn. 18), certain *Poskim* maintain that a *bedikah* should be performed following the subsequent intercourses (until one intercourse takes place with neither pain nor

discovered anyway, it is self-understood that she is *temei'ah*.

18. According to the latter opinion, if blood was discovered following the first intercourse or if it is certain that it had been completed, she remains *tehorah* following the subsequent intercourses even if a *kesem* was discovered on her sheet after the intercourse (if it is a *kesem* that can be rendered *tahor*, as per the criteria enumerated in Chapter Four). This is true even if pain was felt during the intercourse. It is therefore advisable to cover the bed with a colored sheet before the subsequent intercourses (i.e., those following a complete intercourse) or to place a colored towel beneath her (see Chapter Four §§48ff.).

However, this applies only if what was discovered following the intercourse was merely a *kesem*. But if she wiped herself or performed a *bedikah*, she is *temei'ah* even if a minute drop of blood was discovered and even if it was found on a colored garment or the like. It is therefore advisable to refrain from wiping herself or performing *bedikos* unnecessarily following the subsequent intercourses.

19. As stated above (§16), the *kallah* remains *tehorah* following the subsequent intercourses if no blood was discovered. This is true even if the first intercourse had not been completed but blood was discovered when she examined herself following the intercourse (see §2). In such a case, she

---

blood). Others have ruled that there is no need to perform a *bedikah*, but her sheet should be examined. Yet others have stated that although there is no *halachic* requirement to do so, a *bedikah* should be performed to remove all doubts. However, certain noteworthy *Poskim* are of the opinion that there is no need to perform a *bedikah* at all, and the Tzemach Tzedek appears to share this opinion.

is *tehorah* even though the subsequent intercourse is the first one to be completed, because we presume that the entire *besulim* (hymen) fell apart at the first intercourse.

However, this assumption cannot be applied if no blood was discovered following the first intercourse (and it was incomplete). In such a case, even according to those opinions who hold that she becomes *temei'ah* anyway (see §3), she will become *temei'ah* once again following the subsequent complete intercourse.

Dam Besulim Vs. Blood Caused by Marital Relations

20. It is quite common to discover blood following the subsequent intercourses as well. This blood is assumed to be *dam besulim* (hymenal blood) if pain was felt and blood was discovered at each intercourse.

21. However, if one intercourse took place without blood being discovered and blood was discovered at a subsequent intercourse, the blood is not assumed to be *dam besulim* and is viewed as blood caused by marital relations (see Chapter Two §§24ff.). This is true even if pain was felt during the intercourse.

22. This applies in the converse case as well: if blood was discovered at each intercourse but she did not feel pain during one intercourse, the blood cannot continue to be associated with *dam besulim*.

In these cases, an expert rabbi should be contacted immediately to determine how they should proceed. They should not wait to see if it will reoccur (see ibid.).

23. As stated above (§21), if one intercourse took place

without blood being discovered, any subsequent blood is not assumed to be *dam besulim*. This is true even if the intercourse without blood was the first complete intercourse, and even if pain was felt at that time. (See note for additional details.[3])

Bedikos Before and After Marital Relations

24. Once blood is no longer assumed to be *dam besulim*, the couple can begin performing *bedikos* before and after three marital relations (to create a *chazakah* that marital relations do not cause her to bleed—see Chapter Fifteen §1; §3). The details of how and when these *bedikos* should be performed can be found in Chapter Fifteen (§§4ff.).

An expert rabbi should be consulted if one is unsure if the time to begin performing these *bedikos* has arrived.

24*. Whenever there is no obligation to perform *bedikos* after marital relations, they should not be performed even if the husband and wife both desire to do so (see ibid. §17). Accordingly, if the husband is accustomed to wiping himself following marital relations, he should do so with a cloth upon which blood will not be noticeable at all. Alternatively, he

---

3. Although the first complete intercourse renders her *temei'ah* regardless of whether blood was discovered or not (see §2), if no blood was actually discovered at that time, any subsequent blood is not assumed to be *dam besulim*.

However, this only applies if it is certain both that the first intercourse was completed and that no blood was discharged at that time. But if it is possible that the first intercourse was not completed, or if it is possible that blood was discharged (for example, if she did not perform a *bedikah* afterward to determine if blood was discharged or not), blood discharged at subsequent intercourses is considered *dam besulim*, provided they were accompanied by pain.

should wipe himself with a tissue and immediately dispose of it (without glancing at it first).

Shivah Nekiyim Following Dam Besulim

25. As explained in Chapter Seven, a *hefsek taharah* may generally be performed no earlier than the fifth day from the beginning of the *tum'ah*. However, if the *tum'ah* is the result of *dam besulim*, the *hefsek taharah* may be performed on the **fourth** day from the beginning of the *tum'ah*, and she may begin counting *shivah nekiyim* the following day.

An example: If the newlywed couple engaged in marital relations on Sunday night, the fourth day from the beginning of her tum'ah *is Thursday. She may thus perform a* hefsek taharah *on Thursday, begin counting* shivah nekiyim *on Friday, and immerse in the* mikvah *the following Thursday evening.*

26. This is true not only with regard to the first intercourse, but with regard to any subsequent intercourse where blood was discharged as well, as long as the blood is assumed to be *dam besulim* (as per the criteria outlined above [§§20ff.]).

27. This leniency is restricted to a case where the *shivah nekiyim* are being counted **only** due to *dam besulim*. But if she experienced her menstrual period after the intercourse, **five** days must pass before she can perform a *hefsek taharah* (just like any other woman), and the *shivah nekiyim* will begin on the sixth day. However, the five days can be counted from the day she became *temei'ah* as a result of the *dam besulim* (and not from the beginning of her period).

28. An expert rabbi should be consulted if it is difficult

for her to perform *bedikos* during the *shivah nekiyim* (see the *sefer* [Chapter Ten §21 and fns.]).

Removal of *Besulim*

29. If a woman's hymen (*besulim*) must be surgically re-moved (a procedure known as hymenotomy), it should be done when she is *temei'ah* anyways if possible, so that the *halachic* issue of whether she will become *temei'ah* as a result will be avoided. However, if it was removed when she was *te-horah*, the *halachic* ruling is that she does not become *temei'ah* as a result.

30. If the hymen was removed before the first inter-course, she does not become *temei'ah* at the first intercourse if no blood was discovered. However, this is only true if it is certain that the **entire** hymen was removed. The procedure should therefore be done *lechatchilah* by an observant doctor. Alternatively, she should visit a *halachic bodekes* or an obser-vant midwife to ensure that this is the case.

30*. If blood was discovered at the intercourses that fol-lowed the hymen's removal, an expert rabbi should be con-sulted to determine if it can be assumed that the blood is a result of the surgery.

If She Became *Temei'ah* Before the First Intercourse

31. If a woman became *temei'ah* before the first inter-course, the couple may not seclude themselves (*yichud*), just like a woman who marries when she is a *nidah* (see Chapter Seventeen §16). The previous chapter (§§16ff.) should be consulted for the relevant details.

32. If the corona (*atarah*) and a portion of the organ

entered the vagina but she became *temei'ah* before he was able to complete the intercourse, *yichud* is permitted. However, if genital contact occurred but the organ did not enter the vagina in the manner described above, many authorities maintain that *yichud* is forbidden. An expert rabbi should be consulted to assist them in clarifying if the above criteria were met (see note[4]).

Birchas Besulim

33. According to one custom, a special *berachah* known as *birchas besulim* is recited after the first intercourse (if the *kallah* is a *besulah*). *Netilas yadayim* must first be performed, and G-d's name is not mentioned in the *berachah*. However, others have written that this *berachah* is not recited, and one should follow the custom of his community.

The following is the text of the *berachah*:[5] *Boruch asher tzag egoz began eden, shoshanas ha'amakim, bal yimshol zar bemayan chasum, al ken ayeles ahavim shamrah betaharah, vechok lo heifeirah, Baruch habocher bezar'o shel Avraham* ("Blessed [is He] who planted [a bride (Chavah), who is compared to] a nut and a rose of the valleys, in *Gan Eden*. No stranger will dominate [her, as she is compared to] a sealed well.

---

4. According to most authorities, *yichud* is forbidden if no actual intercourse took place. Nonetheless, there is room to consult an expert rabbi if they lay together and attempted to engage in relations but were unsuccessful—either because the *chasan* withdrew upon seeing the *kallah's* pain, or because he was unable to attain proper erection of the organ—and then she became a *nidah*.

5. For a proper understanding of the text of *birchas besulim*, which is replete with Scriptural terminology and allegories, the following sources may be consulted: *Avudraham* (*Birchos Nissu'in*). *Perishah* (*Even Ha'ezer* §63). *Chupas Chassanim* (9:2). *Aruch Hashulchan* (*Even Ha'ezer* 63:10).

Therefore the [bride, likened to a] beloved doe has protected [her virginity] with purity and has not annulled [Jewish] law. Blessed [is He] who chooses the seed of Avraham").

34. A number of clarifications:

While this chapter addresses the **halachic** aspects relating to the beginning of a couple's marriage, it cannot take the place of a private talk with a certified *chasan* teacher regarding the relevant **practical** aspects. This conversation cannot be left out, and one should not presume that he has sufficient knowledge in these matters on his own. Experience has shown that even if doing so initially appears unnecessary, the *chasan* quickly discovers that this is the only way for things to proceed smoothly and successfully!

35. As mentioned, direction should be received from a **certified** *chasan* teacher. This is in contrast to those who believe that any married young man (!) can supply a *chasan* with the necessary practical guidance. Unfortunately, it is possible for a great deal of damage to be caused before the *chasan* realizes his mistake!

36. Similarly, the *kallah* should receive detailed guidance in these matters from a **certified** *kallah* teacher, as the *kallah* plays a large role in the proper fulfillment of this *mitzvah*. (This is in addition to receiving clear instructions how to perform the *bedikos* in the proper manner and in the correct place, along with all the other fundamentals of *taharas hamish-pachah*.)

37. Important words of caution:

In addition to the **practical** elements of marital relations, many laws apply to the manner in which relations should be performed and how the proper holiness should be preserved. In order not to place excessive pressure on the *chasan*, the *chasan* teacher will generally suffice with a number of general guidelines and instruct the *chasan* to return at a later date for a detailed discussion of these laws.

Unfortunately, it is quite common for the *chasan* not to return for this important discussion, assuming that he already knows the necessary information. It then often occurs that at a later point in time, the couple realizes that they have not been conducting themselves properly. The necessity of this important conversation must therefore be emphasized, so that the family to be raised by the new couple will be founded on holiness and purity.

Additionally, the laws themselves must be studied, as explained in *Shulchan Aruch* (*Orach Chaim* §240) and its commentaries, or at least as they have been compiled in contemporary works.[6]

To reiterate: It is vital to be well-informed of these laws and not to rely on one's personal understanding.

---

6. As a suggestion, one who prefers to study these laws in English can make use of an English translation of *Kitzur Shulchan Aruch* §150.

CHAPTER NINETEEN[1]

BIRTH AND MISCARRIAGE

Labor

1. A woman in labor remains *tehorah* if she has not yet reached the point of requesting to lie on the bed where the birth will take place (see the following paragraph).

2. If the labor has intensified to the point that she requested to lie on the bed where the birth will take place, she is *temei'ah*. This is true even if she didn't actually request to do so, but she would have had a midwife been present. Similarly, she is *temei'ah* if it is difficult for her to walk on her own and she requires assistance, even if no blood has been discharged.

3. If her water broke, she remains *tehorah* if it is possible to ascertain that no blood has been discharged as well.

4. If there is a significant need for the husband in particular to assist his wife, he can be allowed to do so even if the labor has reached the point where she is regarded as *temei'ah*, provided it is **certain** that no blood has yet been discharged. In such a case, he should try to limit his assistance to the bare minimum.

If blood has already been discharged, various guidelines apply to how a husband may assist her if there is a great need to do so (see Chapter Six §§127ff.). It is important to study these laws as they apply to this case.

---

1. Corresponding to Chapter Eleven in the *sefer*.

5. If the contractions have stopped and it has been determined that the birth process has been interrupted, she should perform a *bedikah*, and if no blood is discovered, she is *tehorah*. This is true even if the labor had reached the point where she was regarded as *temei'ah*. Once the labor contin- ues and returns to that state, she will be considered *temei'ah* once again.

(Certain families act stringently in such a case, and they must follow their custom.)

6. If the physician or midwife examined her and stated that her womb has dilated as a result of the contractions, she is *temei'ah*. However, if it was open on its own, she is *tehorah*. (Such a phenomenon often occurs to women who have already experienced a number of births, and sometimes it can occur by earlier births as well during the last few weeks of the pregnancy. The physician or midwife should therefore be asked whether the dilation is indeed the beginning of the birth process.)

Harchakos During and After Birth

7. The laws of a *yoledes* are equal to that of a *nidah* in all their details. This includes both the *harchakos* and the entire *taharah* process (the *hefsek taharah*, *shivah nekiyim*, *chafifah*, *tevilah*, and so on).

8. As a rule, the husband may not be present in the room when his wife is giving birth.[2] If an expert rabbi allowed the

---

2. See *Responsa Minchas Yitzchak* (vol. 8, §30 par. 2). See also letter of the Lubavitcher Rebbe (printed in *Sha'arei Halachah U'Minhag Even Ha'ezer* p. 39): "It is obvious that you should not be present [in the room during birth], and I am surprised that you even asked regarding this."

husband to be present (due to an irregular circumstance), he must turn away so that he will not see the areas of her body that are normally concealed.

9. One should refrain from giving gifts to his wife when she is *temei'ah* due to childbirth (see Chapter Six §106). Accordingly, he should tell her that he will buy her a present shortly or the like if doing so will not cause her to take offense. An expert rabbi should be consulted if it appears that this will not be sufficient.

Taharah Following Birth or Miscarriage

10. One may *halachically* not immerse following the birth of a male until seven days have passed, and by a female or miscarriage, until fourteen days have passed. Practically, however, the bleeding generally extends for more than this amount of time, and the *taharah* process can only begin once the bleeding has stopped. But once it has stopped, there is no need to wait and she can immediately begin the *taharah* process. Not only is it not necessary to wait more than is required by *halachah*, but to the contrary, one should try to immerse as soon as possible.

11. Certain women have the custom to refrain from immersing until forty or eighty days have passed since the birth, for a male or female child respectively. If one's family is accustomed to doing so, an expert rabbi should be consulted to determine whether they should continue following this practice. In any case, there is no need to wait additional time after a miscarriage, and she may begin the *taharah* process as soon as *halachically* possible.

11*. Many miscarriages are followed by a procedure

known as D&C (dilation and curettage, involving the removal of the remaining tissue from the uterus), in which case the woman may not enter a new pregnancy for medical reasons until her first menstrual period arrives after the miscarriage. If such a procedure was performed, one should consult an expert rabbi who is also proficient in the relevant medical aspects to direct her how to act.

12. In certain situations, it may be necessary to use contraceptive methods to delay further pregnancies for a period of time (due to illness, weakness, or the like). In such a case, with the consent of both husband and wife, an expert rabbi **must** first be approached to assess the situation with all its details. He will then decide whether they may indeed do so and which contraceptive method should be used.

Vestos Following Birth or Miscarriage

13. Blood discharged during birth is not taken into account with regard to *vestos*, and only once the bleeding has stopped and a regular menstrual period occurs must the relevant *vestos* be kept. When it appears that the bleeding has stopped, it is preferable to perform a *bedikah* (and not suffice with the fact that she does not notice any further discharge of blood) even if she will not be counting *shivah nekiyim* at this point (due to post-partum weakness or the like). This will allow her to know with certainty that the subsequent discharge is indeed a new menstrual period.

(See Chapter Sixteen [§47* par. 4] for how her *vestos* should be calculated in the event that she did not perform a *bedikah*.)

14. During the 24 months following the birth, a *veses*

kavua cannot be established. Even if she experienced three discharges on the same day of the month or at the same *haflagah*, the discharges are to be viewed as a *veses she'eino kavua*. She must therefore keep all the *vestos* that apply to a *veses she'eino kavua*, namely, the *veses hachodesh*, *veses hahaflagah*, and *onah beinonis*. (See Chapter Sixteen [§§93ff.] for additional details.)

15. A miscarriage that occurred over 40 days from the beginning of the pregnancy has the same *halachic* status as a birth, and the laws outlined in the previous paragraphs apply to her as well. The 40 days are calculated from the night of her *tevilah* after the last menstrual period that occurred before the pregnancy.

Caesarean Section

16. For medical reasons, a woman who gave birth through a caesarean section may generally not enter a new pregnancy for a certain period of time. A physician should be asked regarding the matter, and an expert rabbi should then be consulted to determine the correct contraceptive method that should be used.

An expert rabbi should be consulted if such a woman experienced discharges of blood during the 24-month period following the birth that would normally constitute the creation of a *veses kavua* (see the *sefer* [Chapter One, *Biurim* §3].)

Lighting Shabbos Candles After Birth

17. The *yoledes* herself should light Shabbos (or Yom Tov) candles before the first Shabbos after birth as well. If she is

weak and must remain in bed, the candles should be brought
to her to light.[3]

~೧ۿಲ೯~

---

3. Although the Alter Rebbe cites a custom in *Shulchan Aruch*
(§263:5) according to which the husband lights the Shabbos candles on
the first Shabbos, he himself instructed Rebbetzin Chaya Mushka (the
wife of the Tzemach Tzedek) to light them herself. This instruction was
reiterated by the Tzemach Tzedek to Rebbetzin Rivkah, the wife of Rabbi
Shmuel of Lubavitch (see *Shulchan Menachem*, vol. 2, §157).

CHAPTER TWENTY

YICHUD

Introduction

1. It is extremely important to be well-versed in the laws of *yichud*. As the Rambam writes (*Issurei Bi'ah* 22:18ff.): "There is nothing in the entire Torah that is more difficult to abstain from than forbidden relations.... One should therefore control his inclination in this matter and accustom himself to added holiness, pure thoughts, and wise judgment so that he will be spared from [such relations. Additionally,] one should take care [to refrain] from *yichud*, as it is the major cause [of forbidden relations]."

2. The Alter Rebbe writes that women are obligated to study laws which are essential for them to know. As an example, he lists (among others) the laws of *yichud*.

3. According to the majority of *Poskim*, the prohibition of *yichud* is **mid'oraysa**.[1] The Talmud deduces this prohibition from Scripture, and additional details were added by Dovid Hamelech and later by Shammai and Hillel. Additionally, the Talmud relates a number of stories illustrating how our Sages were careful to refrain from *yichud*.

This chapter will outline the laws of *yichud*, based on the

---

1. According to the majority of opinions, the prohibition of yichud with an unmarried woman is *mid'oraysa* as well.

rulings of the *Shulchan Aruch* (*Even Ha'ezer* §22) and the *Poskim*.

Definition of *Yichud*

1. A man and woman may not seclude themselves in a place where they cannot be seen by others. This prohibition is known as *yichud* (lit., seclusion).

The prohibition of *yichud* is not limited to seclusion in a closed house or room. Even if they are in an open field, public garden, or highway, if it is uncommon for other people to pass by at random and notice them, it is considered *yichud* according to all opinions. (The laws outlined below [§§8ff.] are based on this premise.)

Individuals With Whom *Yichud* is Forbidden

2. *Yichud* is forbidden between any man and woman who are not married to each other (with the exception of those listed below [§§6-7]). This includes individuals who are both married or unmarried, young or old, Jewish or non-Jewish, and related or unrelated.

3. A man may not seclude himself with a girl aged three and above, and a woman may not seclude herself with a boy aged nine and above. However, *yichud* is permitted between a boy and a girl until they are *bar* and *bas mitzvah*.

4. The *Poskim* unanimously agree that the laws of *yichud* fully apply to a fiancé and fiancée (see §60).

5. Although *yichud* is permitted between a husband and wife even when she is a *nidah*, *yichud* is forbidden if a bride became a *nidah* before they had a chance to engage in

marital relations (see Chapter Seventeen §§19-20 for additional details).

6. *Yichud* is permitted between the following individuals: A father and daughter; a mother and son; a grandfather and granddaughter; and a grandmother and grandson.

7. *Yichud* is permitted temporarily between a brother and sister; however, they may not live alone in the same residence permanently. Some opinions hold that less than thirty days is still considered temporary, while others rule that they may not live alone in the same residence for more than three nights.

If they live together permanently with their parents, they may remain alone in the house together even when their parents are presently not home (see note[2]).

If the Door is Open or Unlocked

8. As stated above (§1), the prohibition of *yichud* is not limited to seclusion in a closed room, rather it includes any place or situation where it is uncommon for other people to pass by and disturb them. The laws outlined in the following paragraphs are based on this premise.

9. A man and woman may seclude themselves if the door is open to the street, provided it is possible for someone to enter the room without prior warning. This leniency can therefore only be applied during those hours and in those

---

2. However, they should not be left home alone often at night for hours at a time, as this can be viewed as a permanent *yichud*. Exact guidelines cannot be given in this regard; rather, each set of parents must act according to the nature of their children.

places where people are passing by in the street or public staircase. But if it is late at night when people are no longer passing by, or if the street or staircase is not frequented by passersby, they may not seclude themselves even if the door is left open.

10. If an individual with whom *yichud* is forbidden entered the house and is unaware that a door has been left open, the person inside must notify the visitor that this is the case.

11. If the door is closed but unlocked, they may seclude themselves if it is possible for someone to enter without prior warning. But if this is not the case, it is forbidden.

If people usually knock and wait for permission before entering, one should not act leniently even if they sometimes enter after a short knock without waiting for permission. However, one can act leniently in challenging situations—i.e., where no other alternative is available—or if it is uncertain if the current situation constitutes a forbidden method of *yichud*.

12. If the door is locked and other individuals have copies of the keys, they may seclude themselves if it is possible for these individuals to enter without hindrance and prior warning.

This leniency may often apply in offices and the like where men and women work together in a closed room and no one else is present to preclude the issue of *yichud*. In such situations, if it is indeed practically possible for other individuals with keys to enter the office without prior warning, there is no issue of *yichud* even if the door is locked.

13. Similarly, they may seclude themselves if it is possible for outsiders or neighbors to see what is taking place inside the house via the windows.

In such a case, they may only seclude themselves in those areas of the room that can be viewed from the outside; they may not seclude themselves in the corners of the room where they cannot be seen.

Two Rooms of a House

14. *Yichud* is forbidden even if they are each in separate rooms, if it is possible to go from one room to the next without encountering others. But if one must first enter a hallway where it is possible to be seen by others, there is no issue of *yichud*.[3]

15. Certain authorities rule that they may be in separate rooms if they each lock the door of their respective rooms from the inside. However, one should not rely on this opinion except in extremely challenging situations. In any case, locking the door from the inside is ineffective if they do not each have a separate restroom and must leave the room for this purpose.

16. There is no issue of *yichud* if one of them locks the door from the inside and gives the key to another individual, and he or she cannot leave the room without first summoning the individual with the key.

---

3. An example is if they are each in a separate room of a hotel and it is impossible to go from one room to the next without first entering the hallway.

Yichud in an Elevator

17. A man and woman may not ride an elevator alone if it cannot be stopped by someone outside until it reaches its destination. Although certain authorities rule leniently if the trip is extremely short (see note[4]), it is advisable to refrain from doing so if possible, because others rule that it is forbidden in any case. However, it is permitted to ride together if the elevator can be stopped on any floor by someone outside who wishes to enter.

Yichud for a Short Amount of Time

18. As stated in the previous paragraph, certain authorities allow a man and woman to ride an elevator together for an extremely short amount of time. However, this is only true with regard to an elevator or the like where it is impossible for the yichud to extend itself for longer (because the doors of the elevator will open shortly). But in a situation where it is possible for the yichud to extend itself for longer, it is forbidden to be secluded even for an extremely short amount of time.

It is therefore forbidden to enter a house if it constitutes yichud even if he is planning to stay there just for a moment and then leave immediately, because it is possible for the yichud to extend itself for longer.

Traveling in a Car

19. If there is a great need to do so, a woman may travel in a car with a male driver if the following conditions are met:

---

4. One authority defines this as a three-minute trip, while another authority extends the time to five minutes.

1. The windows of the car are transparent and the trip will take place by day or in lit streets, so that it is possible to see what is transpiring in the car from the outside.

2. The trip will take place in areas and at times when people or cars are passing by constantly.

If these two conditions are met, the car can be compared to a room with a door that is open to the street.

If the road is dark, she may travel in such a car only if the car light is turned on so that they can be seen by the people or cars who are passing by.

20. If the above conditions are not met (i.e., if there is either insufficient lighting or lack of passersby who can see what is transpiring in the car), she must bring a *shomer* along with her who will preclude the issue of *yichud* (see §§25ff. for the relevant details).

21. The following laws apply if a woman must travel somewhere urgently or for an extremely important purpose, and the trip will take place at times or in places where there is an issue of *yichud* (such as a trip to the *mikvah* late at night): If her husband or a *shomer* cannot accompany her, one can rely on the opinions who allow traveling in a taxi that belongs to a well-known company. If possible, it is preferable to travel in a taxi with a female driver. (See also §37.)

Public Transportation

22. If a woman was riding on a public bus or the like and all the passengers got off, causing her to remain alone with the male driver, she must get off as well if the conditions

detailed above (§19) are not met. However, there is room to act leniently if doing so will involve much difficulty and discomfort. Similarly, she may remain on the bus if it might be dangerous for her to get off at that point (see the following paragraphs).

In Dangerous Situations

23. In some areas it can be dangerous to stay outdoors at night—and perhaps even during the day—especially for a woman. If one is in such a situation, one may *lechatchilah* board a public bus or the like, even if there are no other passengers on board to preclude the issue of *yichud*. If she entered a taxi with a male driver, she should mark down the name of the company and the taxi driver's license number in a conspicuous manner so that the driver will notice.

24. One must try to avoid dangerous situations which will require entering a **private car,** because the *Poskim* differ whether *yichud* is allowed in such a case. However, if such a situation did arise, it appears that one can rely on the lenient opinions. This applies both to a woman entering a car with a male driver and vice versa. Similarly, a male driver may offer a ride to a woman who is in a dangerous area (and vice versa).

Yichud When a *Shomer* is Present

25. A *shomer* (lit., "guard"), refers to an additional individual whose presence precludes the issue of *yichud*.

A number of clarifications:

1. Even in situations where the presence of a *shomer* is effective to preclude the issue of *yichud*, it is preferable to leave

the door unlocked, because certain authorities maintain that *yichud* is forbidden even between a woman and a number of men.

2. In cases where the presence of a *shomer* is effective, he does not need to be in the room the entire time; rather, it is sufficient if he enters occasionally, provided there is no set time for him to enter. But if there is a set time when he enters, his occasional entry does not preclude the issue of *yichud*, because the man and woman are not afraid that he might enter at any moment and see what is transpiring.

More Than One Man

26. A woman may be secluded in the city by day with two **upright** men, as each one is embarrassed of the other. An individual is assumed to be upright unless it is known otherwise. (See below [§28] for the laws that apply in an uninhabited area or at night.) But she may never be secluded with **immoral** men, even if they are more than two. She may also not be secluded with two men if one is upright and the second is immoral.

27. If there is a need, a woman may be secluded with two men if one is upright and the second is a non-Jew, even if the non-Jew is immoral.

28. The presence of two individuals precludes the issue of *yichud* only in the city and by day, but in uninhabited areas or at night, three individuals must be present. This includes the early morning when people are still sleeping, even if it is already light outside.

29. If there is a great need, a woman may be secluded

at night together with two men if the area is illuminated, provided they are not planning to spend the night together.

More Than One Woman

30. A man may not be found alone together with two women, even if they are extremely upright and G-d-fearing. The *Poskim* differ whether a man may be secluded with three women or more, and one should act stringently whenever possible. Sephardic Jews may not act leniently, as R. Yosef Karo rules stringently in this regard.

31. As explained below (§§41ff.), if certain criteria are met, a man may be secluded with a woman if her husband is in town. If there is a great need, he may be secluded with an additional woman as well; however, *lechatchilah* one should act stringently (see §§54-55).

32. At night, one should try to make sure that four women are present if possible. But if there is a need, one may be secluded with three women at night as well.

33. A certain authority has stated that if one is found in an uninhabited area, he should also try to make sure that four women are present if possible.

34. Even the opinions who allow *yichud* with three women or more agree that it is forbidden if the man's business dealings involve women. This includes someone who sells women's or children's clothing, jewelry, or the like. Certain authorities add that this also applies to someone who interacts with women in an open manner, for example, if he calls them by their first name or the like.

35. A man may not be secluded with immoral women,

even if they are three or more. However, if one of them is upright it is permitted.

36. The authorities differ whether three upright women may be secluded with an immoral man, and one should only act leniently in challenging situations.

37. In light of what has been explained in the previous paragraphs, if three women must travel in a taxi with a male driver in a manner that constitutes *yichud* (see §19), they should try to travel in a taxi that belongs to a well-known company. (See also §21.)

Wife

38. A wife is considered to be the most effective *shomer* and precludes *yichud* in any situation. A woman may therefore be secluded with a man if his wife is present, even if the man is unobservant. Similarly, a man may be secluded with another woman if his wife is present.[5]

39. A man's wife can serve as a *shomer* even if she is not in the same room as them, as long as she is in the house, yard, or anywhere else in close vicinity. However, being in town is insufficient; she must be in the same area as her husband and the other woman. Certain authorities allow *yichud* with two women if the man's wife is in town.

39*. As explained below (§52), a wife can serve as a *shomer* even if she is sleeping. Additional details can be found there.

_____

5. However, a *kallah* cannot serve as a *shomer* (to allow *yichud* between the *chasan* and another woman) if she became a *nidah* before they had a chance to engage in marital relations.

40. A woman may not be secluded with a non-Jew even if his wife is present. However, a man may be secluded with a non-Jewish woman if her husband is present (see §41*).

Husband

41. A man and woman may seclude themselves if the woman's husband is in town. However, it is preferable to leave the door unlocked in every case (if possible), because there are various opinions regarding when this leniency applies (as will be explained in the following paragraphs).

41*. If her husband is in town (as per the criteria outlined in the following paragraphs), a woman may be secluded with a non-Jew as well.

The *Poskim* differ whether a man may be secluded with a non-Jewish woman if her husband is in town. The consensus is that it is permitted.

42. According to many opinions, this leniency only applies if her husband might appear unexpectedly, but if she is in another house and it is unlikely for her husband to appear, *yichud* is forbidden.

43. If the city is large and her husband is far away, certain noteworthy *Poskim* are of the opinion that *yichud* is permitted only if it is possible for him to appear unexpectedly at times without notifying her first (see note[6]).

---

6. According to one authority, a differentiation can be made between a hired employee and a self-employed worker. While the former cannot leave his job during work hours, the latter can leave whenever he desires and come home unexpectedly (even if doing so will result in financial loss).

44. Even if her husband is in town, a woman may not be secluded with a man with whom she is exceedingly familiar, such as an intimate relative and the like (with the exclusion of parents and grandparents with their children and grandchildren—see §6). One authority adds that the same law applies to a maid or co-worker with whom one is exceedingly familiar.

45. Accordingly, if a woman receives a visit from her father-in-law, brother-in-law, son-in-law, or the like when her husband is not home, they must take care that *yichud* is not transgressed, as the above leniency does not apply in such a case. The same is true if a man receives a visit from his mother-in-law, sister-in-law, or daughter-in-law.

Children

46. A boy or girl no younger than five and no older than nine can serve as a *shomer* as well, and a man and woman may seclude themselves if such a child is present. This includes a son or daughter of the above age in the presence of their mother. (See [§49] for the law of *yichud* with an adult daughter in the presence of her mother.)

47. Although when traveling an additional *shomer* is generally required (see §28; §33), one may travel together with a mother and young child who is afraid to leave his mother.

48. However, a young child cannot serve as a *shomer* late at night when he will probably fall asleep (see §52).

Relatives

49. A man may be secluded with a woman in the pres-

ence of one of the following relatives: (1) Her mother-in-law. (2) The wife of her husband's brother.[7] (3) Her husband's sister. (4) Her stepdaughter (i.e., her husband's daughter). (5) The *Poskim* differ whether a man may be secluded with a woman and her daughter (or granddaughter). Accordingly, *lechatchilah* one should avoid doing so, except when necessary and in challenging situations.

50. The above women can only serve as a *shomer* if the marriage that creates the relation is still in existence. But if they are divorced or widowed, they share the status of a regular woman.

51. Certain *Poskim* hold that the presence of one of the above women is not effective at night or when traveling, and an additional *shomer* is then required. Others, however, are of the opinion that they are effective in such situations as well. The *halachic* conclusion is that one should not rely on the lenient opinions unless there is no other choice.

If the *Shomer* is Sleeping

52. A single *shomer* who is sleeping is ineffective, with the exception of a wife who is in the same area as her husband (see §39*). However, certain authorities state that she cannot serve as a *shomer* if she is taking sleeping pills.

52*. A woman may be secluded with three men (as is required at night—see §28) even if two of them are sleeping.

---

7. There is reason to believe that one should act stringently in one of the following cases: (1) if the two women are sisters; (2) if they have children; and (3) nowadays (when *yibum* is not performed). However, it appears from the wording of the *Shulchan Aruch* that *yichud* is not an issue in any case.

Similarly, a man may be secluded with three or four women (see §§30ff.) even if some of them are sleeping.

53. A *shomer* is effective even if they are unsure whether he is awake or sleeping.

A Woman With Whom *Yichud* is Permitted

54. The *Poskim* differ whether a man may be secluded with a woman with whom *yichud* is generally forbidden, if another woman is present with whom *yichud* is permitted (such as the man's mother, sister, or daughter [see §§6-7], or a woman whose husband is in town). In other words, the question is if it is only permitted to be secluded with such a woman herself, or if she can serve as a *shomer* to allow *yichud* with a second woman as well.

55. The *halachic* conclusion in the above case is as follows: Although one's wife can serve as a *shomer* to allow *yichud* with additional women (see §§38ff.), any other woman with whom *yichud* is permitted cannot serve as a *shomer lechatchilah*. However, if there is a great need, one can rely on the lenient opinions. Certain contemporary authorities have written that although there is room to act stringently out of piety, such a woman can *halachically* serve as a *shomer*.[8]

---

8. However, if a *kallah* became a *nidah* before they had a chance to engage in marital relations (in which case *yichud* between the *chasan* and *kallah* is forbidden—see Chapter Seventeen §§16ff.), they may not seclude themselves even if another woman is present. This is because in such a case the *kallah* cannot serve as a *shomer* to allow *yichud* with the other woman (see fn. 5), and consequently the presence of the other woman cannot allow *yichud* between the *chasan* and *kallah* either.

Babysitters and Private Tutors

56. As stated above (§3), *yichud* is forbidden between a man and a girl from the age of three and above and between a woman and a boy from the age of nine and above. Accordingly, if one must babysit or tutor a child of this age, care must be taken that *yichud* is not transgressed (by keeping a door open or making sure that a *shomer* is present).

Yichud When Visiting a Doctor

57. If a woman is visiting a doctor in a **public** venue, it is preferable to be accompanied by a *shomer* so that the issue of *yichud* will be avoided. If this is not possible, she may remain in the same room as the doctor if the following conditions are met:

1. The visit is taking place during regular hours.

2. The door remains unlocked, and it is a common practice for nurses or other doctors to enter after a short knock on the door, without waiting to receive explicit permission.

3. Alternatively, other patients are present in the waiting room, and it is an accepted practice for them to sometimes enter to ask a question without first waiting for permission.

If these conditions have not been met, the laws described below (§58, regarding a private clinic) apply.

Even when these conditions are met, *yichud* is only permitted due to the assumption that the doctor will be afraid to ruin his image as a result of improper conduct. But if she sees that he is acting in an immodest manner, **she must leave the room immediately.**

58. If a woman is visiting a Jewish doctor in his home, she may be in the same room as the doctor if his wife is at home (even if she is not in the same room as them). If the doctor's wife is not at home or if the doctor is a non-Jew, she must be accompanied by another male individual (such as her husband, brother, or father), a child, or a woman who can serve as a *shomer* (see §§26ff. §46. §§49ff.). In challenging situations where this is not possible, one can rely on the fact that her husband is in town (see supra (§§41ff.).

Stepchildren and Adopted Children

59. The laws of *yichud* apply **without exception** to a parent and a stepchild or adopted child. Furthermore, one must be aware that one may not hug or kiss such a child when he or she reaches a certain age. The Lubavitcher Rebbe's words on the topic appear in the footnote.[9]

Fiancé and Fiancée

60. Jewish leaders over the course of the generations have vehemently opposed any leniency relating to *yichud* between a fiancé and fiancée, which is the result of a sheer lack of knowledge. They have also sharply expressed the severe

---

9. The following is a quote from a lengthy letter penned by the Lubavitcher Rebbe on the matter (printed in *Sha'arei Halachah U'minhag*, vol. 4 p. 44, and in full in *Igros Kodesh*, vol. 23, pp. 310-311 and *Otzar Haposkim* [*Even Ha'ezer*], vol. 9, pp. 130-132): "I have witnessed many cases where parents who are scrupulous [in fulfilling] even the slightest rabbinic matter have not paid attention to the fact that all the issues of *yichud*, kissing, and much more fully apply to adopted children."

negative outcomes that can result from acting leniently in this matter.

This is especially common when they are going some-where by car and she is the only passenger. Often, they are unaware of the issues that might be present—i.e., if the roads are dark or if cars are not constantly passing by (see §§19ff.). *Yichud* can also be an issue if they are taking a walk in the countryside, riding on a boat, or the like, if it is a place or time when people are not in the area.

* * *

It is appropriate to conclude with the words of the Rambam (*Issurei Bi'ah* 22:21):

"The most effective [method of protecting oneself from sin is] to devote himself and his thoughts to the words of Torah and broaden his mind with wisdom, for immoral thoughts do not increase unless one's heart is bare of wisdom. [Indeed,] the verse states with regard to wisdom [Mishlei 5:19]: *A beloved doe and a graceful mountain goat, her breasts will constantly satisfy you; you will always be intoxicated with her love.*"

GLOSSARY

akirah (pl. *akiros*): The uprooting of a *veses*. An *akirah* is achieved when the day of the *veses* passes without a discharge of blood.

alos hashachar: A *halachically*-defined point of time preceding sunrise when the day begins for many *halachic* purposes.[1]

Alter Rebbe: R. Schneur Zalman of Liadi (1745-1813), founder of Chabad Chassidism and widely-accepted *halachic* authority (see Alter Rebbe's *Shulchan Aruch*).

Alter Rebbe's *Shulchan Aruch*: Code of Jewish Law authored by R. Schneur Zalman of Liadi (1745-1812) and first published in 1814-1816. The decisions codified in this work are followed by Chabad adherents as well as by many others.

amah (pl. *amos*): A *halachic* measurement equivalent to approximately 0.5 m. or 19 in.

Av: Hebrew month that occurs around the months of July-August.

bar/bas mitzvah: The age when a boy and girl respectively are held fully responsible for religious observance. This occurs at age thirteen for a boy and age twelve for a girl.

be'ilas mitzvah: The first marital act to take place after the wedding.

becher: Goblet used when reciting *Kiddush*.

bedi'eved: A *halachic* term signifying the after-the-fact status of an act which should have ideally not been performed or been performed differently.

---

1. One can visit chabad.org/zmanim to find out the exact time of *alos hashachar* in any location.

bedikah (pl. *bedikos*): Internal examination performed to determine a woman's cleanliness from blood.

bein hashmashos: The time from sunset until *tzeis hakochavim*, viewed as a transitional stage between the preceding day and the following day.

berachah: Blessing. In the context of this book, this refers to the blessing recited when immersing.

besulah: Virgin.

besulim: Hymen.

birchas besulim: Blessing recited by some after a couple's first intercourse (see Chapter Eighteen §33).

birchas eirusin: Betrothal blessing recited as part of the marriage ceremony.

bodekes: Observant woman certified to perform gynecological internal examinations.

bris: Circumcision ceremony performed when a baby boy is eight days old.

chafifah: Preparation for immersion by thoroughly cleansing all parts of the body and removing any possible *chatzitzah* (see Chapter Eleven).

challah: Bread customarily eaten as part of a Shabbos or Yom Tov meal.

chasan: Groom.

chatzitzah (pl. *chatzitzos*): Intervening substance between one's body and the water of the *mikvah* which may render the immersion invalid.

chazakah: *Halachic* assertion.

Cheshvan: Hebrew month that occurs around the months of October-November.

Chol Ha'moed: Intermediate days of the Pesach and Sukkos holidays.

chupah: Marital canopy under which the marriage ceremony takes place.

dam besulim: Hymenal bleeding.

dam chimud: The *halachic* concern that the pre-wedding emotional feelings may have resulted in a minute discharge of uterine blood. This concern obligates the bride to perform the *taharah* process before the wedding (see Chapter Seventeen §§2ff.).

dam leidah: Blood discharged at birth.

dilug: Skipping (see *veses hadilug*).

Dovid Hamelech: King David.

eiruv tavshilin: A *halachic* procedure that allows one to prepare for Shabbos on the Yom Tov directly preceding it.

eiruv: A structure (commonly consisting of string and poles) that allows the area enclosed within it to share the laws of a private domain (see *reshus harabim*).

Elul: Hebrew month that occurs around the months of August-September.

erev: The day preceding, as in *erev Shabbos* (i.e., Friday), *erev Yom Tov*, etc.

etzba'os: Plural form of *etzba*, a *halachic* measurement equivalent to 2 cm. or 0.78 in.

Geonim: Babylonian scholars of the seventh to tenth centuries C.E. (See *Rabbeinu Tam*.)

gris ve'od: An area larger than a *gris*. This measurement is used to determine if a *kesem* is *tamei* (see Chapter Four §§5ff.; §§28ff.).

gris: A *halachic* measurement (see addendum to Chapter Four).

haflagah (pl. *haflagos*): Interval between one menstrual period and the next.

halachah (pl. *halachos*): Jewish law. (*Halachic, halachically*: Pertaining or according to Jewish law.)

Hamotzi: Blessing recited before eating bread.

harchakos (sing. *harchakah*): The various types of separations kept by a husband and wife when she is *temei'ah* (see Chapter Six).

hargashah (pl. *hargashos*): Sensation of fluid trickling from the uterus.

Havdalah: Prayer recited on *motza'ei Shabbos*, which includes blessings over wine, spices, and a candle.

hefsek taharah: A *bedikah* performed as part of the *taharah* process to verify that the menstrual bleeding has stopped (see Chapter One §5; Chapter Eight).

heker (pl. *hekerim*): A difference in conduct employed by a husband and *nidah* wife when eating together (see Chapter Six §§51ff.).

hiddurim: Plural form of *hiddur*, a praiseworthy method of performing a *mitzvah* not actually required by Jewish law.

Hillel: Mishnaic scholar of the Second Temple period.

Isru Chag: The day following the festivals of Pesach, Shavuos, and Sukkos.

Iyar: Hebrew month that occurs around the months of April-May.

iyun: Inspection of body and hair before immersing (see Chapter Eleven §1).

kallah (pl. *kallos*): Bride.

kesem (pl. *kesamim*): Stain of blood, specifically one that is unrelated to a menstrual period, *bedikah*, or *kinuach* (see Chapter Four).

Kiddush: Prayer recited over wine at the beginning of a Shabbos or Yom Tov meal.

kinuach: External wiping of the vaginal area.

Kislev: Hebrew month that occurs around the months of November-December.

lechatchilah: A *halachic* term signifying the ideal way in which an act should be performed.

lechem mishneh: Two loaves of *challah* upon which the blessing of *Hamotzi* is recited at the beginning of a Shabbos or Yom Tov meal.

Maariv: The evening prayer.

mar'eh (pl. *mar'os*): Stain on a *bedikah* cloth, garment, sheet, and the like.

mayim acharonim: Ritual performed before reciting Grace after Meals in which the fingertips are rinsed.

mekabel tum'ah: Capable of entering a state of ritual impurity. Only certain materials and objects belong to this category.

mesulekes damim: A woman who *halachah* establishes as not being expected to experience menstrual periods (see Chapter Two §9).

mid'oraysa: By Biblical law.

mid'rabanan: By rabbinic law.

mikvah (pl. *mikva'os*): Ritual bath in which a woman immerses as part of the *taharah* process (see Chapter One §5; Chapter Fourteen).

minchah ketanah: 2½ *halachic* hours[2] before sunset.[3]

Mishnah Berurah: A highly-recognized *halachic* work authored by R. Yisrael Meir Kagan (1838-1933) and first published in 1873.

mitzvah: One of the 613 commandments; in more general usage, any religious obligation or praiseworthy act.

moch dachuk: A cloth inserted and left in the vagina as part of the *hefsek taharah* procedure (see Chapter Eight §16).

motza'ei: The night following, as in *motza'ei Shabbos, motza'ei Yom Tov*, etc.

muktzeh: Rabbinic ordinance that prohibits the handling of certain objects on Shabbos and Yom Tov.

netilas yadayim: Ritual washing of the hands.

nidah: A woman who is ritually impure due to blood assumed to have been discharged from her uterus. Commonly refers to a menstruating woman.

Nissan: Hebrew month that occurs around the months of March-April.

nittel: The night preceding December 25. It is customary to refrain from certain activities on this night.

onah (pl. *onos*): Lit., "period of time." 1. Reference to half of a twenty-four hour period, either the day (from sunrise until sunset) or the night (from sunset until sunrise). 2. Conjugal obligations of husband toward wife.

---

2. A *halachic* hour (or *sha'ah zemanis* in Hebrew) is calculated by dividing the daylight hours into twelve equal portions. Consequently, in the summer when the days are long an hour may consist of more than sixty minutes, and in the winter it may consist of less than sixty minutes.

3. One can visit chabad.org/zmanim to find out the exact time of *minchah ketanah* in any location.

onah beinonis: A *veses* kept on the thirtieth day from the beginning of one's menstrual period (see Chapter Sixteen §§27ff.).

pelag haminchah: 1¼ *halachic* hours[2] before sunset.[4]

Posek (pl. *Poskim*): *Halachic* authority.

Purim: Festival observed on the fourteenth day of the Hebrew month of Adar.

Rabbeinu Tam: Moniker of R. Yaakov ben Meir (1100-1171). According to the view of Rabbeinu Tam, *tzeis hakochavim* is calculated 72 minutes later than it is calculated by the *Geonim*. Although the view of the *Geonim* is accepted by most segments of Orthodox Jewry, certain circles follow the opinion of Rabbeinu Tam. (Such individuals should consult the Rabbis of their communities for the practical applications of this view.)

Rambam: Acronym for R. Moshe ben Maimon (1135-1204), a renowned medieval scholar.

Ramban: Acronym for R. Moshe ben Nachman (c. 1194-c. 1270), a renowned medieval scholar.

reshus harabim: Lit., "Public domain." One may not carry an item from a private domain to a public domain on Shabbos.

Rosh Chodesh: The first day(s) of a Hebrew month.

sefer: Book. (In the context of this book, "*sefer*" usually serves as a reference to the book titled *Taharah Kahalachah* by the author—see Introduction.)

Sefiras Ha'omer: The forty-nine days from Pesach until Shavuos when the Omer is counted. These days are distinguished by various laws that express mourning, including refraining from taking a haircut. This is done to commemorate a mass epidemic that occurred during these days in Mishnaic times.

---

4. One can visit chabad.org/zmanim to find out the exact time of *pelag haminchah* in any location.

segulos (sing. *segulah*): Actions or items that provide spiritual protection.

selichos: Penitential prayers recited during the days preceding the High Holidays.

Shabbos: The Sabbath.

shalom bayis: Marital harmony.

Shammai: Mishnaic scholar of the Second Temple period.

sheloshim: The thirty days following the death of a close relative during which various laws are kept that express mourning.

sheva berachos: Marital blessings recited as part of the marriage ceremony.

shinuy: Unusual manner in which an activity is performed.

shivah nekiyim: The seven clean days counted as part of the *taharah* process (see Chapter One §5; Chapter Nine).

shivah: The seven-day period of mourning following the death of a close relative.

shomer (pl. *shomrim*): An individual whose presence precludes the issue of *yichud*.

shul: Synagogue.

Shulchan Aruch: Code of Jewish Law, authored by R. Yosef Karo (1488-1575) and first published in 1565. The *Shulchan Aruch* serves as the basis of Jewish law and observance until day.

Sivan: Hebrew month that occurs around the months of May-June.

taharah: Ritual purity.

taharas hamishpachah: Lit., "family purity"; reference to the impurity and purity of a woman based on her menstrual state.

Talmud: Major, classic work comprising the teachings of the Babylonian scholars of the first to fifth centuries C.E. The Talmud serves as the basis of Jewish law and thought until today.

Tamuz: Hebrew month that occurs around the months of June-July.

tehorah (pl. *tehoros*); *tahor* (pl. *tehorim*): Ritually pure.

temei'ah (pl. *temei'os*); *tamei* (pl. *temei'im*): Ritually impure.

Teves: Hebrew month that occurs around the months of December-January.

tevilah: Immersion in a *mikvah*.

Tishah B'Av: Fast day observed on the ninth day of the Hebrew month of Av, commemorating the destruction of the First and Second Holy Temples in Jerusalem. Tishah B'Av and the days that precede it are distinguished by various laws that express mourning. They include refraining from washing oneself or wearing leather shoes on Tishah B'Av itself; refraining from cutting one's nails during the week of Tishah B'Av; refraining from washing one's clothing or enjoying a shower during the nine days that precede it; and refraining from taking a haircut during the three weeks that precede it.

Tishrei: Hebrew month that occurs around the months of September-October.

tum'ah: Ritual impurity.

tzaddik: Righteous individual.

tzeis hakochavim: A *halachically*-defined point of time following sunset when the night begins for many *halachic* purposes.[5]

Tzemach Tzedek: R. Menachem Mendel of Lubavitch (1789-

---

5. One can visit chabad.org/zmanim to find out the exact time of *tzeis hakochavim* in any location.

1866). Author of numerous works, including a set of *halachic* responsa with this name.

veses (pl. *vestos*): 1. Day when one's menstrual period is expected to arrive, based on the calculations defined by *halachah*. 2. Menstrual period.

veses hachodesh (pl. *vestos hachodesh*): A *veses* calculated based on the Hebrew date of the previous menstrual period (see Chapter Sixteen §§34ff.).

veses hadilug (pl. *vestos hadilug*): A *veses* that "skips," i.e., a *veses* in which the subsequent discharges of blood occur at later dates or at longer intervals than the previous discharges (see Chapter Sixteen §§81ff.).

veses hahaflagah (pl. *vestos hahaflagah*): A *veses* calculated based on the intervals between earlier menstrual periods (see Chapter Sixteen §§45ff.).

veses hasirug (pl. *vestos hasirug*): A *veses* that alternates between one week or month and the next (see Chapter Sixteen §§77ff.).

veses kavua (pl. *vestos kevu'im*): Permanent *veses*; a *veses* that recurs on a set day.

veses kavua lechodesh (pl. *vestos kevu'im lechodesh*): A *veses kavua* that recurs on the same date of the Hebrew month.

veses kavua lechumra: A *veses kavua* that is kept for stringent purposes but must be viewed as a *veses she'eino kavua* as well.

veses kavua lehaflagah (pl. *vestos kevu'im lehaflagah*): A *veses kavua* that recurs at equal *haflagos*.

veses she'eino kavua (pl. *vestos she'einam kevu'im*): Temporary *veses*; a *veses* that does not recur on a set day.

Veyiten Lecha: Prayer recited on *motza'ei Shabbos*, customarily together with another individual from the same prayer book.

yad soledes bo: A *halachic* measurement of heat, equivalent to 40-45°C or 104-113°F.

yahrtzeit: Anniversary of the passing of a relative.

yichud room: Room where the groom and bride seclude themselves following the marriage ceremony.

yichud: Prohibition for a man and woman to seclude themselves in a place where they cannot be seen by others (see Chapter Twenty).

yoledes: Woman who has given birth.

Yom Kippur: Day of Atonement, observed on the tenth day of the Hebrew month of Tishrei. It is forbidden to wash oneself or wear leather shoes on Yom Kippur.

Yom Tov: Jewish festival.

INDEX

Baby: See *children*.

Babysitters: 20:56 (*Yichud*).

Bag: 6:16 (Removing from/putting into bag held by spouse when *nidah*).

Bandages: 11:72:10 (Removing and replacing on Shabbos/Yom Tov). 11:72:14 (Using bandages to wipe off blood on Shabbos/Yom Tov). 12:98 (*Chatzitzah* status).

Band-aids: 11:72:10 (To fasten bandage on Shabbos/Yom Tov). 11:72:11 (Removal on Shabbos/Yom Tov). 12:96 (*Chatzitzah* status).

Basket: 6:16 (Removing from/putting into basket held by spouse when *nidah*).

Bath, before *hefsek taharah:* 8:6 (If she cannot take a full bath; if no water is available). 8:7 (Warm water). 8:7* (Baby wipes instead of bath). 8:8 (If she did *hefsek taharah* without bath). 8:9 (Does she need to take a bath before *hefsek taharah* if she stained during *shivah nekiyim,* or if she found blood during *shivah nekiyim* when doing *bedikah* or wiping). 8:10 (Taking a bath earlier in the day). 8:11–13 (On Shabbos or Yom Tov). 8:14 (On Yom Kippur or Tishah Be'av). 8:15 (During the Nine Days or when mourning).

Bath, other: 6:116 (Preparing bath for spouse when *nidah*). 14:34–36 (Taking bath after immersing). 16:23 (Taking bath on day of *veses*). See also *chafifah: shower.*

Bathroom: See *restroom*.

Be'ilas mitzvah: 16:106 (*Be'ilas mitzvah* on day of *veses*). 17:09 (*Bedikos* between wedding and *be'ilas mitzvah*). 18:1 (Definition). 18:8 (Importance of trying to complete intercourse on night of wedding; speaking to *chasan* teacher or rabbi for guidance). 18:10 (Bride should assist groom in completing intercourse). 18:11–12 (Guidance from *chasan* teacher regarding *be'ilas mitzvah*). 18:13 (Guidance from *kallah* teacher regarding *be'ilas mitzvah*). 18:15 (Separation after *be'ilas mitzvah*). 18:31 (If she became *nidah* after wedding but before *be'ilas mitzvah*). 18:32 and fn. 4 (How much genital contact is necessary to allow *yichud* if she became *nidah* afterward). 18:33 (*Birchas besulim*). 18:34–36 (Importance of receiving guidance from certified *chasan* and *kallah* teacher). 18:37 (Importance of studying

felt). See also *hefsek taharah; moch dachuk; shivah nekiyim: bedikos; vestos: day of veses.*

Bedikah, unclean *bedikah:* 1:3 (When *tamei,* full *taharah* process must be kept). 2:12 (*Tamei mid'oraysa* regardless of size of stain, color of cloth, etc.). 2:13 (If cloth was not examined before *bedikah,* but it was washed). 2:14 (If she merely glanced at the cloth quickly before *bedikah*). 2:15 (If stain may be from another source). 2:16 (If cloth was not examined before *bedikah*). 2:17 (If in doubt whether cloth was examined before *bedikah*). 2:18–9 (Misplaced *bedikah* cloth). 7:5 (Waiting five days after unclean *bedikah* during *shivah nekiyim*). 8:9 (Does she need to take a bath before *hefsek taharah* if she found blood during *shivah nekiyim* when doing *bedikah*). 8:45 (*Hefsek taharah* before *minchah ketanah* after unclean *bedikah*). 16:5 (Calculating *vestos* from unclean *bedikah*). 18:18 (After intercourses following *be'ilas mitzvah*). See also *mar'os.*

Bedikos before and after marital relations: 2:25–26 (If blood was discovered after previous relations). 15:1–2 (General laws of doing three sets of *bedikos*). 15:2* (If she was married before). 15:3; 18:24 (Only once there is no more *dam besulim*). 15:4–5 (Only on days when her period might begin). 15:6–7 (How to calculate these days). 15:8 (If they did the *bedikos* when her period will certainly not begin). 15:9 (It might take a few months to do these *bedikos*). 15:10–11 (How and when to do *bedikah* before marital relations). 15:12 (How and when to do *bedikah* after marital relations). 15:13 (Husband's examination after marital relations). 15:14–15 (Pregnant woman; nursing woman; woman who suffered miscarriage). 15:16 (If a couple did not do these *bedikos*). 15:17–18; 18:24* (Continuing to do *bedikos* after having done them three times).

Bedikos during *shivah nekiyim:* See *shivah nekiyim: bedikos.*

Bedikos on day of *veses:* See *vestos: day of veses.*

Bein hashmashos: 7:8 (How to calculate the five days if bleeding began during *bein hashmashos*). 9:4 (If she did second daily *bedikah* of *shivah nekiyim* during *bein hashmashos*). 13:22–23 (If she immersed during *bein hashmashos*). 8, fn. 9 (If she bled a second time during *bein hashmashos* and did a *hefsek taharah* the next day before *minchah ketanah*). See also *moch dachuk.*

Cervix: 5:7 (Attributing blood to wound created by physician grasping cervix with tongs).

Chafifah, bath: See chafifah: shower.

Chafifah, combing: See chafifah: hair.

Chafifah, ears: 11:36 (Cleaning the ears; if she only cleaned outside area of ears; using cotton balls). 11:55 (Removing earrings). 11:56 (Cleaning pierced ears). 11:72:16 (Removing earrings on Shabbos/ Yom Tov). 12:30 (If dirt was discovered in ears after immersion). 12:32 (If she did not clean pierced ears; if dirt was discovered in holes after immersion). 12:33 (If she did not remove earrings).

Chafifah, eyes: 11:19–20 (Untangling eyelashes and eyebrows). 11:36 (Cleaning the eyes; using cotton balls). 11:45 (Removing eye shadow; if she did not remove it). 11:48 (Removing dye from eyelashes and eyebrows). 11:55 (Removing eyelash extensions). 11:57 (Removing contact lenses). 12:19 (Eyelash or eyebrow extensions). 12:23 (Mucus in eyes). 12:24 (Eye cream). 12:25 (Eye drops). 12:26 (Eye shadow; eyebrow or eyelash tint). 12:27 (Contact lenses).

Chafifah, general: 7:15 (Waiting five days if that will cause separation between chafifah and immersion). 10:1 (Best time to do chafifah; interruption between daytime chafifah and nighttime chafifah). 10:2 (What should be done by day). 10:3 (Length of chafifah). 10:4 (If being done only at night). 10:5–7 (If being done only by day). 10:8 (Preference of day over night). 10:9 (Separation between chafifah and immersion). 10:10–11 (Where to do the chafifah). 10:12 (When to go to mikvah if she did chafifah at home by day). 11:2 (Definition). 11:16–17 (Length of chafifah; not to rush). 17:07 (Time of bride's chafifah before wedding). See also iyun.

Chafifah, hair: 10:15; 10:24 (Keeping hair untangled after chafifah done on erev Shabbos). 11:19; 12:5 (Definition of hairy areas). 11:20 (Obligation to comb; relevant details). 11:21 (Combing during or after shower). 11:22; 12:10 (If she used fingers instead of comb). 11:23 (If she is not sure whether she combed her hair; if she combed her hair but not for chafifah; if she braided her hair after combing). 11:24; 12:11 (Untangling hair of armpits/pubic hair with fingers instead of comb; if she did not untangle them at all). 11:47; 12:12

(What to do during *chafifah* of *erev Shabbos;* when to do it; applying makeup and the like in honor of Shabbos). 10:15 (Avoiding sticky substances; keeping hair untangled). 10:16 (Eating on Shabbos; meat). 10:16* (Eating/drinking on *motza'ei Shabbos* before immersion). 10:17–18 (What to do during *chafifah* of *motza'ei Shabbos*). 10:19 (If she didn't do *chafifah* on *erev Shabbos*). 10:20 (Immersion on *motza'ei Yom Tov*). 10:21 (Immersion after Yom Tov that followed Shabbos or vice versa). 10:33 (Mourner whose *shivah* concluded on Shabbos/Yom Tov). 11:73 (Cutting nails on Chol Ha'moed if immersing *motza'ei Yom Tov*). 11:76 (Cutting hair on Chol Ha'moed if immersing *motza'ei Yom Tov*). See also *chafifah: when immersing on second night of Yom Tov or on the night between Shabbos and Yom Tov.*

Chafifah, when immersing on second night of Yom Tov or on the night between Shabbos and Yom Tov: 10:29 (*Chafifah* of *erev Shabbos/erev Yom Tov;* avoiding sticky substances and keeping hair untangled; eating before immersion). 10:30–31 (What to do before immersion). 10:32 (Do not prepare on first day of Yom Tov for immersion of second night).

Chair: 6:31 (Sitting on spouse's chair when *nidah*).

Challah: 6:56 (Use as *heker*). 6:91 (Giving piece of *challah* to spouse when *nidah*). 11:61 (Kneading *challah* dough on day of immersion).

Chasan teacher: 18:8 (Speaking to *chasan* teacher for guidance). 18:11–12 (Guidance from *chasan* teacher regarding *be'ilas mitzvah*). 18:34–35 (Importance of receiving guidance from certified *chasan* teacher). 18:37 (Importance of discussing with *chasan* teacher laws relating to sanctity of intimacy).

Chasan: See *groom.*

Chatzitzah, ears: See *chafifah: ears.*

Chatzitzah, eyes: See *chafifah: eyes.*

Chatzitzah, general: 11, introduction (Importance of consulting rabbi with *chatzitzah* questions). 11:1 (Definition). 12, introduction (Complexity of laws of *chatzitzah;* taking care of *chatzitzah*-related issues in advance; consulting rabbi if *chatzitzah* was discovered after

mersion). 11:73 (Cutting nails on Chol Ha'moed before immersion). 11:76 (Cutting hair on Chol Ha'moed before immersion.)

Chupas nidah: See wedding: if bride is nidah at the wedding.

Cigarette: 6:18 (Igniting cigarette from flame held by spouse).

Clothing, colored: See kesamim: colored garment.

Clothing, non-mekabel-tum'ah: See kesamim: non-mekabel-tum'ah item.

Clothing: 6:7 (Touching spouse's clothing when nidah). 6:8 (Clothing of both spouses touching each other; touching clothing when they are not being worn; touching clothing stained with nidah blood). 6:9 (Blowing lint off spouse's clothing when nidah). 6:40 (Wearing spouse's clothing when nidah). 6:121 (Wearing specific clothing when nidah). 13:9 (Covering herself with husband's garment as segulah when immersing without relations). See also undergarments.

Coffee: 6:94 (Preparing for spouse when nidah).

Cold cuts: 11:31 (Eating on day of immersion).

Comb: 11:20 (Combing hair as part of chafifah). 11:22 (If she does not have a comb).

Conception: See pregnancy.

Conditioner: 11:15 (Using conditioner when showering before immersion).

Contact lenses: 11:57 (Removing before immersion). 12:27 (If she immersed with contact lenses).

Contraception: 5:9 (Consulting halachic authority). 19:11*–12 (Following miscarriage or birth). 19:16 (Following caesarean section). See also contraceptive patch; IUD; pills; vaginal ring.

Contraceptive patch: 12:96 (Chatzitzah status).

Convert: 17:14 (Counting shivah nekiyim after three-month separation of couple who converted).

Corn: 11:35 (Eating on day of immersion).

Cotton balls: 4:54 (Kesem found on cotton ball). 8:21 (Using cotton ball

directly from the bottle). 6:86 (Eating after immersion from earlier leftovers). 17:22 (Drinking wine from the same cup as bride at wedding if she is a *nidah*).

Harchakos, general: 1:2 (Effects of leniency in keeping *harchakos* on *shalom bayis*). 1:4 (Displaying *harchakos* as cause of *nidah* status). 4:2 (Must also be kept if one is *nidah* due to *kesem*). 6:1 (Definition of *harchakos*; must be kept no matter how she became *nidah*). 6:2 (Keeping *harchakos* after finding questionable *mar'eh* or after questionable *tevilah*). 6:3 (Acting stringently with *harchakos*). 6:4 (They apply to both spouses). 6:5 (Importance of not acting leniently due to embarrassment or other reasons). 6:50 (Not to add new *harchakos* or be lenient with existing ones). 13, introduction (Must be kept even if immersion is delayed).

Harchakos, heker: 6:51 (Definition of *heker*; when holding food in hand; when not sitting at table). 6:52 (Types of *hekerim*). 6:53 (If only one spouse is eating). 6:54 (Item not usually on table). 6:55 (Moving item's usual location). 6:56 (Food or drink as *heker*). 6:57 (In embarrassing situations). 6:58 (Height of *heker*). 6:59 (Separate tablecloths; one spouse on tablecloth and other on table or folded tablecloth; napkin, place mat, or wide plate beneath plate). 6:60 (Separate place mats). 6:61 (When others are present). 6:62 (When others are sitting between them). 6:63 (When eating separate from family at their own table). 6:69* (Required even when eating from separate plates). 6:87 (Required even if food is not her leftovers).

Harchakos, other: 6:122–126 (If husband is ill). 6:127–134 (If wife is ill). 6:141 (On Yom Kippur). 6:143 (On Tishah Be'av). 6:144 (On ninth of Av which occurs on Shabbos). 16:16 (On day of *veses*). 17:16 (If bride is *nidah* at wedding). 19:4 (During labor). 19:7 (After birth). See also *affectionate speech; body: areas usually covered; frivolity; gifts; jewelry; perfume; singing; traveling*.

Harchakos, passing: 6:10 (Passing or throwing object to spouse). 6:11 (Passing child to spouse). 6:122 (Passing to husband if he is ill).

Harchakos, serving: 6:89 (With a *shinuy*). 6:90 (If spouse turns away). 6:91 (Water; *challah*). 6:92 (If food will only be eaten later). 6:93 (If spouse was not present when food was put on plate; if food was

Mucus: 11:36 (Cleaning mucus from eyes, nostrils, and ears before immersion). 12:23 (If mucus was discovered in eyes after immersion). 12:28 (If mucus was discovered in nostrils after immersion).

Muktzeh: 3:10 (*Mar'eh*). 11:72:5; 11:72:9 (Nail polish remover).

Music: 6:24 (Listening to wife playing music when *nidah*).

Nail extensions: See *artificial nails.*

Nail polish remover: 11:72:5 (Usage on Shabbos/Yom Tov). 11:72:9 (To remove stains on Shabbos/Yom Tov).

Nail polish: 10:14 (Applying nail polish on *erev Shabbos* if immersing on *motza'ei Shabbos*). 11:45 (Removing before immersion). 11:72:5 (Removing nail polish on Shabbos/Yom Tov). 12:80–81 (*Chatzitzah* status).

Nails: See *chafifah: nails.*

Napkin: 6:59 (Napkin beneath plate as *heker*).

Navel: 11:25–26 (Cleaning before immersion). 11:68 (If she did not do so).

Negel vasser: See *netilas yadayim.*

Neon lighting: 3:13 (To examine *mar'os*).

Netilas yadayim: 6:119 (Preparing water for spouse to wash hands when *nidah*). 6:130 (Helping wife wash hands if she is ill).

Nickel: 4, addendum (To measure *kesem*).

Nidah: 1:4 (If she says that she is *nidah*, it might be required to consider her as such). 6:121 (Wearing specific clothing when *nidah*). 6:135–139 (Customs kept when menstruating). 6:140 (Passing between two men when *nidah*). 6:142 (Light in bedroom on Yom Kippur night when *nidah*). See *menstrual period; wedding: if bride is nidah at the wedding.*

Night of *veses:* See *immersion: on night of veses; vestos: day of veses.*

Night table: 6:29; 6:30* (Placing night table between beds).

Nightlight: 6:142 (In bedroom on Yom Kippur night).

Nine Days: 8:15 (Taking bath before *hefsek taharah*). 8:46 (Washing undergarments or sheet). 11:74 (Cutting nails during week of Tishah Be'av).

Nits: 11:53 (Removing before immersion). 11:72:8 (Removal on Shabbos/Yom Tov). 12:13 (*Chatzitzah* status).

Nittel: 13:14 (Immersion on *nittel*).

Non-Jew: 14:31 (Immersing again if she met a non-Jew when leaving *mikvah* before meeting a Jewish person). 14:33 (If she did not do so). 20:2 (*Yichud* with non-Jew). 20:27 (*Yichud* with one Jew and one non-Jew). 20:40 (*Yichud* with non-Jewish man if his wife is present; *yichud* with non-Jewish woman if her husband is present). 20:58 (*Yichud* when visiting a non-Jewish doctor in his home).

Non-kosher animal: 14:31 (Immersing again if she met a non-kosher animal when leaving *mikvah* before meeting a Jewish person). 14:33 (If she did not do so).

Nose: See *chafifah: nostrils.*

Nostrils: 12:29 (How to immerse if nostrils may not get wet for medical reasons). See also *chafifah: nostrils.*

Nursing woman: 2:9; 16:93 (Status as *mesulekes damim;* includes any woman after birth or miscarriage, even if she is not nursing). 2:10 (*Bedikah* after feeling *hargashah*). 5:1; 5:3 (*Nidah* status due to medical procedure). 6:22 (Nursing a baby when *nidah* and husband is home). 15:14; 15:18 (*Bedikos* before and after marital relations). 16:96–97 (How a nursing woman keeps *vestos*). 16:97* (Keeping thirty-first day and/or *onah* of *Ohr Zarua* if she is nursing). 16:98 (Combining periods of first 24 months from birth and afterwards to create *veses kavua*). 16:99 (Keeping *vestos* from before pregnancy after birth).

NuvaRing: See *vaginal ring.*

Nylon: 4:54 (*Kesem* found on nylon).

Ocean: See *sea.*

Office: 20:12 (*Yichud*).

Passing: See *harchakos: passing.*

Patch: See *contraceptive patch.*

Perfume: 6:19 (Smelling wife's perfume when *nidah;* applying perfume when *nidah*).

Period: See *menstrual period.*

Pessary: 8:32 (How to do *bedikos*). 12:120 (*Chatzitzah* status).

Physical exertion: 2:1 (If caused uterine bleeding).

Physician: See *doctor.*

Pictures: 17:24 (Avoiding touch during wedding pictures when *nidah*).

Pillow: 4:24 (*Kesem* on pillow). 6:39 (Using spouse's pillow when *nidah*). 6:111 (Preparing spouse's pillow when *nidah*). 8:46 (Unstained pillow during *shivah nekiyim*). See also *bed.*

Pills: 16:100 (How to keep *vestos* if taking pills).

Pimples: 12:94 (*Chatzitzah* status of pus in pimple).

Pins: 12:21 (If she immersed with pins in her hair).

Place mat: 6:59–60 (Eating on separate place mats as *heker*).

Plaque (teeth): 12:64 (*Chatzitzah* status).

Plate: See *harchakos: eating from same plate.*

Popcorn: 11:35 (Eating on day of immersion).

Pregnancy: 2:9; 16:89 (Status of pregnant woman as *mesulekes damim*). 2:10 (*Bedikah* after feeling *hargashah*). 5:1; 5:3 (*Nidah* status due to medical procedure). 7:15 (Waiting five days if she has difficulty becoming pregnant). 9:12–13 (Difficulty doing *bedikos* during pregnancy). 15:14–15; 15:18 (*Bedikos* before and after marital relations). 16:90–92 (How a pregnant woman keeps *vestos*). 16:97* (Keeping thirty-first day and/or *onah* of *Ohr Zarua* if she is pregnant). 16:98 (Combining bleeding during first three months of pregnancy and afterwards to create *veses kavua*). 16:99 (Keeping *vestos* from before pregnancy after birth).

she only did *bedikos* on first and seventh day). 9:11 (Only on first day; only on seventh day; only during middle days). 9:12–13 (If it is hard for her to do *bedikos*). 9:14 (If she has a vaginal wound). 9:15; 13:11 (Between end of *shivah nekiyim* and delayed immersion). 9:16 (Evening *bedikah* of *shivah nekiyim* in place of new *hefsek taharah*). 16:54–58 (How unclean *bedikos* during *shivah nekiyim* affect *vestos* calculations). 18:28 (If it is hard for her to do *bedikos* following *dam besulim*).

Shivah nekiyim, general: 7:1 (Must be preceded by minimum of five days). 8:4–5 (Separation between *hefsek taharah* and *shivah nekiyim*). 8:53 (Day of *hefsek taharah* is not included in *shivah nekiyim*). 9:15 (Separation between *shivah nekiyim* and immersion). 9:16 (Bleeding, unclean *bedikah*, unclean wiping, or stain during *shivah nekiyim*). 13:11 (Counting *shivah nekiyim* on time, even if immersion will be delayed).

Shivah nekiyim, other: 4:61 (*Kesem* found during first three days of *shivah nekiyim*). 6:135 (Visiting cemetery during *shivah nekiyim*). 6:136 (Visiting the *Ohel* during *shivah nekiyim*). 9:18 (If she is not sure which day of *shivah nekiyim* it is). 9:19 (If she changed time zones). 9:20 (If she crossed the International Date Line). 16:54–58 (How bleeding/unclean *bedikos* during *shivah nekiyim* affect *vestos* calculations). 17:02–3; 17:12–15 (Counting *shivah nekiyim* before wedding).

Shivah nekiyim, white undergarments and sheet: 4:52; 8:49 (Colored undergarments or non-*mekabel-tum'ah* material if she often finds *kesamim*). 4:58 (Pads if she often finds *kesamim*). 8:46 (Washing them during Nine Days or when mourning). 8:47 (If she has no white undergarments). 8:48 (Stained undergarments or sheet). 8:50 (No need to change undergarments and sheet after unclean *bedikah*). 9:5 (Examining undergarments and sheet daily).

Shivah: See *mourning*.

Shower: 6:116 (Preparing shower for spouse when *nidah*). 14:34–36 (Taking a shower after immersing). See also *chafifah: shower*.

Shul: 6:138 (Going to *shul* when menstruating).

Siblings: 20:7 (*Yichud* between siblings).

Tichel: See *kerchief.*

Time zones: 9:19 (If she changed time zones during *shivah nekiyim*).

Tishah Be'av: 6:143 (Intimacy and *harchakos* on Tishah Be'av; delaying immersion). 6:144 (Intimacy and *harchakos* on the ninth of Av that occurs on Shabbos). 6:145 (Intimacy on the night following Tishah Be'av). 8:14 (Washing vaginal area before *hefsek taharah*). 10:34 (*Chafifah* if immersing on *motza'ei Tishah Be'av*). 10:35 (*Chafifah* if immersing on *motza'ei Tishah Be'av* which is Sunday night).

Tissues/toilet paper: 2:22; 5:18; 9:6 (Looking at tissues used for wiping). 2:23 (Showing tissue with stains to a rabbi). 3:12 (Misplaced tissue with stain). 4:54 (*Kesem* found on tissue). 8:23 (Using for *bedikah*). 8:49 (Placing between vagina and undergarments during *shivah ne-kiyim*). 11:72:12 (Using to remove cream on Shabbos/Yom Tov). 12:116 (*Chatzitzah* status of pieces of toilet paper in vagina). See also *wiping.*

Toenails: See *chafifah: nails.*

Toes: 4:30 (*Kesem* on toe). 11:25–26 (Cleaning between toes before immersion). 11:60 (Washing between toes if she walked barefoot to the *mikvah*). 11:68 (If she did not clean between toes).

Toilet paper: See *tissues.*

Toilet: 5:17 (Blood found in toilet).

Toothbrush: 11:72:6 (Usage on Shabbos/Yom Tov).

Toothpaste: 6:20 (Using same toothpaste when *nidah*). 6:80 (Using her leftover toothpaste). 11:72:6 (Usage on Shabbos/Yom Tov).

Towel: 11:72:12 (Using towel to remove cream on Shabbos/Yom Tov).

Trauma: 1:11 (Requirement to perform *bedikah* upon experiencing sudden trauma).

Traveling: 6:45–48 (Traveling together when *nidah*). 7:15 (Waiting five days if husband or wife will be traveling and that will cause her to be unable to immerse beforehand). 13:2–4 (Traveling on day of immersion). 16:104 (Marital relations on night before trip if it is day of *veses*). 16, fn. 9 (Length of trip that obligates marital relations).

Vaginal ring: 8:33 (Removal before *hefsek taharah*). 9:2 (Removal before *bedikos* during *shivah nekiyim*). 12:118 (Removal before immersion).

Vaginal wound: See *wound*.

Vase: 6:55 (Use as *heker*).

Vaseline: 8:24 (To moisten *bedikah* cloth).

Veses hachodesh: 16:34 (Definition; how it is calculated). 16:35 (If she began bleeding on the 30th day of the month, and the next month only has 29 days). 16:36–37 (Establishing a *veses kavua* for days of the month). 16:38 (How to uproot a *veses hachodesh*). 16:39 (If new bleeding occurred before *veses hachodesh*). 16:40–41 (If new period began before *veses hachodesh* and continued until day of *veses*). 16:43–44 (If she saw twice on same day of month; uprooting *veses hachodesh* if she did not do *bedikah* on day of *veses*). See also *veses kavua*; *vestos: day of veses*.

Veses hadilug: 16:74 (Importance of being familiar with *veses hadilug*). 16:66 (Not kept unless it becomes *kavua*). 16:81 (Definition). 16:82–83 (*Veses hadilug* with days of the month). 16:84 (*Veses hadilug* with *haflagos*). 16:85–86 (If she only bled three times in a *dilug* pattern). 16:86* (Other *dilug* patterns). 16:87 (*Dilug* pattern of earlier dates of the month). 16:88 (*Dilug* pattern of shorter intervals).

Veses hahaflagah: 13:11 (Performing *hefsek taharah* on time so that *haflagos* will be accurate). 16:45 (Definition). 16:46 (Establishing a *veses kavua* for *haflagos*). 16:47 (How it is calculated). 16:47* (Opinion of Alter Rebbe; if she did a *bedikah* before end of five days; if she will not begin counting *shivah nekiyim* until later; if she did not do a *bedikah* to determine that bleeding had stopped). 16:47** (Opinion of other *poskim*). 16:48–48* (Calculating with *onos* vs. days). 16:49 (How to uproot a *veses hahaflagah*). 16:50–51 (If new period occurred before *veses hahaflagah*). 16:52 (Possibility for a *haflagah* to remain for a long time; possibility for a *veses kavua* to be established over an extended period of time). 16:53 (Uprooting *veses hahaflagah* if she did not do *bedikah* on day of *veses*). See also *veses kavua*; *vestos: day of veses*.

Veses hasirug: 16:74 (Importance of being familiar with *veses hasirug*). 16:66 (Not kept unless it becomes *kavua*). 16:77–78 (Weekly *veses*

that it is day of *veses*). 4:60 (*Kesem* found on day of *veses*). 7:12 (Waiting five days if she became *nidah* on day of *veses* and day before was *onah beinonis*). 7:15 (Waiting five days if that will cause immersion to be on day of *veses*). 13:5–6 (Delaying immersion if it is day of *veses*; delaying immersion if that will cause immersion to be delayed even more). 13, fn. 2; 16:16 (Affectionate touch on day of *veses*). 13:17 (Delaying immersion on day of *veses* if that will cause immersion to take place on Shabbos). 16:9–10 (Length of separation on day of *veses*; *onah* of *Ohr Zarua*). 16:16 (Affectionate touch on day of *veses*; *harchakos*). 16:17 (*Bedikah* on day of *veses*). 16:18–19 (When to do *bedikah*; wearing white undergarments). 16:20 (If she did not do *bedikah*). 16:21 (Asking wife if she did *bedikah*).16:22 (If *bedikah* cloth was misplaced). 16:23 (Taking bath, swimming, etc. on day of *veses*; *chafifah* on day of *veses*). 16:104 (Traveling on day of *veses*; marital relations on night before trip if it is day of *veses*). 16:106 (Marriage on day of *veses*). See also *immersion: on night of veses.*

Vestos, general: 16:1 (General concept). 16:2 (Usage of Hebrew dates; *vestos* associated with physical sensations; importance of knowing uncommon *veses* calculations and how to uproot a *veses kavua*; all Hebrew dates begin the previous evening). 16:3–4* (Keeping a calendar). 16:5–8 (Types of bleeding for which *vestos* must be calculated). 16:11 (Day and night defined by sunrise and sunset). 16:12–13 (If she is not sure if her period began by day or at night). 16:14 (If the bleeding extended only a few hours into second *onah*). 16:15 (Status of days corresponding to continuation of period). 16:75; 16:107 (Keeping note of periods and *haflagos* on a separate sheet to assist in noticing significant patterns). 16:101–103 (If she is not sure when her *veses* dates are). 16:107 (Keeping a calendar).

Vestos, other: 16:54–56 (If bleeding/unclean *bedikah* during *shivah nekiyim* requires new calculations). 16:57 (Doubtful *bedikah* during *shivah nekiyim*). 16:57* (Unclean *bedikah* during *shivah nekiyim* if she is *temei'ah* due to *kesem* or *dam besulim*). 16:58 (Establishing a *veses kavua* through bleeding during *shivah nekiyim*). 16:89–92 (How a pregnant woman keeps *vestos*). 16:93–97 (How a nursing woman keeps *vestos*; miscarriage; caesarean section). 16:100 (How to keep *vestos* if taking pills). 19:13 (Keeping *vestos* from blood discharged during birth). 19:15 (Keeping *vestos* from blood discharged during miscarriage).

rooms of a building; if door of one of the rooms is locked from the inside.) 20:17 (Elevator). 20:19–20; 20:24 (Car). 20:21; 20:23; 20:37 (Taxi). 20:22–23 (Bus).

Yichud, with more than one individual: 20:26 (With two men). 20:27 (With one Jew and one non-Jew). 20:28–29 (With two men at night or in an uninhabited area). 20:30 (With two women; with three or more women). 20:31 (With two women if husband of one of them is in town). 20:32 (With three women at night). 20:33 (With three women in an uninhabited area). 20:34 (With three or more women if his business dealings involve women or if he interacts with women in an open manner). 20:35 (With three or more immoral women). 20:36 (Three women with an immoral man). 20:37 (Three women in a taxi). See also yichud: shomer.

Yom Kippur: 6:141 (Intimacy and harchakos on Yom Kippur; delaying immersion). 6:142 (Candle or nightlight in bedroom). 8:14 (Washing vaginal area before hefsek taharah). 10:34 (Chafifah if immersing on motza'ei Yom Kippur).

Yom Tov candles: See Shabbos/Yom Tov candles.

Yom Tov: 8:11 (Washing vaginal area before hefsek taharah). 8:12 (Opening hot water). 8:13 (Using soap; washing body with sponge or washcloth). 8:25 (Smearing gel on bedikah cloth). 8:26 (Moistening bedikah cloth with water). 8:39 (When to do hefsek taharah and moch dachuk before Yom Tov). 8:52 (Replacing sheet on Yom Tov). 10:12* (Preparing for motza'ei-Yom-Tov immersion on Yom Tov; washing body on Yom Tov). 10:32 (Preparing on first day of Yom Tov for immersion on second night). 11:33 (Eating meat on day of immersion). See also chafifah: when immersing Friday night or Yom Tov night; chafifah: when immersing on second night of Yom Tov or on the night between Shabbos and Yom Tov; challah; havdalah; immersion: Friday night or Yom Tov night; kiddush; motza'ei Yom Tov; muktzeh.

DEDICATED IN LOVING MEMORY OF

Mrs. **Miriam** bas R. **Eliyahu**

ע"ה

Althaus

Shabbos Nachamu, 11 Menachem Av, 5783

ת'נ'צ'ב'ה'

may she rest in peace

◆

Mrs. Althaus was a devoted Chabad educator,
who particularly assisted kallahs in preparing for their special day,
and was especially active in the Family Purity Campaign

◆

BY HER SON AND DAUGHTER-IN-LAW

Pini & Sary Althaus

and family

לעילוי נשמת
הרה"ת ר' **מרדכי צבי** בן הרב ר' **חיים יוסף שלמה** ז"ל
גרינוולד

היה חייל נאמן של כ"ק אדמו"ר מליובאוויטש זצ"ל
והתייצב בגאון בכל מקום בו נדרש:
בקיבוצים, יישובים, ערים, בפני חוגים שומרי מצוות
ובפני אנשי קיבוצי השומר הצעיר.
ובכל מקום הביא את דבר ה' ודבר החסידות
בנועם-שיח, במתק שפתיים ובדוגמה אישית אצילית.
לצד זאת, הייתה דמותו של 'המורה צבי' לסמל ודוגמא
עבור אלפי התלמידים שלמדו אצלו במשך עשרות שנים
ומתגעגעים לקולו החם וליחסו המיוחד.

נלב"ע ביום רביעי ג' אייר ה'תשע"ח
ת.נ.צ.ב.ה.

מצבת זכרון

לכבוד אבינו היקר באדם
הרה"ח התת' מו"ה **צבי דב** [**הערשל**]
ב"ר יהושע מנחם מענדל הלוי ע"ה
שיינער

מתלמידי ישיבת תומכי תמימים ליובאוויטש
מקושר בלו"נ לכ"ק אדמו"ר מליובאוויטש
קבע עתים לתורה על ימים, במסירה ונתינה
ובעזרה ליתומים עולי רוסיה
אהוב ונוח לבריאות וביתו פתוח לרווחה
נפטר בשם טוב ביום ד' ניסן ה'תש"פ
תנצב"ה

❦

הונצח ע"י בני משפחתו שיחיו

R|KI'S
M|KVAH

מקוה טהרה עין רבקה

In loving memory of Rivkah bat Harav Yekutiel Farkash

ת.נ.צ.ב.ה.

Issaquah, WA